SINGING THE GLORY DOWN

SINGING THE GLORY DOWN

Amateur Gospel Music In South Central Kentucky 1900-1990

WILLIAM LYNWOOD MONTELL, *1931-*

THE UNIVERSITY PRESS OF KENTUCKY

Copyright © 1991 by The University Press of Kentucky

Scholarly publisher for the Commonwealth,
serving Bellarmine College, Berea College, Centre
College of Kentucky, Eastern Kentucky University,
The Filson Club, Georgetown College, Kentucky
Historical Society, Kentucky State University,
Morehead State University, Murray State University,
Northern Kentucky University, Transylvania University,
University of Kentucky, University of Louisville,
and Western Kentucky University.

Editorial and Sales Offices: Lexington, Kentucky 40508-4008

Library of Congress Cataloging-in-Publication Data

Montell, William Lynwood, 1931-
    Singing the glory down : amateur gospel music in south central
Kentucky, 1900-1990 / William Lynwood Montell.
      p. cm.
    Includes bibliographical references and Index.
    ISBN 0-8131-1757-7 (alk. paper)
    1. Gospel music—Kentucky—History and criticism. I. Title.
ML3187.M66   1991
782.25'09769'6—dc20   91-8688

This book is affectionately dedicated to all the
shape-note music teachers, gospel song writers,
singers, and musicians from south central
Kentucky, including those whose time to cross over
the river they wrote and sang about came before
their involvement in gospel music was documented
in print.

CONTENTS

ACKNOWLEDGMENTS

I began field research on this project during the summer 1985 and continued on a regular basis through the summer 1989, as my teaching schedule at Western Kentucky University permitted. Some research was conducted later that fall and during the spring 1990, when I was visiting professor at the University of Notre Dame and heavily involved in writing the manuscript. During this five-year period, many people gave me invaluable assistance and support. The Faculty Research Committee of Western Kentucky University provided financial support during the early stages of this project. Department head Carol P. Brown, departmental secretary and part-time teaching colleague Laura Harper Lee, Folk Studies program coordinator Burt Feintuch, and Dean Ward Hellstrom deserve a special note of thanks, as they supported and encouraged me in many ways. Personnel in the cartography laboratory of Western's Department of Geography and Geology provided the map of south central Kentucky, and Carl Kell, professor of Speech Communications, suggested the title for the book. Joel Hemphill of Nashville, who in 1974 wrote the very popular gospel song "Sing the Glory Down," granted permission to use the sound-alike title for this book. Thanks also to Donald P. Costello, chairman of the Department of American Studies at the University of Notre Dame, for inviting me to teach during the 1989-1990 academic year and to Dean Michael Loux and the Notre Dame administration for granting me access to the university's stenographic pool and computer lab.

My debt is also heavy to undergraduate and graduate students at Western Kentucky University, especially Amy and Beth Watt, who entered transcripts and manuscript drafts on the word processor, and Chad Berry, Xiaoge Cai, Callie Dalton, and Kim Schmitt, all of whom worked as my graduate assistants during this period. I want, above all, however, to thank the countless gospel singers and musicians for their untiring cooperation and unflagging interest in my work. All persons whose interviews were tape-recorded are listed in Appendix A. A host of other singers, musicians, and gospel music fans provided information, photos, records and tapes, and memorabilia during short informal interviews or in letters. A very special word of thanks is due, however, to those who made special efforts in one way or another to assist me. Without their help my labors would have been of little avail.

In alphabetical order, by county, these research assistants are Paul Curry, Hartsell Hodges, and Curtis and Mildred Wilson from Adair County; Erlis D. Austin, Glen Conner, Buell Gibbs, Roger and Diane Goad, Arlis O. Harmon, David Holder, Corbin Napier, Ronnie and Teresa Williams, and Jessie Johnson Young (now living in Illinois) from Allen County; Rex Agers, C.E. Deweese, Bill and Margaret Jones, J.T. Light, Bill and Nedie Martin, Debbie Reece, Clovis Sadler, Eva Strode Speer, and Richard Tinsley from Barren County; Eulema "Jimmie" Keith of Butler County; Rick Cooper, Hobart Haste, Jason Haste, Lois Perry, and Mrs. R.C. Weddle, Jr., of Casey County; Johnny Howard (now of Elizabethtown), and Ray and Libby McWhorter Mullinix from Clinton County; Morris and Norma Butler, Gary Cash, and Shirley Wray from Cumberland County; Georgie and Willowdean Childress, Lowell Davis, and Johnnie Lindsey of Edmonson County; Buddy Lowe, Garry Polston, and Elois Thompson of Green County; Christell Bennett, Don and Jim Cottrell (now of Elizabethtown), Elmo Dorsey, Haskell and Annette McCubbins, Guy Templeman, and Lucille Wells from Hart County; Anne Rose, and Tom and Audrey Webb of Logan County; Jack and Patty Hurt, Sherman and Mary Hurt, Stanley and Lourine Syra, and Mary Thrasher of Metcalfe County; Zilpha Hume, Hazel Montell, and Wayne Strode from Monroe County; Lewis Adams, Bob and Mathael Foster, Bob Sears, Norma Sears, and June Smith from Pulaski County; Grace Bertram Foley Hall, Ernest McKinley, Doyle and Reva Rexroat, Ivis Roy, and Woodrow Wilson of Russell County; Edna Swift of Simpson County; Clarence Bertram, Imogene Muncie, Mary F. Neely, Bryan Newton, and Maurice Wethington of Taylor County; Hazel Bryson, Edwin Dye, Lyndell Graven, Ed and Roberta Grimes, Mike Lindsey, Lana Miller, James and Sandy Pennycuff, Chris Reynolds, Noble

Stuart, Brodus Tabor, and Frank Weaver, all of Warren County; and Jean Guffey Crabtree of Wayne County.

Finally, to my wife, Barbara, goes a special word of thanks, praise, and admiration. She traveled thousands of miles to attend singing events with me; took notes on the singers, their performances, and their songs; assisted me with tape-recording, video-taping, and photography; and, on the way home, offered suggestions and interpretations of what we had just witnessed. And although she was busy with her own research and writing, she took time to offer positive criticism of my manuscript in its various stages.

INTRODUCTION

To most people, the term "gospel music" conjures up images of groups of black professionals who travel the concert circuit from one big city to another, and the music genre they sing. The stereotype prevails, whether the performers are black or white, that gospel music is a form of big business that utilizes radio and television broadcasts to reach and cultivate the interest of people who are easy touches for sales promotions. But not all gospel music is performed by professionals for monetary gain. As folklorist Burt Feintuch observes, "Gospel music thrives in a number of settings, where it is practiced by nonprofessional, non-commercially motivated performers . . . who perceive and practice a 'gospel life.'"[1] Kip Lornell, folklorist and ethnomusicologist, went a step further by commenting on the need for in-depth studies of local amateur singing groups: "Perhaps the most pressing concern is the decided lack of research on community quartets, which are the backbone of the gospel quartet tradition. . . . Community quartets have had a strong local and regional impact, tend to reflect regional styles of singing, and are the wellspring for nearly all of the commercially successful groups."[2]

This study looks at the rich history and performance aspects of community-based shape-note gospel music and its offshoots—church singings, singing conventions, and four-part southern harmony quartet music. My own purpose in writing about amateur gospel music in south central Kentucky is to convey to the reader how very important this rich, traditional form of religious music is and has been in the lives of its practitioners and aficionados. Like nothing else I have encountered in thirty-plus years of regional research, old-time southern gospel music is woven into the emotional fiber of the people who loved it as children and have continued to nurture it through the years. The story of this music cries out to be told as a testament to an artistic, religious force that exhilarates, comforts, and extends a promise of wonderful things to come in another life that awaits Christian believers "on the other side of Jordan."

This study of old-time gospel music does not include consideration of its African-American counterpart. While white and black singing traditions in the South exhibit affinity in terms of song content, the history and performance styles of these two religious song traditions are quite different. I talked with several black gospel singers during the course of my research but have chosen not to include the information here, as African-American gospel music is deserving of a separate volume entirely.

I spent five years investigating shape-note schools, singing conventions, and amateur quartet music in a nineteen-county area of the Commonwealth of Kentucky. I found this area to be the center of white southern gospel music in the state,[3] based on the large number of former and presently active gospel music ensembles in the area compared with the number of those based in other portions of the state. Very few quartets are found in the rest of Kentucky's 120 counties. Thirty-four of the forty-three Kentucky state singing conventions have been held in south central Kentucky, and seven of ten present State Convention board members are from the south central region. The remaining three members are from Hardin and Grayson counties, which are adjacent to the study area.

Gospel music is the term commonly used to describe southern vernacular religious music, a genre that exists outside the formal hymnals published by denominational presses of most Protestant churches. A. Doyne Horsley defines gospel music as "the popular music of American Christianity."[4] James R. Davidson is more specific. He refers to a gospel song as "a simple harmonized tune in popular style combined with a religious text of an emotional and personal character in which the individual . . . is usually the center rather than God."[5] While there are certain lyrical exceptions to Davidson's definition, it is true that, unlike hymns, most gospel songs are typically not songs of praise. By strict definition, "gospel" songs should address biblical themes and carry only biblical messages spoken by Jesus and His Apostles. Not all of them do this. While gospel songs as described in this volume do focus on the individual's relationship with God, they also address a wide variety of secular themes, including family. Some of the more popular compositions are

SOUTH CENTRAL KENTUCKY

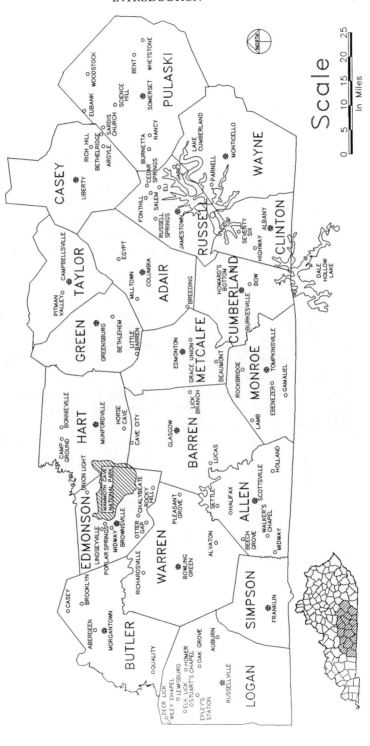

Scale

In Miles

0 5 10 15 20 25

NORTH

associated with hearth and home—Mother and Father, the old home-place, and the good old days when times were not so fast. Such "home" songs are more sentimental than religious, and belong more appropriately in an inspirational song category. Perhaps "sacred" or "Christian" is a better term than "gospel" for this entire body of religious songs; it is the latter term, however, that stuck and is used today by those who sing the music, and those who listen to it.

Gospel music is alive and vibrant today in south central Kentucky, especially in rural areas and small towns where the church is still very much the focal point of community life. For Protestant residents of these locales, gospel songs express their real theology, a theology that is based on the democratic Christian ideal that "the ground is level at the foot of the Cross." Gospel music as sung by the community-based ensembles described in this study knows no denominational boundaries. People of all evangelical Protestant denominations can come together and sing or listen to gospel music and not experience the tug of doctrinal divisions. Gospel is religious music, not denominational. It is ecumenical and bond-forming, never divisive.[6] Gospel music is the strongest agent at work today in binding the local evangelical communities together.

Gospel music as described throughout this work is in every way a vernacular music genre. It lives through performance. Seeing and hearing it performed in churches, schools, outdoors, and at home, endears it to listeners. Furthermore, the artistic rendering of this music is a creative outlet for the singers, who often rework the lyrics and music to suit their own tastes and needs. Through performance, the songs become the vicarious property of all the people involved in gospel music—singers and listeners alike—as the song lyrics embody the democratic Christian ideals of these Anglo-Protestant worshipers.

Many of the older songs still being performed are familiar to the singers and listeners, who "grew up with them" and view the songs as part of their cultural heritage. Some of the songs are passed along orally from one generation of singers to the next. For this reason, it is not uncommon for the songs to exist in several slightly different versions. This characteristic was demonstrated as recently as March 1990, when one member of a family quartet sang the chorus to a song all three times using two or three words that were different from the words sung by other members of the ensemble. Many of the gospel songs are composed in a formulaic manner, using traditional themes, well-known metaphors, and commonplace words and phrases. Perhaps it is by using these stylistic devices over and over in different songs that composers, regardless of their own denominational affiliation, are able to turn out songs that do not violate doctrinal beliefs of others.

Early shape-note singings were vernacular events in the purest sense of the term. Although the songs and the songbooks they came from were new, the much-loved, time-tested manner of singing the notes and words in a distinctive style was something these people treasured and shared.

I am still at a loss for an answer when people ask why I chose to investigate gospel music. My research began in mid-1985, immediately after I had completed a book-length manuscript on homicidal behavior. Perhaps my decision was a reaction to the negative aspects of killings and other forms of criminal behavior. I wanted a research topic that was more in touch with day-to-day living in south central Kentucky. Recalling my former student Shirley Bowman Hammer's 1984 research into gospel music as sung by members of her own family and their neighbors in the Metcalfe-Monroe County area, I decided to investigate the history and contemporary performance aspects of this interesting phenomenon throughout south central Kentucky. I did not know at the time that this geographical area was the hotbed—past and present—of gospel music activity in Kentucky. Nor did I have any notion then that, in the process of documenting gospel music in the region, I would eventually account for at least 825 quartets, trios, and family ensembles that sang actively in and beyond the region.[7]

Over 200 groups are active today, if we define an active group as one that performs at least four times each year outside the singers' home church(es). Some of these singing ensembles have existed for over thirty years. Many of them, like their predecessors in the sixties and seventies, have issued one or more commercial recordings. While information is not available for comparison, perhaps no other similar portion of the South or Midwest can lay claim to such a great number of community-based gospel groups.

Preliminary library research, including an on-line database search, revealed virtually nothing written about small-ensemble white gospel music. This volume thus represents the first known book-length effort to portray white amateur gospel music in regional, historical, and social context.[8] In order to focus carefully on the field research that lay ahead, I began to jot down questions for which I needed answers. What were the real parameters of the gospel music "heartland" in Kentucky? How could the boundaries best be determined? How many gospel music groups were active through the years? How could they be identified and documented? Were they more numerous at certain times? What was the ratio of family-based groups to groups comprised of individuals who were unrelated? To what extent were early quartets the products of shape-note singing schools? When and where were these schools taught and by whom? What factors were at work in causing changes in the sounds and performance of gospel music? When did these changes occur and which groups were movers in this regard?

With these questions as a beginning point, I sent letters to the editors of numerous daily and weekly newspapers in central, southern, and western Kentucky. Eastern Kentucky was omitted because of the paucity of southern harmony groups there, and its long-standing involvement with an older hymnody tradition that is not common to the rest of the state. Also, the Kentucky State Singing Convention, which has been a "quartet convention" since the early 1950s, has never been held farther east than Somerset and Richmond. The letters asked for readers' help in identifying and documenting shape-note singing schools, music teachers, and local singing groups past and present. My plea for help was also broadcast numerous times over WGGC, a 100,000-watt radio station in Glasgow. The response to my request was not overwhelming, but it was adequate in helping to define the geographical area to be targeted for intensive investigation.

I responded to each letter or telephone call by sending a questionnaire that asked for detailed information relative to the respondent group's personnel, years of active service by both the group and the individual performers in it, tapes and albums issued, and other items of information. The questionnaire also asked for a listing of names and addresses of other ensembles and individuals who should be contacted. This was a fruitful venture, and names began to pour in. More questionnaires were sent out and the response rate was probably in excess of 85 percent. For the first time in these musicians' lives, it seems, somebody was interested in writing about them and the thing they loved most.

I began receiving handwritten notes and telephone calls inviting me to "come hear our group sing this Sunday night." I also listened to radio announcements, usually on a weekly, one-hour gospel music program, and watched for announcements of singings published weekly in most area newspapers. During this phase of the research, I drove in excess of 30,000 miles to music events in all parts of the region. My goal was to hear firsthand every active gospel music group in the nineteen-county study area. I was able to document about 95 percent of these ensembles during actual singing performances, which were held at churches, schools, outdoor functions, fund-raising efforts, and at the Kentucky State or Ohio Valley singing conventions.

With the assistance of my wife, Barbara Allen, I tape-recorded, photographed, and made descriptive notes about the groups' performance styles and song repertoires. Numerous singing events were videotaped. Some of the groups sent me copies of their self-recorded videos and audio tapes, knowing that all such items were to be donated to the Kentucky Library at Western Kentucky University, as part of a gospel music collection.[9]

Researchers who embark upon fieldwork involving people and their time-honored traditions are never fully able to gauge the effects of their labors on the traditions being studied. Some scholars feel that such fieldwork has a negative impact, perhaps even to the point of creating an unhealthy self-consciousness in tradition bearers. In other words, a tradition, once disturbed by exterior factors, may never again be the same; those persons who have thus far preserved the tradition as a matter of in-group routine, may now do things to stimulate it artificially and, in so doing, change it markedly.

Such has certainly not been the case in my own research into white gospel music in south central Kentucky. In no known way have I altered the tradition that sustains this form of religious music. Instead, the singing stream that I investigated between 1985 and 1990 is so well established that it absorbed my research and documentation efforts into its very fiber. The singers totally accepted me, viewing me as one of them. They drew me into the round of activities that I had set about to document, not as a singer but eventually as an officer in both the Ohio Valley Singing Convention and the Kentucky State Singing Convention. I was honored to serve as president of the latter organization in 1989.

I began the process of writing this book in midsummer 1989. It was finished a year later. The final product contains nine chapters in addition to the Introduction and Conclusion. Chapter 1 describes the shape-note singing schools and the culture heroes who taught them during their heyday from 1900 to the 1950s. Chapter 2 provides a look at church singings and country-wide singing conventions that sprang organically from the shape-note music schools, and Chapter 3 describes what has been called the golden years of quartet music. Those fondly remembered years, covering the period 1910-40, featured four-part southern harmony sung the way it was written in the songbooks issued by such publishing giants as Vaughan and Stamps-Baxter.

Chapter 4 deals with quartet music in the 1940s, a period marked

by a gradual shift away from the songbook format to a more innovative, somewhat flashy style of stage presentation. Chapters 5 and 6
continue with the small-group singing tradition, focusing on the
significant changes that quartet music experienced from roughly
1950 through the 1980s. Chapter 7 takes an inside look at singing
groups, focusing on singers and musicians as human beings who are
expected to live lives that are free of all human foibles and imperfections. Chapter 8 moves inside the singing arenas and offers descriptions of these gospel music groups in performance contexts. Chapter
9 considers the importance of the family group in gospel music, and
offers a lengthy description of the extended Haste family of Bethelridge in Casey County. This historic family provided the very first
gospel quartet in the region. It has so far produced five generations of
quartet singers; youthful representatives of the sixth generation are
already taking active parts in church choirs and as solo performers.

Southern gospel music remained vigorous at the community
level in south central Kentucky at the beginning of the 1990s. It is a
music current that, in spite of certain changes in sounds, lyrics, and
performance styles, is still fed by older traditions with origins in the
singing schools at the beginning of the twentieth century.

1

THE SHAPE-NOTE ERA

Georgie Childress stood up, looked out over the twenty-five singers and ten or so visitors chatting in the small, rural church sanctuary in northern Edmonson County. He cleared his throat and announced that it was time for the singing to begin.

The singers moved quickly to the altar area, picked up their songbooks, and formed a closed circle in which they grouped themselves according to their respective vocal parts. In clockwise order were the sopranos, made up of both men and women; the altos; the tenors; and the bass vocalists, who stood with their backs to the audience. David Taylor, song leader, stood in the middle of the circle facing the audience. He directed the singing of each song, but it was Childress who selected the songs to be sung, called out the numbers from the book, and vocally pitched the tunes in the appropriate key without benefit of a musical instrument, tuning fork, or pitch pipe.

"Tonight we'll start off by using our new song book," he announced. "Let's sing number twenty-four. Number twenty-four. Sing the notes, then the words."

Childress, born in 1919, has been singing for forty years. With near perfect pitch, he intoned the opening notes, and the other singers joined in as together they keyed the tune. Their "do, re, mis" filled the sanctuary with enthusiasm, volume, and authority. Clearly, these shape-note singers knew what they were doing and loved doing it.

Another weekly choir practice at the Union Light Missionary Baptist Church was under way. Such has been the case every Friday night since Charlie Sturgeon conducted a seven-note singing school at the church in 1950. Even before that, choir practice had been held

I attended this practice of the Union Light Church's shape-note choir in 1986.

off and on since 1905, according to Childress, who recalled such singing events during his late teenage years.

Following the first song, Childress took time out to explain to those of us in the audience that the Union Light Church frequently purchases new shape-note songbooks. "We love the new song," he told us. "Get tired of singing the same old songs all the time. We meet here and pick out new songs together. Most of us have been singing the shape-notes for a long time," he said proudly, and then added without apology, "I don't know anything about the round notes [i.e., regular musical notation]."

"Number eighty-four, number eighty-four," he called out to the singers. "Let's sing the notes to 'Just Over Yonder,' then we'll sing the words." Their voices made the church sanctuary echo with the beautiful four-part harmony that characterizes shape-note music.

Pausing only once for brief personal testimonies, prayer requests, and then simultaneous individual prayers said aloud, the singers continued for almost two hours. They concluded the session by singing "Amazing Grace," while the singers and the audience moved around the altar area, single file, shaking hands with all those present as a gesture of love and fellowship. Thus ended a Friday evening choir practice in April 1986.

The singers who congregate weekly at Union Light are moving along in the shape-note gospel music singing stream that flowed wide and long until the 1940s, when technology began to take a heavy toll on this genre of American religious folksong. The seven shape-notes are used to teach a system in which the pitch of each note corresponds to its shape, independent of lines and spaces on the musical staff. (Notes for soprano and alto voices are on the top staff; tenor and bass notes are located on the lower staff.) This particular music tradition is a direct descendant of the four-note system that began in the early 1700s in New England and, although now diminished in importance, continues to act like a rivulet of fresh water that refuses to dry up entirely.

The popularity of shape-note music can be attributed to many factors, but its roots are deeply embedded in the religious zeal that swept through the American colonies following the Great Awakening in the mid-eighteenth century. Until that time, it had been common practice in England and America to sing only the Psalms during worship services. Psalters and hymnals containing the Psalms were brought to this country from England and generally contained no music. Only six to twelve different tunes were used, and these were sung quite slowly. But with the tide of emotional revivalism that swept through the colonies in the latter years of the eighteenth century, many Protestant denominations began to sing a body of religious songs that were written, published, and sold by contemporary, educated tunesmiths. These new compositions attempted to eliminate the practice of singing hymns in a slow monotonous fashion.[1]

The new hymns were set to traditional folk melodies that members of the congregation knew and loved. Examples of these hymns and melodies are still alive today in some southern churches, mainly in the mountains. Sung by ear and from memory, such songs are performed without musical score. Georgie Childress recalls revivals at Union Light Baptist Church during the early 1920s in which some of the old-timers sang strictly from memory certain songs that were designed to bring sinners to their knees in repentance. "I'll never forget the one about the dying girl on her way to hell," Childress reminisced; she "chewed her tongue as she felt the flames of hell."

Other older religious songs employed the stylistic device of incremental repetition (repeating words and verses) to aid the singers in recalling the lyrics. For example, a song might contain many verses that were identical in wording except that brother, sister, father, mother, and so on, were interchanged as the chief actors in the verses. Many of the early singers could not read at all, and still fewer of them could read music. Musical illiteracy, coupled with an inadequate supply of songbooks, led to the practice of "lining out" the songs. The song leader in each local congregation often had the only songbook in the church. He selected the tune, chanted aloud one line at a time, then joined the congregation in singing the words. Responsorial hymn singing was practiced in some early churches of south central Kentucky before the advent of hymnbooks containing musical scores. Bob Sears, a Pulaski County native, recalled hearing his grandfather describe how the song leader at Clifty Grove Baptist Church lined out hymns during religious services.[2]

Lewis Adams of Science Hill, Pulaski County, was confronted early in his music-teaching career by Madison Roy, who staunchly defended the use of words-only hymnals. Roy, a member of the Bethlehem Baptist Church, "could sing any of the songs in that old book," Adams recalled. "The old fellow said, 'If a man can sing at all, he can sing these songs without the music,'" Adams continued. "He went by the name Uncle Matt. Had a great, long white beard. As a child I heard him sing one solo after another from that kind of book. And when they had an altar call [pastor's invitation for individual sinners' responses to the sermon], he'd sing several of them old songs."

Early churches in the Lindseyville area of Edmonson County are known to have used songbooks "that didn't have any music, only the words," according to singer Johnnie Lindsey. Both he and his wife, Chloie, recalled "hearing the old folks talk about the little books" that were used in local churches during the late nineteenth and early twentieth centuries. Allen Countian Jonas Britt, born in the late 1890s, told me that his father "used to sing out of a little black book that had about 200 songs in it but didn't have any music." The Ebenezer Baptist Church near Tompkinsville continued to use such songsters until around 1912-14. Zilpha Hume, widow of gospel music teacher and singer Archie Hume, recalled, "We used these little hymnals without music until I was a good-sized girl. Jerry Elzie Adams, a school teacher, was the song leader back then."

By 1805, books were published that contained both the well-loved, traditional hymns and the new pieces. At the same time, both publishers and music reformers addressed the problem of the key in which the songs were to be sung. Among the solutions offered by the reformers was the notion of using scale degree numbers rather than note heads on the staff. Such numerals were the signs of sounds. Punctuation marks used either before or beneath the numerals indicated the note's length. Thus, :1 represented a whole note, .1 represented a half note, and 1 stood for a quarter note. A comma beneath the 1 indicated an eighth note, two commas a sixteenth, three commas a thirty-second note, and four commas a sixty-fourth.[3]

It may be that such figure-face songbooks were used across south central Kentucky to one degree or another. Curtis Savage, who grew up in north Logan County and taught singing schools there in the 1930s, recalled that old timers in the area told him about "songbooks that had numbers that stood for the tunes."

The sight reading system that caught on best everywhere in the South among rural people with minimal education was the shape-note system, a method designed to help singers read music easily by assigning a specific shape to each note of the scale. This system insured that even if the note itself moved from one key to another, alert singers knew how to sound their parts at all times, as no mental transposition of keys was necessary. In the words of folklorist Daniel Patterson, "To say that singers who learn the shape-note system *well* are marvelously adept singers would be an understatement of reality."

The first of the shape-note systems was developed by William Little and William Smith in 1798 and published in Philadelphia in 1802 under the title *Easy Instructor; or A New Method of Teaching Sacred Harmony.* They employed the triangle, oval, square, triangle, oval, square, diamond, triangle to represent the musical notes. These shapes corresponded to fa, so, la, fa, so, la, mi, fa, and were recorded on four staffs, one for each voice.[4]

Interestingly enough, music reformers in New England vigorously opposed this new shape-note system of sight reading almost as soon as it was introduced. They urged people to sing the fa, so, la syllables from round notes instead. In so doing, these reformers were eventually successful in eliminating shape-note music from urban religious life in the North. "Shape-notes came to be regarded in the cities as the musical notation for country bumpkins," writes music historian B.F. McLemore.[5] Shape-note songbooks containing the four syllables became extremely popular in the South, however. They are

A page from James D. Vaughan's 1938 *Happy Praises* shape-note songbook, which was called "Our annual 1939 book for Sunday-Schools, Singing-Schools, Revivals, Conventions, and General Use in Christian Worship," shows the use of shape-notes in a song by C.E. Deweese. Used by permission.

still in limited use in far western Kentucky and in portions of the Cotton Belt states where the music is commonly called "Sacred Harp" or "Southern Harmony."[6]

The extent to which the four-note system was utilized in south central Kentucky will never be known. No formal records exist to indicate the degree of acceptance of four-note music, and time has taken its toll of personal recollections about this music genre. A few people recall that it did at one time exist in the study area, however. Bobby Sears told of a "family named Phelps that moved to Pulaski County from extreme western Kentucky into the Bent community in the mid-1800s. They were all members of the New Hope Baptist Church," Sears said. "There were a father and mother and several sons. All of the boys were fa, so, la, fa, so, la, mi singers. The most noted of the bunch was Obediah Phelps. A lot of the old people around here remember Ob, as they called him. He had a strong singing voice. A man I'm a little bit of kin to says he remembers hearing Uncle Ob's singing a mile away each morning. And my granddaddy, John Wesley Sears, lived a mile away on the other side. And he could hear Ob, too! That was shortly after 1900."

Glen Roy of western Pulaski County recalled that the Cumberland Quartet, which he described as the first in his memory, "sang on a different cleft from the way today's songs are written. It was not seven-note; not round note either." This may have been a local Sacred Harp quartet.

Lucinda Simpson, pioneer resident of Wayne County, mentioned in her memoirs what may have been a four-note singing school there. Born in Virginia in 1791, she was brought to Kentucky at the age of six months. In later years she wrote, "About the year 1812, Philip Denham taught the first singing school ever taught in this county, and I learned to be a splendid singer, in which I took great delight."[7] The Rev. A.B. Wright, a Methodist circuit-riding minister from adjacent Fentress County, Tennessee, wrote in his diary, "In the winter of 1848, I taught a singing school on Cumberland Mountain, eight miles southeast of Jamestown,"[8] but he did not specify what type of music school he taught.

Everett Jewell Butrum, accomplished pianist for the John Daniel Quartet and other early professional quartets, told me that his grandfather, Hewlett Butrum, taught both Sacred Harp music and the seven-note variety in the 1880s and early 1890s in Macon County, Tennessee. His teaching duties often took him across the state line into Allen and Monroe counties, Kentucky. Hewlett's son L.E. Butrum, later a resident of the Allen-Barren area, could also teach the

four-note system. Although L.E. began teaching as early as
following attendance at music publisher James D. Vaughan
seven-note music school, he was never called on to teach Sacred Harp
music in area churches. Arlis O. Harmon told me that a music teacher
had a copy of *The Sacred Harp* with him at a 1909 music school in
Allen County. If Sacred Harp music was ever popular here, however, it
was swept away by the floodtide of interest in the seven notes that
inundated the region prior to World War I.

An expansion of the four-note system to seven was undertaken as
early as 1810 by Nathan Chapin and Joseph L. Dickerson in *The Musical Instructor.* The transition was not fully successful, however,
until Jesse B. Aiken revised the system in 1846. Aiken adopted three
new shapes—a pyramid-shaped triangle, a half-circle, and a cone—to
represent the notes do, re, and ti and to supplement the original four
shapes. The seven shapes that he devised gradually supplanted the
traditional four and remain unchanged to this day, despite intense
early competition from rival seven-note systems. By the late 1870s,
Aiken's shapes represented the only seven-note system in use, and
numerous songbook publishers sprang up to meet an increasing
demand for new books using his system.[9] Such books contained
compositions that the music teachers themselves wrote, a practice
that was to last into the 1960s.

Much of the South came under the influence of itinerant shape-
note teachers during the first three quarters of the nineteenth century, including some teachers from New England, but relatively few
of these music masters moved across south central Kentucky con-
ducting schools. An elderly Hart County woman, born in 1887,
recalled one such itinerant teacher who taught a music school there
as late as 1900. "This singing school teacher, who looked like the
fragments of hard times, came through the country," she recalled.
"He wanted to teach a school," she continued, "so he put up in Uncle
Joe Logsdon's cabin and carried on a singing school."[10]

Instead of being organized by traveling music teachers, most area
schools were taught by local persons. In addition to the early seven-
note schools taught in Allen and Monroe counties by Hewlett
Butrum, Harvey D. Hall of Clay County, Tennessee, also conducted
music schools in southern Monroe County before the turn of the
century. Hall's granddaughter wrote that he "taught music at local
schools and churches in Monroe County sometime between 1884
and 1890. His wife died in 1887 and about 1890 he left for Texas. He
told us years later when he visited us that he had taught music in

Music teacher C.E. Deweese illustrates the basic C scale for the seven shape-notes on the treble and bass clefs. *Photo by Dianne Watkins.*

northern Texas and in Arkansas in the rural areas around Little Rock."[11]

Several other turn-of-the-century instances of seven-note music schools in south central Kentucky should be mentioned. Professor Jim Riggs of Hart County taught a school at the Campground Methodist Church near Bonnieville in those early years. An extant group photograph of that class bears the inscription "c. 1898-1899." Another landmark music school was held along the banks of Fishing Creek, on the Casey-Pulaski border near the Bethelridge community. It was there, at the end of a singing school in 1900, that four Haste brothers, who were taught music by their neighbor, Mark DeBord, organized the now legendary Haste Family Quartet. A Logan County school was also conducted in 1900 at the Oak Grove Baptist Church by Watt Gilliam.[12] Elsewhere in the region, the Howard's Bottom Methodist Church in Cumberland County sponsored a singing school in 1902. It was taught by Dan Wray, a resident of Bow, a community still heralded for its excellent congregational singing.

A significant bit of information concerning the introduction of shape-note music instruction in the region was provided by Glen Roy, a third generation music teacher from the west Pulaski County community of Bernetta. Roy told me that his father, Bob Roy, his grandfather Tolbert Roy, and Sid Beasley, all of whom taught music schools at the time, "would get together at Grandfather's house and talk about nothing but religion and music." Roy said: "They argued the Book of Revelation and about the rudiments of music. And they put in full time arguing whether the chromatic scale was for human voices, or for instruments only. They were in the process of changing over from the minor scale back then that had a folk sound to it, when "la" was the key note. I've got a feeling that it was Vaughan's [shape-note] songbooks that were causing the debates between the ones that liked the old way of singing best and the ones that liked the new." [13]

These isolated examples of early shape-note instruction in south central Kentucky were harbingers of the rush of activity still to come. But singing schools by and large were not instituted in the region until around 1912 when the Vaughan Music Company began to send its representatives into the area to teach music schools and to peddle the company's seven-note songbooks, a practice that continued until the mid-1950s. The influence of the singing schools swept across the hills, hollows, and flatlands like a wild fire fanned by a strong wind, and seven-note instruction touched every rural church in the region during this period like nothing before or since. It was as though the millennium had come. People fell in love with the new music and zealously sought recognition for the quality of their congregation's singing through word of mouth testimony and in open competition at singing events.

During the zenith years of shape-note schools, the singing school teachers were just a notch below God in the eyes of local residents. They were respected, appreciated, and admired beyond all measure, both for the specialized nature of their own training and for the knowledge they were able to instill in people who sat spellbound night after night listening while they unraveled the various threads of this wonderful new music. Ivis Roy of Russell County remembered his music school days with considerable fondness. "I set my mind to be a gospel singer when I was ten years old," he said. "I'd walk two and a half to three miles to an old country church to study music under an old music director by the name of Sid Beasley."

In rural areas, where specialists were few and far between, it was only natural for local residents to view shape-note music teachers as very special persons and to accord them a hero-like status. In some

A singing school held in eastern Casey County, c. 1915. *Photo courtesy of Mrs. R.C. Weddle.*

instances, shape-note music tutors became legendary within the geographical area they served and are still described in larger-than-life terms to this day. Because these teachers moved freely across county boundaries to fill engagements, it was not at all uncommon for residents of two, three, or four counties to claim a certain teacher as a native son. For example, Warren, Allen, and Barren counties all claim L.E. Butrum; Sid Beasley is claimed by Russell, Casey, and Pulaski counties; and Frank Spencer is reputedly a native of McCreary, Wayne, Pulaski, and Russell counties.

Most recollections about these old-time music teachers include comments about their modes of transportation. Although later teachers traveled by automobile, earlier ones had to move about on foot or on horseback. Lewis H. Gilpin recalled that, as a young lad in the Breeding section of Adair County, he always watched breathlessly as a local singing school master rode by on a handsome white stallion. "I thought that that was the finest horse I had ever seen," Gilpin reminisced. "Brother Grimsley looked like a king passing by on that horse."

Some people remembered the teachers boarding in area homes while the singing schools were in session. Woodrow Wilson of Jabez, a Russell County community now isolated from the county seat by the waters of Lake Cumberland, recalled an early singing master who always stayed in the Wilson home: "I remember as a child seeing William Rexroat [of Parnell, Wayne County] walking up the road here with his music chart rolled up under his arm. I remember that just as well as anything. He'd stop here at the house and leave his music chart here. He'd stay with us. Rexroat was the first music teacher ever to come into this country."

The teaching methods employed by the music teachers were also a topic of fond remembrance among the persons interviewed. Standing tall in front of the students, and typically with wooden pointer in hand, the music master began each school by stressing that the foundation of all music is the diatonic scale, or ladder, and that it is made up of eight syllables—do, re, mi, fa, so, la, ti, do.[14] Most of the students had a real desire to learn to sing. Garnet Cassaday of Allen County recalled that even in the early stages of a school, the children lined up and sang the notes of the scale with keen interest. "The teacher would go over them every night with the kids for the first four or five nights. They would just eat that up. They learned the do, re, mis, and sang them until they wore a rut in their voices."

The next area of instruction involved measures, which most teachers referred to as timing. Students were called upon to learn how long and to hold each note, and what was meant by the dots, double dots and other markings they might encounter. In the final stages of the ten- or twelve-day singing school, the teachers introduced students to relative and absolute pitch for each note, and to the concept of sharps, flats, and naturals.

Teachers often employed mnemonic devices to help pupils learn the sharps and flats. Students were told that one sharp signified the key of G, two sharps stood for D, three for A, four for E, five for B, and six sharps designated the F key. Albert and Leonard Norris of Cumberland County favored the following memory prompt in teaching the sharps: "**G**o **D**own **A**nd **E**at **B**reakfast **F**irst." J.W. London of the Savoyard community in Metcalfe County preferred "**G**o **D**own **A**nd **E**at **B**ugs **F**reely," while C.E. Deweese suggested the biblical theme "**G**od **D**estroyed **A**ll **E**arth **B**y **F**lood."

In teaching the flats, the Norris brothers and London alike jokingly employed this catchy statement: **F**at **B**oys **E**at **A**pple **D**ump-

This music school was held at Mt. Lebanon Church in Allen County, c. 1915. *Photo courtesy of Jesse Young.*

lings **G**reedily. Again, sticking to a more serious approach, Deweese preferred the words **F**or **B**eing **E**vil **A**nd **D**isobeying **G**od.

Recollections of these singing masters also include humorous anecdotes. The following apocryphal story about L.E. Butrum told by Noble Stuart of Bowling Green illustrates the humorous side of these task masters while stressing the qualities that their students were expected to demonstrate:

L.E. Butrum was teaching this singing school over in Logan County. And there were people there who would just sit and listen but not partake of the school itself. L.E. was strong at that time! And Buddy don't you forget it!

So he was practicing this group. And there was a pause in the song for a couple of beats. Nothing. Not a sound was to be made. And they's not using music yet. He was trying to beat that time into them so they could learn to do it.

So they was going along here, singing. And then they's suppose to cut it off; hold it, and then go again.

Well, these two old women were sitting back there visiting. And everybody was singing loud, you know. Of course these two had to be talking a little bit loud [to hear each other over the singers' voices]. And when Butrum cut the singing off at the pause, one of the women was saying to the other [in a high-pitched voice], "I always fry mine in lard."

Ernest McKinley of the Eli community in Russell County recalled with considerable nostalgia the manner in which his teacher-grandfather assisted him as a youngster in learning to sing by the shapes of the notes and, in the same breath, told how he and his sister sang with the old fellow in his final moments of life:

My grandfather, C.L. McKinley, was an old music teacher. When I was just a little boy, I'd try to sing bass. And I don't reckon my voice ever changed. Back then, they'd set the bass singers back on the back seat of the choir. And he'd be up in front directing the choir.

He had a big long, white beard that reached way down to his belt. And I could tell just as well as anything if I'd missed a note. He'd start walking backwards and singing until he was standing beside me. Then, when we'd come to my part, he'd get the bass part and sing it. Then he'd look at me and I could see him smile through his whiskers. And he'd stroke his beard, and on back up front he'd go.

And then for my benefit, the next day at his repair shop, when I'd be playing around and in his way while he was working, he'd be a-singing that song for me. And I'd be listening.

And the saddest thing, he passed away right there [points to the spot] in this room. And just before he died, he told me to go across the road and get my sister. He wanted to sing. And he died with me and him and my sister a-singing together. Just a minute after we finished singing, he was gone.

During the advanced sessions of each music school, when the emphasis was on actual singing, teachers stressed the correct articulation of words. Eva Strode Spear, now of the Jubilee Singers but then of the Strode Family Quartet, illustrated the importance of proper enunciation with the following story involving J.T. Light of Glasgow, who was both a music teacher and a quartet singer for many years:

I never will forget one thing that J.T. taught us. He came to one of our singings one night and after it was over he asked me if it would make me mad to tell me something. And I said "No."

And he said, "I want to tell the Strode Family that there's not a 'me chew' in a song anywhere."

And that always stayed with me. When I hear somebody sing a song and they say "me chew" instead of "meet you," that's the first thing I notice.

Virtually all persons interviewed agreed that the real purpose of singing schools was to improve the quality of congregational singing. Garnet Cassaday observed that "churches held singing schools so that members of the congregation could learn the new songs. They'd pick out all the good songs," he continued, "and teach them to people." Hazel Bryson claimed that an essential component of the singing schools of her childhood years in Simpson County was to train church members to become congregational song leaders. Jeff McKinney of Logan County supported Bryson's position, stating flatly that "the purpose of singing schools was to teach teachers," who could then lead congregational singing after the schools were over and the teacher had departed the scene. The importance of a well-trained leader and church choir in earlier times was always apparent during the pastor's invitation following the sermon. At that point, the choir assembled in the altar area to sing while worshipers made their responses to the sermon. That was neither the time nor the place for mistakes by the singers.

Some churches in the early years of the twentieth century sponsored as many as two or three singing schools each year, but most were content with only one. These schools were typically held in churches or schoolhouses in early spring before planting time, during the summer when the crops were laid by, or in late fall when the farm families had extra time. The teacher was generally selected from the pool of teachers in the county, or from nearby communities in adjacent counties. It was not uncommon for some of the better teachers to serve a three- or four-county area. The selection process was made largely on the basis of teacher availability, proximity, and prior record of success.

After the local congregation had made its decisions regarding which teacher to invite, how much money he would be paid, how long the school would last, and how best to prepare for the school, word was spread from the pulpit and by word of mouth throughout the community and into adjoining areas. In later years, notices were published in local newspapers and aired over radio stations. The publicity was intended to attract a large attendance beyond the boundaries of the congregation, including members of other denominations, who were welcome to take part in the classes. Attendance at a singing school usually began to decline after the first few days. On the first day, some people in the community attended, whether or not they wanted to sing. They went to see the teacher, visit with their friends, and demonstrate community spirit. Only the most interested persons attended every night, however. Chester Whitescarver of Logan County, who taught music schools there in the 1940s and 1950s, estimated that an average of thirty-five to forty people of all ages attended the first few sessions. Rarely, however, did more than twenty people attend the full two weeks.

The final evening of the school was devoted to group singing before a community-wide audience. That was the night for the proud students to show off their abilities to sing by the shapes of the notes without the aid of an instrument or another voice to lead them. Often the music teacher formed a "scrap iron quartet" (a frequently employed affectionate term that was sure to bring chuckles from the other singers) on the spot by choosing a soprano, alto, tenor, and bass. Their performance provided a grand finale to the school, and these handpicked individuals knew they were on the spot. They were expected to sing in near-perfect harmony, time, and pitch. Many quartets formed in this manner became official foursomes, offering their services to area churches.

Because singing schools were rooted in conversion-centered religion, many people attended them fully expecting an emotional experience while learning to sight-read music or reviewing skills learned previously. The teacher determined the extent to which religion entered into a singing school. Some chose not to use prayer at all in their sessions, but those were an extreme minority. Folklorist Drew Beisswenger writes that "a teacher who did not occasionally bring religious messages into his sessions would no doubt cause skepticism among some church members as to his religious sincerity." Locally born C.E. Deweese, who was for years a teacher on the faculty of the Vaughan School of Music, noted that Vaughan himself was much in tune with the personal spiritual needs often manifested at a singing school. He always instructed his teachers to "take time for someone to be saved at a singing," Deweese recalled and then added, "We'd lay the singing aside and pray with them."

Professor Jim Riggs of Hart County looked upon his teaching as a service to God. "Instead of preaching, he was teaching; to him, this was a religious calling," according to Riggs's grandson, Hartsell Hodges of Columbia, who taught music schools himself in the Lake Cumberland area in the 1940s and 1950s. "I've seen my grandfather Riggs be teaching and all of a sudden he'd quit. He was full emotionally. He'd stop teaching or singing and rejoice a little bit. And everybody'd shake hands and the like."

Opening and closing music schools with prayer was a standard part of the singing school tradition. After the initial prayer, a member of the local congregation typically gave a ten or fifteen minute Bible-based devotional. Many teachers tried to prevent this worship period from consuming an undue amount of time. They did, however, allow the devotional to continue if the Spirit seemed to be present. When that happened, the seasoned veterans extended the length of the evening's music lesson to compensate for time spent in this matter.

While applause was not encouraged by the teachers, shouting during the song sessions was a positive sign that the Holy Spirit was using the singing school as a channel for reaching those present. Thus, the opening prayers, devotions, personal testimonies, exclamatory words of affirmation (such as "Amen" and "Praise God"), and episodes of shouting, were all viewed as positive means by which people could express emotional, heartfelt religion.

Besides providing musical education and meeting religious needs, singing schools gave rural people and small town residents a chance to come together for companionship and fellowship. The need to socialize was crucial and often prompted people to travel great distances to attend each session. Andrew Jackson Adams, born in western Pulaski County in 1857, serves to illustrate this aspect of singing schools. As a fiddle player who was well versed in shape-note music, Adams never missed a chance to learn new songs and to attend singing schools. "When he'd get a new shape-note hymnal," recalled his son, Lewis, "he'd lock himself in a room and play the new songs on his fiddle in order to learn them. He could really read the notes. You couldn't keep my dad away from any singing school that was within twenty miles. He'd get on the old black mare and go. And most of the time, I'd get on behind him and go with him."

Singing schools acted as social magnets in drawing young people together. In the words of Woodrow Wilson, "people wanted some place to go. It wasn't like it is today when you can jump in your car and go to town every day. Didn't have no way to go unless you rode on a horse, went in a wagon, or on foot. Back in them days around here, when something started at the church—singing or revival—people went. Wanted somewhere to go. Wanted to meet people."

Virgil Ware, legendary teacher from eastern Casey County from 1914 to 1920, taught an annual singing class at the Rich Hill Church near his home. These events were anticipated with excitement and enthusiasm. "It was customary," writes Mrs. R.C. Weddle, "for people to walk for miles to hear good singing, participate in clean fellowship, and give the fellows a chance to walk the girls home." [15]

Some of the men who went to the singing schools chose to remain outside the building. They generally listened to the proceedings through an open window or door. Typically, these people were not troublemakers, although they did become loud and boisterous on occasion, and fights sometimes occurred. When altercations took place, they almost invariably involved two fellows who were waiting for the same girl to emerge from the night's music session, hoping to escort her home.

All the people I interviewed agreed that the shape-note singing phenomenon was at its height from 1915 until the early 1940s. This important socioreligious activity began to decline rapidly by the late 1940s and virtually vanished in the 1950s. Its demise cannot be blamed on any one factor, however. Indeed, the change in gospel music tastes in south central Kentucky was a composite of many forces ranging from the simple to the complex. Garnet Cassaday claimed that interest in gospel singing declined irretrievably "when all of this other kind of music [rock and roll] come around and attracted the attention of young people." Lewis Adams likewise blamed the demise of shape-note music on the fact that the younger generation of the postwar years had a broader range of activities to occupy their time. With specific emphasis on the singing school, Adams offered the following commentary:

Interest in singing schools began to decline in the 1940s. The younger generation had something else to do. Too many [picture] shows. And television was the worst thing, later on, that tore things up. The younger people just wouldn't get interested in singing. Too many other things to occupy their time.

Transportation got to be too good and too fast and too quick. Too many places for younger people to go besides singings. That's when the singings and even the churches started going down—the country churches.

I really quit teaching because I got older and there just wasn't too much interest in singing. I went out to teach a school at the Old Cuba Church out beyond Eubank. There used to be the biggest crowds there ever was. Had an excellent singing teacher there by the name of Jim Mercer.

That's when I quit, for when I got there, there was only one real old woman there; couldn't hardly walk, and a younger woman and two men. That's all I had to start the singing school. Well, I didn't start. That kind of got me. That was in the early 1970s.[16]

Curtis Wilson of Columbia, one of the region's finest tenor singers, and Earlis Austin, old-time music school teacher and quartet singer from Scottsville, both felt that the demise of singing schools was likely due to the introduction of music instruction in the public schools. In a similar vein, Doyle and Reva Rexroat, members of the Twilight Singers of Russell Springs and proponents of shape-note music as well, observed that too many activities at school have taken away children's interests in learning the seven-note system.[17] They also noted that two annual revivals at their home church have taken the place of singing schools. "You can tell it in our singing," Reva commented. "These young kids aren't learning to sing now."

Brodus Tabor and Hartsell Hodges, quartet singers from Bowling Green and Columbia, both felt that shape-note singing schools died out when gospel quartets came onto the scene and replaced class singing. It became more difficult to get choir members together to practice on a regular basis. Forrest Rexroat of Russell Springs echoed their sentiments. "I like good quartet singing," he commented, "but usually the four best singers in a church are in a quartet. And when they go to going everywhere to sing and stop attending church, they've messed up the singing at home." Frank Weaver of the Bowling Green-based Southern Harmony Quartet continued that line of thought. "You can take the best singer out of each part in the choir and maybe they won't have good quartet harmony and won't stay together," he observed, "but you've hurt the choir in the process."

When the quality of a church's singing declines, the overall quality and success of the church as a whole suffer. If singing school teachers are to be credited with a single important contribution, it was in helping to keep the quality of music high in rural and small town churches. They strengthened these venerated institutions like nothing before or since.[18]

Singing schools were products of the final years of the period when area residents looked inward for the means to sustain life and culture. That period in south central Kentucky began in the shadow of the eighteenth century when there were no automobiles and no roads on which to drive them. Travel was still by horseback, in horse-drawn conveyances, or on foot. The shape-note singing era declined drastically in the late 1930s when automobiles and battery-powered radio sets found their way into virtually every rural household. Area

Above: Curtis Wilson and his young music students pose in Russell Springs in the 1940s. *Photo courtesy of Curtis Wilson.* Below: A few churches still sponsor shape-note schools. McNeal VanMeter taught this one at Otter Gap in Edmonson County in 1987. *Photo by the author.*

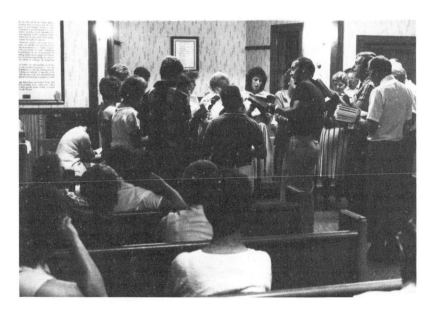

residents no longer needed singing schools and family gatherings by the fireside as social and creative outlets. They could now look beyond their families and the local community for ways to meet their needs.

In retrospect, singing schools may be viewed as important social events that took advantage of an existing institution—the church. The schools simply elaborated on the religious aspects of church and community life. The fact that the music was religious in nature made socialization at church a wholesome activity. It was perfectly acceptable by community standards for young people to go to singing schools and see each other on the side. Anything that was church related was all right. As an arm of the church, the singing school functioned as a powerful influence in shaping local culture.

Postwar technology must assume its share of the blame in turning people's attention away from shape-note singing schools. Yet, ironically, it was this venerated musical institution's own offshoot that triggered the decline and ultimate demise of shape-note music. Here I refer to the local singing conventions and the quartet movement, both of which came into their own as concomitants of shape-note instruction and people's love for this music. County singing conventions remained strong through the 1940s and well into the 1950s, at which time they became performance-oriented and were themselves subsumed by the gospel quartet movement, which thrives on performance. The historical roots and widespread popularity of singing conventions, along with the decline of their own vitality, will be examined in chapter 2. Quartet groups will be described and analyzed in subsequent chapters.

2

THE SINGING
CONVENTION
MOVEMENT

Shape-note singing schools conducted during the first four decades of the twentieth century were directly responsible for significant improvement in the quality of congregational singing across south central Kentucky, both in the small-town churches and the sister institutions that dotted the adjacent rural landscape. There were three direct descendants of those golden years of four-part harmony, all of which were introduced as concomitants of congregational singing. The first of these was church choir performances called "singings," held in area churches and rotated regularly among participating congregations. The second natural offspring of the singing schools was the county-wide singing conventions that originated beginning in 1912. The third descendant of singing schools was the amateur quartet movement, a phenomenon that did and still continues to do more to unify rural Protestantism in the study area than any other single ecumenical force. Quartet singing, in its infancy from 1900 to 1940, grew to a magnificent maturity by the late 1950s. Soon after, local quartet music was influenced by media-disseminated gospel music that took it far from its singing school roots.

Shape-note based congregational singing, church choir singings, and singing conventions will be described in this chapter. Because quartet music in its present form and style continues to serve widespread worship needs in area churches, its history, characteristics, and contemporary performance aspects will be dealt with in the remaining chapters.

Folklorist David Stanley writes that the proliferation of singing schools in south Georgia "seems to have led directly to the founding of singing conventions as public events for the performance of singing classes."[1] The same can be said of the influence of shape-note instruction in south central Kentucky on area singing conventions. There was an intermediate stage in Kentucky, however, not mentioned by Stanley, which local people referred to simply as "singings."[2]

Local singings, perhaps descended from eighteenth-century New England singing societies,[3] were held in many area churches on Sunday afternoons or evenings one or more times each year. Such singings generally assumed the form of all-day events, interrupted only by "dinner on the ground" at noon. While these relatively informal events were firmly rooted in evangelical religion, their major purpose was to provide people with the opportunity to sing and to socialize. There was an opening and closing prayer, but no sermons. Perhaps an absence of the sermon explains why visitors from other denominations were invariably present and felt comfortable in neighboring houses of worship. Garnet Cassaday recalled that, in the late 1930s, the Allen County community of Settle had four churches that rotated Sunday night singings to ensure a regular weekly gathering that several hundred area residents could attend. And Noble Stuart said that all of the Methodist churches on the same circuit in Logan County rotated Sunday afternoon singings in the 1920s and 1930s. "We'd sing until milking time," Stuart recalled. The church pews were typically packed a full hour in advance of the singings. Children sat on window sills and on the floor. Due to the popularity of these events and the limited space available, especially in rural churches, the number of people outside often exceeded the number of those inside the church.

Overflow crowds at church singings were, in fact, the rule rather than the exception from the early 1920s to the 1950s. Singings were held at the Grace Union Baptist Church in Metcalfe County every Sunday night for five or six years in the late 1940s and early 1950s. People came from miles around in such numbers that it was often necessary to set up a public address system to accommodate those forced by seating limitations to remain in the church yard. Although a different guest quartet, generally non-professional, was featured each Sunday evening, the bulk of the program was devoted to congregational singing and choir specials that were selected from shape-note songbooks. The emphasis on congregational participation during those years was evident in an announcement carried on the pages of the *Green County Record* on February 1, 1927. The notice read: "Singing at Bethlehem every Sunday night. The public is welcome to come and bring songbooks."

Pulaski Countians were likewise excited and challenged by the presence of new songsters. "Back then before singing conventions came along, we'd have a week's meetings of nothing but singing," recalled Glen Roy of the Bernetta community. "When a new songbook would come out in February, we'd all get together here and practice that new book," he went on. "Every night, people'd come from 20 to 30 churches. All of them were shape-note readers. We'd sing for two to three hours. The house would be full to running over."

New songbooks were in evidence everywhere at such events. People talked incessantly about the new compositions as they tried to guess which titles would be chosen for the evening by the various song leaders. As would be the case with the county singing conventions, the major attraction at these singings was, according to Stanley, "the challenging opportunity to sight-read and sing a large number of new gospel songs printed in small paperback songbooks published annually or semiannually by about a dozen music companies specializing in gospel music, ranging from small family-owned businesses to the two giants, James D. Vaughan of Cleveland, Tennessee, and Stamps-Baxter Music of Dallas."[4] All songs were written to be sung in shape-notes and in four-part harmony.

In early years, the physical positioning of the singers was of utmost importance. They often stood in a circle in the open space between the front pew and the pulpit (the altar area). Like the Union Light singers described in chapter 1, they were grouped in the circle according to their vocal parts. Singers assembled in vocal groupings even in churches where they remained seated. Leaders and singers were extremely proud of their musical expertise. "Choir leaders liked songs with alto leads and bass leads," reminisced Noble Stuart. "The choirs could really get with such songs as 'Give the World a Smile Each Day.' If you could sing those difficult songs, you've kinda 'showed out' a little," Stuart went on. "To the singers, that meant the difference in walking and running." So, too, with their leaders.

Some music masters in southern Kentucky pursued their teaching and singing interests for a lifetime, not so much for the money as for the sheer love of gospel music and the opportunity to mingle with others who shared their fondness for four-part singing. Archie Hume, song leader, singing school teacher, and hillcountry farmer from the Ebenezer community near Tompkinsville, provides an excellent case in point. Born July 21, 1892, to tenant farmer parents, Hume acquired a keen interest in gospel music and song at an early age. He told on numerous occasions how, as a boy, he was required to sit in the back of the church during a singing school because he was unable to pay the seventy-five cent tuition charged by the teacher. It was then he vowed that, given the same situation, he would never charge any person who was unable to pay. He never did.

In June 1912, he led congregational singing at Ebenezer, in what was to mark the beginning of one of the most illustrious music careers in south central Kentucky—a career that would span fifty-one years and touch the lives of countless people in the process. I personally remember Archie Hume from my childhood years at the Skaggs Creek Baptist Church in northern Monroe County. He was a large, dark-skinned man with a round face and bald head. He wore his eyeglasses on top of his head when they were not in use. I recall vividly how he would twist his face while teaching, causing the glasses to slip down from his sweat-beaded forehead onto his nose, perfectly in place and ready for immediate use.

Beginning in 1948, Hume kept a diary of his singing and teaching activities, a practice that he continued until his death on December 14, 1963. Zilpha, his widow, shared his diaries with me in August 1989. These historically valuable documents revealed that when he was not teaching a music school, Hume was engaged in a singing somewhere in northern Tennessee or southern Kentucky every week-end, often on both Saturday and Sunday. The entries for August 1952 illustrate the typical extent of his singing activities during any given month: August 3, "Singing at Plum Point [Metcalfe County]"; August 10, "Singing at Mosbys Ridge [Metcalfe County]"; August 17, "Singing at Oak Forest in Green County"; August 24, "Singing at Wells Chapel [Metcalfe County]"; August 30, 31, "Singing at Gladeville Tenn. Sat. and Sun."

Hume's singings were all-day affairs, replete with dinners on the ground. All denominations were welcome and usually present at these events, and song leaders from different churches took turns leading congregational singing. For his labors, Hume usually received a "free-will" love offering, plus the income derived from the sale of songbooks, usually those published by Vaughan and by Winsett. According to Mrs. Hume, he felt called by God to do this type of work and often cried when he had to miss an engagement due to sickness. His last singing was scheduled for late December 1963 at a church near Columbia. Death struck him down before he could fulfill the appointment.

Closely akin to these church singings led by Hume and a host of other area singing masters were county-wide shape-note singing conventions that developed across south central Kentucky in the early years of the twentieth century.[5] County singing conventions were

This singing school was led by Archie Hume in Ebenezer in Monroe County in the 1930s. *Photo by Zilpha Hume.*

much like regular singings except that they covered larger geographical areas and were almost always scheduled at regular intervals. Some of them met biweekly, others monthly, and a few convened on an annual basis only. Sharon S. Lawrence points out that "these were county-wide events that were sponsored by shape-note advocates but there was no teaching of the shapes during the convention."[6] Sight-reading skills had already been acquired. The early county conventions were thus public events that came into being to show off the abilities of church choirs and singing classes. This was the case in south central Kentucky by the 1940s, when some of the counties here boasted of the largest, most vigorous conventions in the South.

Singing conventions were and still are, first and foremost, religious events. The themes and lyrics of the songs are always religious in nature. During the heyday of congregational singing it was not uncommon for song leaders to comment on the words to the songs. It is a rare singing event even today that does not include personal testimonials by two or three singers about God's blessings on them during the past week. They often explain why the song is important to them and admonish those in the congregation to "listen to the words of the song."

It would be difficult to overestimate how central the county singing conventions were to virtually every aspect of gospel music, especially before the 1950s. Most singing school teachers, songbook publishers, and professional quartets, not to mention the local choirs and quartets, used these conventions as readily available and accessible platforms from which to promote or present their products, schools, and skills to interested individuals and church congregations.

The music companies were the dominant forces at the conventions. These companies sent representatives to the local conventions to mix and mingle with the song leaders and singers. Representatives often included a company quartet that had one or more locals in the ensemble. For instance, the original Vaughan Kentucky Quartet (1936-38), composed of C.E. Deweese, Billy Carrier, Herman Luttrell and Jesse Gilbert, all Edmonson Countians, carried the Vaughan banner into numerous counties in southern Kentucky and northern Tennessee. The group moved to Knoxville in 1938, where they continued to sing as the Vaughan Four through 1941, although Stacy Abner of Tennessee had replaced Gilbert by then.

Allen, Simpson, and Logan counties, located along the western edge of the region, appear to have been the first area counties to organize county-wide singing conventions—in 1912, 1914, and 1918, respectively. Allen County has been a bastion of four-part harmony singing from earliest times to the present day. A large singing class organized about 1911 by Dr. Andrew J. Dixon and led by Warner D. Holloway indicates that the popularity of gospel singing here dates from around the turn of the century. It was at the Beech Grove Baptist Church that Dr. Dixon, a country physician, formed the Pioneer Singing Class, consisting of about eighty singers, an ensemble described by composer Arlis O. Harmon as the "best trained group of singers that Allen County has ever had."

On Thanksgiving Day 1914, the Pioneer Singing Class went to the Chapel Hill Modern Woodmen Hall to sing in concert. It is reported that there were not enough hitching trees in a three-acre lot to accommodate the horse-drawn conveyances present. The large hall quickly filled up, leaving a large number of people outside the building. In September 1915, the increasingly popular Pioneer Class sang to an overflow crowd at the Simpson County fairgrounds in Franklin.

Thanks to the instant popularity of the Pioneer group in particular, and of singing schools and church singings in general, the Allen County Singing Convention was founded on the second Sunday in October 1912. James D. Vaughan, founder of the Vaughan School of Music and Vaughan Publishing Company, was present in Scottsville that day, along with such local teaching notables as L.E. Butrum, W.T. Steenberger, Daily C. Gaines, Abraham B. Willoughby, Virgil McGuire, and Charlie Lamb. A Mr. Taylor was selected as the convention's first president.

Although those early Allen County conventions consisted largely of church choirs, two local quartets were soon a familiar part of the convention scene. The West Allen Quartet and the Beech Grove Ladies Quartet were both formed about 1912 out of the Pioneer Singing Class. While these quartets were both present for the Allen County convention in May 1914, that event was still very much in the hands of the visiting church choirs and area song leaders. Present at the convention that year were J.W. Gaines of the Gaines Music Company, Mac D. Weems and Joe M. Allen of the Vaughan Music Company, and a score of choir directors and hundreds of singers from Allen and adjoining counties. One person who attended the convention penned the words, "My how they sang the song 'Away to the Harvest Field,' by S.W. Beasley. The hundreds or more voices led by Vernon Conner made this a red letter day and a great song feast never to be forgotten."[7]

The West Allen and Beech Grove Ladies quartets notwithstanding, quartets were generally not present at these early Allen County conventions. The same was also true of other area conventions. In the words of Garnet Cassaday, one of the best-remembered early quartet singers, "There was no place for quartets. It was song leaders that got all of the attention. Back then, the president would call for so-and-so and his choir to come up." And Buell Gibbs of Holland, who at present sings with the Kentuckians, recalled that in early times, "Everybody sang with everybody else, led by a song leader, who was a really big cheese if he was good."

A boost to local gospel music like nothing before or since took place at the turn of the century with the construction of a building in Scottsville known as the Tabernacle.[8] The May and September singings at the Tabernacle throughout the late 1910s, 1920s, and 1930s attracted the largest crowds of any public events in Allen County. "The choir loft was filled with singers," Gibbs recalled. "They'd raise the roof off. Anyone was welcome to sing in the choir."

By the mid-1930s, as many as six thousand people attended each

People in attendance at the formation of the Allen County Singing Convention in 1912. James D. Vaughan is in the center, wearing the white vest. *Photo courtesy of E.D. Austin.*

Allen County convention. More than that were present at each Tabernacle singing until the late 1940s. Even the monthly singing conventions held around the county in local churches continued to attract more people than their sanctuaries could accommodate. In light of such intense interest in gospel singing, it is little wonder that Vaughan's *Family Visitor* was mailed to more subscribers in Allen County than in any other county in the entire South, according to C.E. Deweese, who taught for Vaughan in the late 1940s and 1950s.

Little is known about the early years of the Simpson County convention. Records were not kept or have been lost. From all indications, however, it was formed about 1914, blossomed between 1925 and 1940 under the leadership of Cager Gammon, J.B. Howser, J.C. Haliburton, and Tom Patterson, and reached its apex in the early 1950s. By the late 1950s, however, public interest and support had declined measurably. The Simpson County convention languished through the 1960s, then ceased entirely about 1970. In 1986, Kendall Bush, president of the convention and singer with a new quartet called Greater Desire, led an effort to revive the convention. In Bush's words, "The purpose of the new convention will be to better educate people as to what gospel music really is; that it is an art form; that there is a ministry in it." By mid-1990, however, Bush's efforts had yet to garner adequate public support to revive the Simpson County Convention.

Few counties in the South can boast of as rich a gospel singing legacy as that enjoyed by Logan Countians. In 1947, during the zenith years of local singing conventions, a feature article appeared in the Logan County *News-Democrat* summarizing the early years of that county's singing convention. The article states, in part:

Singings first came into prominence in Logan around 1898 and were held at the different churches, each church being host in turn. The very first meeting, as W.B. Smotherman remembers, was at Mt. Pleasant Church near Lewisburg. Another church prominent in singings was Bethel near Oak Grove. It was at this church, according to Mr. Smotherman, where the floor gave way under the weight of such a crowd, at which time the leader with great presents [sic] of mind invited the audience to finish the singing in the grove.

The hymns were lined and tuning forks were used instead of musical instruments.

As the crowds attending these musical gatherings became larger, the county court issued an invitation to the groups to meet at the court-house, about 1920 or probably a few years earlier.

Curtis Savage, formerly of north Logan County, claims that the Logan County Convention began in 1918 or 1919 at Epley's Station as a result of the huge crowds that met there for all-day singings and dinners on the ground. The majority of the singers were Methodists, Savage said, but there were others present from the Presbyterian and Baptist churches as well.

The Epley's Station singings consisted primarily of church class singing, congregational singing, and quartet music by such locally famous groups as the Campbells, Smothermans, Stuarts, and McKin-neys. By the early 1920s, the Logan County Singing Convention was a semiannual event held on the first Sundays in June and October. Dad Speer, founder of the famous Speer Family Quartet, attended the 1923 Logan convention and led the congregation in two songs. Some say that this was his first public appearance as a gospel performer.

A Logan County tradition began about 1931, thanks to the Citizens National Bank of Russellville, of awarding a silver loving cup to the church choir judged to be the best at the convention. The winning church displayed the cup proudly in its sanctuary until another church claimed ownership. The cup went to Stuart's Chapel Methodist Church the first two years and then passed back and forth among Deer Lick Church, Elk Lick Baptist Church, Stuart's Chapel, Bethel Presbyterian Church, and Wiley's Chapel Methodist Church. It was last won in 1967 by Wiley's Chapel, where it is still proudly kept as a sacred trust.

In the late 1930s, changes began to occur in the Logan County Singing Convention. The size of the crowds increased dramatically. In 1939, a newspaper reporter was surprised to find that hundreds of people had filled the courtroom to capacity on Sunday morning well before the first number was sung. Two years later, the newspaper estimated a crowd of eight thousand had gathered, mostly on the courthouse lawn, to listen to the singing over the newly installed public address system. The most influential development during this period, however, was the movement to highlight well-known family quartets from Logan County, most of which had received training at the Vaughan School of Music. Featuring local quartets was a means of generating greater public interest in gospel music in general and singing conventions in particular.

The late 1940s represent the apex of interest in the Logan County Singing Convention, but the interest was generally passive, not active. Although choirs continued to compete for the cup, and congregational and local quartet singing did occur, people mainly came to hear out-of-state big-name quartets such as Wally Fowler and the Oak Ridge Quartet, the Frank Stamps Quartet, and the John Daniel Quartet. The lessening emphasis on church choirs and congregational singing was a portent of a radical decline in public interest and attendance that was soon to plague local conventions across the region.

In 1953, attendance at the semiannual convention in Logan County was still in the hundreds. And on the first Sunday in June 1954, the all-day singing was held in the courthouse, with Roy Shoemaker in charge. "The courthouse was crowded with singers and lovers of gospel singing," wrote C.E. Deweese in *Vaughan's Family Visitor.*[9] "Several quartets were there, a trio of girls [Stuart Sisters Trio], and a lot of directors." By 1956, however, the crowds had diminished to the point that the local newspaper carried a front page article suggesting that the poorly attended event "be kept alive as one of the pleasant happenings of yesteryear." Conventions in Logan County continue to meet monthly, alternating from rural church to rural church, and they show no clear sign of either declining or growing. Some gospel music enthusiasts boast of never missing one. But their numbers are slim.[10]

Singing institutions similar to the Allen, Simpson, and Logan conventions were organized in the 1920s in Russell, Pulaski, Warren, Butler, Edmonson, Monroe and Barren counties. Russell County was the first of this group to bring its singers together on a regular basis. Credit for the convention there belongs to M.F. Upton, who had recently returned from Texas to his native Russell County. Upton, with the assistance of the other convention officers, Claude Harmon, Richard Blair, and W.H. Hopper, organized the event, and singers from across the county assembled at the Russell Springs Methodist Church in May 1923.

Because of an overflow crowd in 1924, the Russell County Convention was moved to the county fairgrounds in 1925. It was then moved to Jamestown about 1928 to take advantage of the facilities jointly offered by the courthouse and the Baptist, Nazarene, Methodist, and Christian churches located adjacent to the public square.

During the 1930s, the crowds increased in size to between five and six thousand at the annual August singings, a situation that continued until the 1940s. Ernest McKinley, who served as the convention's president from 1960 to 1988, recalled some of the early singings:

I remember that the Coffey's Chapel class sang at the 1924 convention. We sang, "I Will Sail Up High Someday," out of a Vaughan songbook.

Back then, there were no refrigerators. Merchants would bring their half barrels of ice and soft drinks and kegs of ice cream out on the sidewalk. This was three or four years after the singing convention first started.

I was there singing; just a little bitty fellow. We'd sing here at the Methodist Church, and we'd go out the back door and we'd start running to the Baptist Church. We'd go in at the back door and the other group would go out the front. We'd get up and sing our same two songs. We'd leave there and go down to the Nazarene; sing two songs then march over to the Christian Church and sing two and back to the courthouse and sing two. And then back to the Methodist with two new songs, and start again. Every building was packed to its capacity, and they were standing down the aisles. You couldn't hardly walk through the courthouse square. I'd hear people say, "Scoot over, get out of the way, here comes the singers."

Road wagons and what few trucks there were would bring in loads of people. And you've never seen such a crowd of people in all your life. But they estimated between five and six thousand people in attendance. And that's the way it was up to World War II. We cut it out for two years during the War—1944 and 1945. After the war we resumed, but it hasn't been the same since.

It is reported that the 1940 singing convention in Jamestown was the largest on record at that time. It was at that event that loud speakers were used for the first time, courtesy of the H.E. Pruitt Funeral Home.

Following a five-year recess during World War II, the Russell County Convention reconvened in 1947 and has met on a continuing basis since that time. Attendance took a nosedive about 1955, however. Like other area conventions, this one has no real hopes for a new vitality. The main singing activity in Russell County takes place at the monthly singings that are held in area churches. But there, too, the crowds have diminished drastically in recent years.

While the year of origin is uncertain, Pulaski County conventions were in full swing by the mid-1920s. Glen Roy described the first county-wide convention in his memory as having taken place in 1922. The date was firm in his mind, for it was the trip to the convention that year that afforded Roy his first automobile ride:

In 1922, my father, Bob Roy, took a choir to Somerset. Wasn't any quartets here then. Used the James D. Vaughan book. He took this choir from Tick Ridge—Cedar Point Church—to a singing convention at Somerset at Crystal Park.

That's the first time I ever rode in an automobile. Hugh Pierce had sold his timber and had bought him a new car. Well, he took Dad to an outdoor singing in that car.

About eighteen people in that choir. My Daddy had them well trained. The older women were generally the sopranos, about four basses, three young girls were altos, and one tenor.

Edna Roy, Alta Beasley Hallmark, and Erie Sullivan were the alto singers. I thought they was the best singers on earth. They was about sixteen and I was five. How good they was!

I remember what song my Daddy had picked out to be the winner's song: "I care not what church you belong to, just as long as for God you stand; If you're my brother give me your hand."

Dad always said he would have won first prize, but a train come along and drowned out part of their song. And they come in in second place.

They was quite a crowd of people there that day; probably five hundred people there. Fred Thompson had a choir there that day. And Willie Wilson had a choir there.

Roy continued his account of early Pulaski County singing conventions by observing that "the biggest crowds we had was in the 1930s and early 1940s in Somerset." Shortly after that, he recalled, "the size of the crowds declined noticeably, even though convention officials began inviting big-time quartets by the late 1940s in hopes of salvaging the old institution."

The Pulaski County Convention experienced renewed vigor in 1950 with the election of James M. Holt to the presidency. Holt, a former school superintendent who led the Pulaski schools through their consolidation phase, was a recognized organization man. More than that, he liked to sing and he liked to lead singing. These attributes undergirded his successful efforts to organize the Pulaski County Singing Association in early 1952. By late 1956, when the noted columnist Joe Creason, writing for the Louisville *Courier-Journal*, attended one of Holt's songfests, the association boasted of 306 consecutive weekly sings in more than fifty different Pulaski County churches. Crowds attending the singings averaged about four hundred persons. The largest crowd ever was in 1954 when one thousand people attended a session held at the Duke Memorial Baptist Church in Somerset.[11] In 1966, when Holt's declining health precluded his taking an active hand in gospel music matters, the Pulaski singing convention came to a virtual standstill. More recent efforts by the Lake Cumberland Gospel Singing Association to recapture local public support have been largely unsuccessful.[12]

The Warren County Convention was organized in the mid 1920s, at the time singings were big everywhere across the region. And, like its counterparts in other counties, the Warren Convention flourished in its early stages. The 1929 event was memorable, as both the Vaughan and Stamps quartets were present for the affair. Public support remained strong through the 1930s. A Bowling Green newspaper dated May 13, 1937, observed that the event that year attracted "one of the largest crowds ever," and that singers were present from Allen, Barren, and Simpson counties, as well as Warren. The paper also noted that Ed Hudson of Richardsville "had been employed by the Adult Education authorities to give music instruction to various churches in Warren County." Hudson's employment indicates that congregational and class shape-note singing were still healthy at that time. Following World War II, however, the Warren County Convention went into decline. It was never able to regain its prewar stature, although the strong leadership offered by Earl and Lorene Norris of Bowling Green kept it viable into the 1970s. The Warren County Convention ceased completely in 1981.

Wradon Fleener, who was born in 1913, recalls attending Butler County conventions as a boy in the 1920s. The convention was in full swing by the mid-1930s, according to Oral Snodgrass and Edwin Dye, who both remembered the sumptuous meals served on the court-house lawn in Morgantown just before the singing began at the adjacent Presbyterian Church. The Butler County conventions were held every fifth Sunday until the mid-1960s when, despite coura-geous efforts by President H. Dye, they succumbed to lack of public interest and support.

The Edmonson County Singing Convention was organized in the late 1920s at the Dripping Springs Church located on U.S. 31W near Smiths Grove. The Convention was planned for the third Sundays in June and September at the courthouse in Brownsville. Through the 1930s, interest ran high and the courthouse was always packed by singers and spectators, who often spilled over into the courtyard. Windows were opened so they could hear the singing.

Some quartet activity was in evidence in the 1930s, but the Edmonson County conventions were made up mostly of congrega-tional singing and church choirs such as the one from Midway Baptist Church. The Midway Choir had about thirty-five singers who used no music while performing. "Man, they could just tear a place all to pieces with their singing!" exclaimed Johnnie Lindsey. "They prac-ticed once or twice weekly, winter and summer. Sang entirely out of new songbooks by Vaughan, Stamps-Baxter, and Hartford."

By the late 1940s, however, interest in congregational singing waned and it was hard for officers of the Edmonson County Conven-tion to book professional groups for the event. Crowds grew smaller and smaller. "Too many other places for people to go," Lindsey noted, "and if you've not got listeners, you'll not have much of a singing." County-wide singing conventions in Edmonson County ceased to be held on a regular basis in the 1960s.

Local conventions came into existence in virtually all remaining counties in the region between 1930 and 1940, during the time the Great Depression choked the local and the national economy. In retrospect, it was the Depression that brought people out to the singing conventions like nothing had before or since. People had no other place to go, save occasional box suppers at the local schools and revival services at the churches. It is little wonder that some newly created county singing conventions were attended by crowds of six to seven thousand people. Casey County is a good case in point.

The Casey County Singing Convention was organized in 1930 under the direction of Virgil Ware, well-known shape-note music teacher from the Argyle community in the eastern portion of the county. The annual convention date was the second Sunday in September. On this day each year through the 1930s, singing groups, generally church choirs, gathered in Liberty from all over Casey and adjoining counties. Because there was no building in town large enough to accommodate the singers and their devout followers, doors to the courthouse, plus those at the Baptist, Methodist, and Christian churches in Liberty, were opened to the public. The choirs and quartets rotated from one building to another to sing for those persons gathered at each location.

No convention was held in Casey County in 1940 because new water and sewage lines were being installed in Liberty. City officials feared that a fire or other disaster might result from such a large gathering of people. With the onset of World War II, the convention ceased entirely. Efforts to revive it in the early 1950s failed.

County-wide singing conventions in south central Kentucky had resulted from the tremendous popularity enjoyed by local singings held in community churches. The desire to show off the talents of the individual church choirs, and the need to engage in fellowship by sharing new shape-note songbooks with people from across the county, led to the creation of big semiannual or annual singings held in the largest sanctuaries and auditoriums, often high school gyms and courthouses. These religious events offered ample opportunity for socializing as well, thus demonstrating their all-important secular nature. David Stanley points out that, as a recurring community event, the singing convention continues to be a major form of recreation and a link between secular and sacred activity in communities across the South.[13]

Interest in shape-note singing and, consequently, in church singings and semi-annual or annual county conventions began to subside by the late 1930s. This decline was due to changing times, coupled with the fact that the singing schools had begun to lose their appeal as social functions.

The onset of World War II was a critical juncture in the development of gospel music in south central Kentucky. In many counties, singing schools and conventions came to a virtual standstill from 1941 to 1945. Broad changes in American culture occurred everywhere following the war. Many of the returning veterans chose to seek factory employment rather than return to the farms. There was a concurrent increase in entertainment options during the late 1940s and early 1950s, which also affected gospel music activities. By then, people had the money and leisure time necessary to seek out different forms of entertainment. In addition, electricity was becoming increasingly accessible to rural areas, and television was growing in popularity.

Concurrent with their shift toward mainstream life and culture, local people gradually moved away from entertaining themselves and sought instead to be entertained. This shift accounts for the virtual cessation of singing schools, the near demise of local singing conventions, and the rapid increase in the number of local gospel trios and quartets. The conventions that once spotlighted congregational singing, choirs, and classes began to feature performances by duets, trios, and quartets. These ensembles were typically local in origin, but touring professionals were common features as well by the late 1940s. Ed Dye commented that "as the conventions began to center more and more on performances by quartets, that took the place of a lot of the classes." Song leaders had to be content with leading no more than three or four songs during the entire song service. Not only were the roles of song leaders rapidly declining in importance, so, too, were local quartets. Johnny Howard, then of the Clinton County-based York Quartet and now of the Heartland Quartet of Elizabethtown, recalled that "people were caught up with listening to big commercial groups. They didn't want to hear a local quartet."

While C.E. Deweese and Edwin Dye, among others, attribute the decline of local conventions to the crowding out of church choirs and increased entertainment options brought by improved transportation and technology, others feel that lack of financial support for visiting quartets signaled the end. Noble Stuart, who was president of the Logan County Singing Convention in 1949, explained that many of the people in attendance looked upon the convention as a free concert and neglected to make adequate monetary contributions: "The thing had advanced enough so that in order to, shall we say, properly entertain the crowd, you needed to bring in guest singers as a highlight. The year I was president, this courtroom in the Logan County Courthouse at Russellville—I don't know how many people it held, pretty good size, standing room only—and naturally we took up a free-will offering to try to compensate visitors. . . . We got a collection of eighteen dollars! Well, I could see right then that this singing was doomed."

Stuart commented that while people would gladly pay to see popular country singers, they often felt uncomfortable paying to hear gospel singers. "Why man, if you would have wanted to really get on the wrong side of the road back in those days, just have a gospel singing and charge admission! People felt that gospel singing was the Lord's work and it ought to be done free."

Stuart believes this attitude is unfortunate and that quality artists who want to devote their lives to singing gospel music deserve the support of the religious community. He stated that a simple lack of ability to continue attracting, or paying, top-name gospel groups was largely responsible for the decline and reorientation of the Logan County Singing Convention at midcentury.

While local county conventions were first characterized by congregational singing and singing classes, their format had been altered in the late 1920s to make room for limited performances by local or touring professional gospel quartets.[14] County conventions, especially in the 1930s, 1940s, and 1950s, served as arenas in which the most current gospel singing styles were performed. Local conventions not only mirrored the development of gospel music styles, but they also influenced that development, first in a positive way and then to its detriment. For as the conventions became more performance-oriented, the music that had once been characterized by audience participation and choir singing was now a spectator art. Participation in singing schools and class singing was a thing of the past.[15]

The same local conventions that eschewed congregational and choir singing in favor of quartets and trios by the late 1940s and early 1950s soon found themselves suffering decreased attendance because of the same forces that had caused a decline in the shape-note genre. Big-name quartets visited virtually every living room in the region, thanks to television sets that were found in abundance by the mid-1950s. The introduction of factory employment in the area provided money that gave people a wider range of leisure possibilities, and improved roads made more distant activities accessible. Young people switched their loyalties from gospel music to rock and roll. But one of the biggest threats to singing conventions was the introduction of full-time churches in rural south central Kentucky.

Congregations that had formerly come together in worship only once a month were suddenly meeting every Sunday morning and Sunday evening. Full-time churches demanded full-time attendance by their members. Monthly attendance at singing conventions in area churches declined radically, and places like the Tabernacle in Scotts- ville and Branstetter Park at Beaumont in Metcalfe County, once famous for their singings, closed down altogether. And while some counties fought to keep alive their once prominent conventions,[16] most of them looked to the still youthful Kentucky State Singing Convention to carry the gospel music banner.

The Kentucky State Singing Convention[17] was founded in Glasgow in 1946, and only twice since 1969 has it been held outside south central Kentucky, both times in nearby Hopkinsville in Christian County. The fact that the State Convention has been so well supported in southern Kentucky demonstrates that this area was and still is the bastion of gospel music activity in the state.

The State Convention was the brainchild of Metcalfe County native John G. Salmon, who spearheaded the move to organize a statewide singing convention. Salmon, who doubled as a Methodist minister and quartet singer, wanted to establish an institution that would serve the best interests of gospel quartets and song leaders alike. In April 1946, an organizational meeting was held in Glasgow, Salmon's home at the time, and his dream became reality. It was agreed by those at the meeting that the convention format would feature three song directors in succession who would lead one song each, followed by a quartet that would sing two numbers, until all leaders and quartets had sung. This format was followed during Salmon's two terms as president at the annual fall conventions held in Bowling Green in 1946 and 1947.[18] Soon afterward, however, the proponents of quartet music, perhaps including Salmon himself, had converted the Kentucky State Singing Convention into a showcase for quartets. L.E. Butrum, who was both a music teacher and a quartet advocate from the Allen-Barren area, frequently and openly accused Salmon of starting a "quartet convention," not a "singing convention." It was a decade before friction and ill-will between the two opposing camps ceased.[19]

The influence of singing schools and singing school teachers ran its course at the State Convention by the mid- to late 1950s. Johnny Martin, a proponent of congregational singing as well as a quartet singer himself, was the Convention's third vice-president in 1955, its first vice-president in 1956, and its president in 1958. But his presence had little effect on the format of the Convention. It was still a quartet convention in spite of the fact that, as late as 1955, Martin, B.C. Frost, Ernest Edwards, C.E. Deweese, and W.B. Walbert of the Vaughan Music Company each led a song at the annual event. In 1956, only Martin participated in this capacity, and in 1957, the last year in which song directors are listed on program, L.E. Butrum and C.E. Deweese led congregational singing. However, songbooks had not been passed out to the State Convention audience since the presidency of Arthur Groves in 1950. It is not surprising that the state convention board voted in 1960 to discontinue the office of convention pianist effective with the 1961 convention. The minutes of that meeting noted that "everyone at the convention usually has their own pianist." Indeed it was a "quartet convention"!

Today's Kentucky State Convention is usually a well-organized event, thanks to year-long planning by the president, secretary-treasurer, and board members. They are dedicated to such pragmatic concerns as finding the right auditorium for the occasion, having a sound system installed, obtaining the right person(s) to run the sound board, and contracting with someone to operate a concessions booth. They also must find people to print the program booklet, to park cars and buses, and to direct and assist visiting singers and patrons. Above all, there is the task of raising enough money through the sale of ads and volunteer donations to defray convention costs.

Nowadays when the big event rolls around, the parking lot adjacent to the convention site begins to swell with the arrival of the singers' cars, vans, and buses by late afternoon. The singers are anxious to mingle with friends in the crowd and strike up conversations with new acquaintances. The first order of business for most of them, however, is to choose a spot in the lobby area where they can set up card tables on which to display cassettes and albums to sell to convention patrons. While one member of the group remains behind with the exhibit, other members of the group wander through the crowd in hopes of engaging old friends and acquaintances in conversation about recent songs and trends in gospel music circles.

What, really, does this annual State Convention mean to present-day singers? Definitions or statements of purpose of this and other area conventions, such as the Ohio Valley Singing Convention held annually in Cave City, were recorded from some of the singers at the 1988 State Convention in Scottsville. All of their testimonials revealed a warm feeling for the convention and expressed an appreciation for its bringing the singers together on a regular basis. Lonnie Cockriel of the Cockriel Family, Bowling Green, commented, "Singing conventions let us see people we maybe haven't seen for years. It's just a good get-together; just sing and have a good time and meet a lot of people for the first time."

Richard Tinsley of the Glasgow-based Canaanland Quartet described a convention as "a kind of homecoming for the singers." In the same vein, 1986 State Convention President Rick Cooper of Liberty, felt that the convention "might be just for diehard fans of gospel music and the singers and their families—a kind of reunion." Wayne Strode of the Jubilee Singers observed that the annual singing convention affords "a time and place when we can all get together and say 'hello,' and see how many groups have re-formed, and how many singers have gone on [died]."

Before the singing is scheduled to begin, at a time announced to the singers several weeks in advance, a representative from each singing group lines up in front of a desk or table positioned near the front door. The order in which an ensemble registers determines when it will sing that evening. Typically, no favors are accorded groups in this regard, except that children's singing groups are invited to go first regardless of their sign-in time. If all members of a group are not present and ready to go on stage when their rotation time comes, the group is moved to the end of the list. They sing only after all other registered groups have performed.

When it is time for the singing event to begin, the president calls all singers onto the stage for a group song, or asks someone to lead the audience in a congregational song. A prayer is then said and the president reads the Convention rules to the audience. Because the rules are of concern only to the singers, the act of reading them aloud reaffirms the notion that the convention serves largely just to bring the singers together again.[20]

Although conventions have provided democratic music forums all along, only in the past fifteen to twenty years have groups of varying abilities felt comfortable performing at the state conventions. There was a time in the 1950s and 1960s when, in the words of Annette McCubbins of the McCubbins Family of Munfordville, "You didn't go to the State Convention and hear a bad group." Her husband, Haskell, reaffirmed her words: "If you couldn't do it right, you didn't stand up to sing," he said. And Noble Stuart, faithful convention attender and former State Convention president, recalled that "it wasn't until the late 1960s that quartet singing began to decline in quality." He then mused a moment before proceeding to offer an explanation as to why the overall quality of gospel music waned about that time:

For a long time, the quartets could sing, unlike the groups now that learn only by ear. You wouldn't believe the groups that today learn their songs from records. They imitate the big groups. They don't know enough music to even try to change it to their own style.

The quality of singing has dropped and that's why the crowds don't come out to hear the groups anymore. Groups back then wouldn't come to the State Convention because they didn't think they were good enough. Well, buddy, they were better than most of the groups today![21]

Above: The first order of business for most gospel groups at a singing convention is to set up a sales display. This one is at the Ohio Valley Singing Convention held in Cave City in 1986. *Photo by the author.* Below: A performance at the Kentucky State Gospel Singing Convention held in Liberty in 1986. *Photo by the author.*

Other observers likewise contend that the democratization practiced by the Convention in recent years has served to bring out some singing groups that are lacking in vocal quality. Bobby Simpson, one-time singer with the Gospel Five, the Melody Makers, and now with the very fine Bowling Green-based Watchmen, prefers not to sing at the State Convention because of the poor quality musical abilities demonstrated by many of the groups that participate. "Some of the groups get together, practice once, go to the Convention, and then not sing together again for a year," Simpson stated.

It may be that most current amateur gospel groups do indeed demonstrate little knowledge of music. The majority of these ensembles certainly lack originality, as they make conscious efforts to imitate the big-name professionals. Yet these same locals continue to attract crowds of eight to twelve hundred at each of the two sessions of the annual State Singing Convention. Most signs are positive for continued public support of these events. The variety of sounds emanating from these gospel ensembles can best be understood by looking at the origins and history of the quartet movement. Subsequent chapters will identify and describe key local singing groups in each of the major gospel music periods from 1900 to the present, and will bring into focus the exterior forces that produced changes in group musical sounds and their performance aspects.

3

SHAPE-NOTES AND EARLY GOSPEL QUARTETS

The gospel quartet movement came to south central Kentucky early in the twentieth century like a breeze that blew softly across an ever-rising current of congregational and choir singing. Both forms of religious music were to become increasingly vigorous over the next four decades, with large group singing maintaining an edge in popularity because of the number of musically-trained persons who could and did participate. During this same period of growth, quartet music and choral singing were never in competition, as both of them were outgrowths of the shape-note schools that left an indelible imprint on area religious life. Strong tensions between the two arose at mid-century, however, creating a rift that was slow in healing.

Area music schools had introduced a uniform singing style in local churches through the use of shape-notes, and encouraged appreciation of this new music and the religious lyrics written to fit its style. Quartets came into existence only to showcase a very small number of individuals who excelled at their vocal parts. Indeed, they produced the finest quality four-part harmony heard in south central Kentucky between 1900 and 1950. During those years, quartets used the same songbooks as the church choirs and everyone sang the songs exactly as the printed music specified. Because shape-note hymnals were so important at county singing conventions, the sounds that emanated from these early quartets was referred to as "convention style music."

The first such group to be formed in south central Kentucky was the Haste Brothers Quartet from the tiny community of Sardis in western Pulaski County. There, just at the turn of the century, James

Above: The Haste Brothers in 1929. For more than a decade, they were the only known quartet singers in south central Kentucky. *Photo courtesy of Jason Haste.* Below: The West Allen Quartet was organized after a singing class in 1912. *Photo courtesy of E.D. Austin.*

Frank (lead), Huston (bass), John (baritone), and Andrew (tenor) Haste formed their now legendary outfit following a shape-note singing school taught by Mark DeBord, a neighbor from nearby Bethelridge in Casey County.

The Hastes were the only quartet singers in south central Kentucky for more than a decade. During the 1910s, however, as shape-note instruction accelerated across the region, eight additional quartets were formed. Like the Hastes, all of these new ensembles are now legendary at home and in adjacent locales. The West Allen Quartet, Beech Grove Ladies Quartet, Liberty Quartet, and Conner-Cassaday Trio were from Allen County; the Smotherman and Campbell family quartets were from north Logan County; the Rock Bridge Quartet was from north central Monroe County; and home base for the McCubbin-Henderson Quartet was Summersville in Green County.

The West Allen Quartet, formed in 1912, was composed of Ewing Hancock, a Spanish-American War vet, who sang the lead; Shirley Caldwell, high tenor; Curtis Newman, bass; and Clair Thomas, baritone and pianist. This group resulted from a singing class taught at Beech Grove Baptist Church by Dr. Andrew J. Dixon, a country physician who did much to create interest in gospel music in the years prior to World War I. The original personnel of the West Allen Quartet, which included members of four different churches, remained intact for seven years, during which time they sang in churches and schools in Allen and adjacent counties in Kentucky and Tennessee. Their most requested song was "Crossing the Bar."[1]

The Beech Grove Ladies Quartet was an outgrowth of that same music school taught by Dr. Dixon. The first all-female ensemble in south central Kentucky, this group was composed of Vona Lyles, soprano; Mildred Ackerman Gent, tenor; Inez McElroy Jones, alto; and Hazel Holland, bass. They sang as a group until the early 1920s.

The third Allen County foursome was organized in 1916 and remained intact throughout World War I, calling it quits in 1920. This was the Liberty Quartet, named for the Liberty Baptist Church at Halifax in northwestern Allen County. Making up the group were Abraham Willoughby, one of south central Kentucky's prominent singing school teachers, who sang lead; John Strait, bass; Vernon Conner, baritone; Carlos Williams, tenor; and Mautie Willoughby (Reynolds), pianist. At some point during the group's active years, Sally Strait (John's wife) sang the alto.[2]

The Homer community in northern Logan County was home to two excellent pioneer singing groups, the Smothermans and Campbells, both family groups and both products of singing schools. The Smothermans, a Presbyterian family, lived just across the Mud River from their friendly singing rivals, the Campbells. The Smotherman Quartet was organized in 1912, consisting of Linnie, Stuart, Duff, and Willie B. Willie B., who was born about 1875, was a top-notch music teacher who taught singing schools all over Logan, Todd, and Simpson counties and in adjacent Tennessee counties. Although memories of Willie B. and the other members of the Smotherman Quartet live on, the group actually disbanded in 1917 or 1918, perhaps because of World War I.

The Campbell Quartet, consisting of Clarence, Henry, Marvin, and Rayburn, was organized about 1918. Their sister Ruth (Cox) played piano for the group, and another sister, Lucy (Chick), frequently sang alto with her brothers. All five of the Campbells went as a group to the Vaughan School of Music in Lawrenceburg, Tennessee. It is said that they came home and sang superb harmony until about 1938, when Henry and Clarence moved to Detroit, where they both organized quartets. Clarence's group, the Guiding Star Quartet, was featured at the 1940 National Singing Convention in Akron, Ohio.[3] Clarence moved from Detroit to Dallas during the late 1940s to take a job as minister of music in a church and to sing with one of the Stamps Quartets.

The two remaining area quartets organized during the pre-World War I era were the McCubbin-Henderson ensemble, formed in 1915 by Emmit McCubbin, Joe McCubbin, John Henderson, and Dr. Arvin Henderson; and the Rock Bridge Quartet. The latter was formed in 1914 as the result of a singing school taught by "Big Jim" Hagan. The group disbanded in 1917 when Herbert Smith, Jesse Bowman, and Millard Hutchens, all neighbors, were drafted for military service. Hazel Montell, Gladys Parrish, and Benton Bowman, all of Rock Bridge, still recall with nostalgia how good the local quartet sounded when singing a song about the "Great Titanic," a ship that by human standards, the song claimed, was unsinkable.

All of these pioneer quartets had certain commonalities. Each was born during the inceptive years of shape-note singing in south central Kentucky and came into being because the members attended one or more music schools. Perhaps not surprisingly, many of these early quartet singers pursued shape-note teaching careers as an adjunct activity to their normal work. The fact that so many of the singers taught music schools on the side helps to explain their dogmatic adherence to singing the music as it was written. Many used only guitars or pianos for accompaniment. Others sang a cappella, using only pitch pipes, tuning forks, or vocal pitches to key the songs.

Early quartets performed rather frequently, even by today's standards, but loyalties to their home church choirs came first. The singers were seldom away from home when their church was holding its own monthly preaching and song service. Perhaps they sang at nearby functions later that afternoon or evening, but travel limitations precluded their going very far from home.

The distances traveled to singing engagements were never very great back then, as such travel had to be done on foot, on horseback, or in horse-drawn conveyances. I have yet to hear mention of the use of automobiles by pre-1920 artists. The truly big events that these groups attended were their local county conventions, and only Allen and Logan counties boasted of singing conventions at that time. Thus, most performance events for these early quartets were staged in churches and schools near home or in immediately adjacent locales.

The pioneer groups (and many of those in later years as well) were largely family units, thus helping to account for their noticeably tight four-part harmony. Many people commented that the best overall harmony is produced by family ensembles, due perhaps to genetic relationships and constant practice at home. Even when a group's personnel were drawn from the larger community, members were still able to come together often to practice. And practice they did, for singing was typically their only form of social diversion. They not only practiced sight reading and singing at home, but song books were sometimes tucked into their pockets when they went to town, to the local country store, or to the cornfield. They sang at every opportunity and often created situations that brought them together.

In spite of the dominance of men in leadership roles in shape-note schools and the singing conventions described earlier, woman were active participants in the movement from the first, as evidenced by their presence in the early quartets. Women frequently sang the alto and soprano parts in mixed gender quartets and, in the instance of the Beech Grove Quartet, all of the singers were female.

Perhaps because only twenty new groups (an average of one per county) came into being during the 1920s, very little change was discernible in quartet composition and performance during that decade. The gender ratio of the singers remained unchanged; singers made no effort to memorize the songs in their repertoires, as they relied totally on shape-note songbooks for words and music; and performances were still held in local churches and schools. While group and individual performance styles varied very little from event to event, some foursomes incorporated novelty numbers into their repertoires. Garnet Cassaday recalled that a Bowling Green group headed by Vernon P. Cassaday came to the Settle community shortly after 1925 and sang "They All Went Down to Amsterdam." Three of the performers sang harmony to "Amster, Amster, Amster," with the fourth member poised to finish the word. When his turn came, rather than say the "curse" word, he always ran off stage, yelling, "No, no, no," to the delight of the audience.

The more prominent foursomes of the 1920s included the McKinney, Stuart, Science Hill, Bowling Green, Friendship, Mabe, and Ward quartets. The McKinneys and Stuarts were from Logan County.[4] The McKinney Quartet, a highly regarded group from the Deer Lick community, was organized in 1920 by Jim, Jeff, and Amos McKinney, along with a Jenkins man. All four members attended the Vaughan School of Music in the early 1920s. Family members say that the McKinneys issued some 78 rpm recordings in the late 1930s or early 1940s.

With the Smothermans, Campbells, and McKinneys, the Stuart Quartet (1925-50) made up Logan County's big four. Indeed, no single county in south central Kentucky can boast of so many families whose reputation for excellent four-part harmony lingers on after a half century or more. Curtis Savage, a Logan Countian and member of the very good Kedron Quartet (1922-27), observed that "the Stuarts were the local gospel music movers in the 1920s and '30s." Comprising brothers Roy (first tenor) and Curtis Stuart (baritone), along with brothers Edgar (lead) and Melvin Stuart (bass)—two sets of double cousins—the Stuart Quartet sang an excellent brand of four-part harmony. They keyed their songs without the benefit of any sort of tuning device.

Due to a lack of adequate transportation during their early years, the Stuarts were confined largely to singing engagements within a few miles of home. As their fame spread with increased mobility in later years, the Stuart Quartet traveled to distant places, including many points out of state. A rather large progeny has kept the Stuart singing tradition alive to the present time.

Across the region in Pulaski County, three new groups came into existence during the 1920s. These were the Whetstone Quartet (1924-28), the Science Hill Quartet (1928-55), and the Sears Quartet (1929-31) also from the Whetstone community. Of the three, perhaps the most highly acclaimed was the Science Hill ensemble comprising S. Ramey Godby (bass), his wife Annie (lead), Ephriam O. Dick (tenor), and Ephriam's wife Ibbie (alto). Vera Fugette was their first pianist. Their home base was the Science Hill Methodist Church, an institution still known for high quality congregational singing and the many singing ensembles produced there. The Science Hill Quartet sang at more than two thousand funerals in their home area, while still finding time to drive to Knoxville for frequent radio appearances over WNOX during the 1940s and early 1950s.

The first foursome to be formed in the Bowling Green area about which adequate information is available is the Bowling Green Quartet (1928-30). The original members, all between the ages of twenty-six and thirty years, included Ward Elkins, Tim Hudson, Earlis D. Austin (of Scottsville), and Neal McElroy, a Bowling Green barber. In 1928, this group introduced the song "Give the World a Smile Each Day" to local audiences. This crowd pleaser, which had been issued on the Victor label in October 1927 by the Stamps All-Star Quartet, had to be repeated three or four times during each concert, Austin recalled.

McElroy and Hudson left the group in 1929 and were replaced by Alfred Dalton and George Shelton. Austin, born in 1897, provided a photograph of both sets of quartet personnel. The 1929 personnel dressed alike in light colored trousers, white shirts, dark jackets, and bow ties. Along with singing the novelty songs mentioned previously, dressing alike is another indication that touring professionals were beginning to influence local tastes and stage mannerisms. The Bowling Green Quartet was also innovative in at least one other regard for, unlike the typical gospel group, some of their songs were committed to memory. The shape-note hymnal was not crucial to their singing performance. These and other changes yet to come—changes that were already affecting the performance styles and marketing tactics of the fledgling gospel music professionals[5]—would alter the local gospel music scene immeasurably. But sweeping innovations were still more than a decade away.

The Friendship Quartet (1928-30) was from the Settle community in northern Allen County. Its members, Gerald Stovall, Joe Howell, Velma Howell, and Garnet Cassaday, sang with guitar accompaniment. The harmony produced by these four "would zizz your ears," according to one person who vividly recalled their singing. The three male members came together again in 1938 to form the Settle Quartet.

The Mabe Family Quartet of Bonnieville in Hart County is numbered among the finest gospel groups ever to come out of south central Kentucky. Four brothers made up the group: Bowers, who

The Bowling Green Quartet in 1929. Their rendition of "Give the World a Smile Each Day" was a crowd pleaser. *Photo courtesy of E.D. Austin.*

sang first tenor; Clarence, second tenor; Willie, the soprano lead; and Charlie, who sang bass. No musical instrument was used by the Mabes throughout their career, which spanned thirty-three years beginning in 1928. When these brothers finally called it quits in 1961, the Mabe mantle was passed to Charlie's children and grandchildren who are still singing gospel music in Hart and adjacent counties.

The final group from the 1920s to be described here is the Ward Quartet of Aberdeen in Butler County. Group personnel included County Sheriff Dewey Ward (first tenor), Mack Smith (second tenor), Pearly G. Kessinger (bass), and Theodore C. Hunt and/or Crennie Hunt (lead). All were members of the Aberdeen Baptist Church. They sang without the benefit of musical accompaniment, producing a sound described by Mrs. Arbie Flener as "the best for their time. Everybody wanted them to sing in their church." The Ward Quartet was active in Butler and surrounding counties between 1929 and 1944, the year Kessinger died.

The 1920s came to a close with the country engulfed in the throes of the Great Depression. South central Kentucky suffered, as people here had very little money throughout the 1930s. But most families, who were accustomed to growing what they ate, did not experience periods of hunger. Gospel singing remained very much in vogue throughout the decade, perhaps in large part helping to sustain local families in times of emotional need. Forty-eight new singing groups emerged between 1930 and 1939.

Nine of these new outfits were family ensembles, four of which were all male. Two community-based groups were made up of all women, but twenty-three groups (including the four family groups) used male singers only. Of the latter twenty-three, twelve sang a cappella, six had women pianists, and four employed a male pianist or guitarist. Eleven additional ensembles, not including the family groups with mixed genders, used both male and female singers. In total, twenty-two groups used both male and female singers and/ or musicians; twenty-five comprised men only, and two had only women members. In an entirely different vein, members of twelve of the groups were music school teachers. In one group, all four male singers were teachers.

These figures provide a basis for three observations. First, family groups comprised roughly one-fifth of all gospel music ensembles during the Depression years. This is not surprising, as they could sing together at home on a daily basis regardless of weather or poor economic conditions. Second, gospel music was dominated by males. Not only were twenty-five of the groups exclusively male, all but two of the other quartets contained men along with women. In the twenty-two mixed gender groups, men typically sang lead, tenor, and bass, while a woman sang alto. Third, singing school teachers continued to maintain a firm hold on the local gospel music scene. They not only taught music schools at which they sold company songbooks under salary or royalty arrangements, they were also in an enviable position to peddle extra copies of the songbooks used by their quartets at scheduled singing events.

These statistics do not reveal the excellent singing skills possessed by most of the quartets that originated in the 1930s. It seems safe to say that this decade represents the truly golden years of four-part harmony in south central Kentucky. Not only did most of the new ensembles possess superior vocal abilities, but so did the still-active earlier groups such as the Campbell, Gray, Holly Springs, Kedron, Mabe, McKinney, Phipps, Powell, Salem, Science Hill, Sears, Sparksville, Stuart, and Ward quartets, which, collectively, represented all portions of south central Kentucky.

The Norris, Bowles, and Davis family quartets were among those that originated in the 1930s. The Norris ensemble, of Bow in Cumberland County, included three brothers, B.R. "Dade" (high tenor),

Albert (bass), and Leonard (lead). A neighbor, Jim Capps, sang tenor with them. The group remained unnamed throughout its eight-year tenure. A 1937 photograph shows the four singers sitting together outdoors in ladderback chairs, songbooks in hand. One wore a white shirt with cuffs turned up, two had on coats and ties, and the fourth member was attired in a black coat and overalls. The original four disbanded in 1940, at which time Leonard, Elwood, and Albert Norris, along with Albert's daughter, Doris, teamed up to form the Norris Quartet. (Dade Norris and Jim Capps sang from 1942 until 1952 with the Riddle Quartet, another of the many singing groups produced in the Bow community across the years.)

The newly formed Norris Quartet, whose members all knew shape-note music and sang from songbooks, remained intact until 1960, except that Ruth Garner replaced Elwood Norris in 1949. The group sang weekly over WAIN radio in Columbia for several years before and after 1949. Their only musical accompaniment was a guitar, first played by Doris and later by Ruth.

The Thompson Quartet, the Sacred Five, the Crusaders, and the Farris Family of Science Hill were four of the singing groups of the 1930s to include at least one female vocalist. The Thompson ensemble was from Eubank in Pulaski County. It was headed up by Fred Thompson, a singing school master who, in the words of Lewis Adams, "was about the best to ever teach in Pulaski and adjoining counties." Thompson sang the lead part with the quartet. He was accompanied by Herbert Todd, bass; Herbert's wife, Bessie, alto; with either Raymond Todd, Herbert's brother, or Fred McDonald singing tenor.

The Thompson group originated in 1931 and remained intact until 1961, serving primarily as a funeral quartet in later years. Thompson himself never gave up singing entirely, even in his final days. To quote Adams again, "Even after Fred was down in bed for good just before he died, when some of his neighbors would come in, he'd say, 'Let's get our songbooks and have a song.' And he couldn't even sit up in bed at the time."

The Sacred Five of Bowling Green has been described by numerous people as possessing the finest array of individual singers of any gospel group ever to come out of south central Kentucky. People who sang at various intervals with the Sacred Five find it difficult to list the group's original members. After weighing available information, it appears that the members in 1936 were Mildred Walthall, alto; Clarence Kirby, tenor; Ernest Marion (perhaps singing concurrently with the Allen County Singers), bass; and Harold West, soprano lead.

The Norris Quartet in 1948 at WAIN radio station in Columbia.
Photo courtesy of Doris Norris McCoy.

Margaret Davis was the group's pianist. Willard Cockrill, formerly
with the Ante-room Quartet, replaced Kirby in 1938. In addition to
his singing duties, Cockrill did a comedy routine with the Sacred Five
until 1940.

In 1941, the Sacred Five was reorganized with an all-male singing
cast consisting of Harold West, lead; Duncan Houchens, second
tenor; Lowell Davis of Lindseyville, tenor; and Stanley Sexton, bass.
Marie Lyle, who later played for the Templeman Quartet of Hart
County, joined the group as pianist. West and Davis left the Sacred
Five in 1942 and were replaced by C.E. Deweese and Ed White.
Deweese, who sang the lead, had quit the Vaughan Four a year earlier.
Ed White, first tenor, likewise had experience singing with other area
groups before coming to the Sacred Five. It was the Houchens-Sexton-
Deweese-White-Lyle configuration that is still widely acclaimed for
its superior four-part harmony. They began singing weekly over WLBJ
radio in Bowling Green on a thirty-minute program sponsored by
Auburn Roller Mills. The group switched station affiliations about
1947, when C.E. Deweese was contacted by WKCT in Bowling Green.
The Sacred Five was promised thirty minutes of free air time until

"THE SACRED FIVE"
W K C T   P. O. Box 26   Bowling Green, Ky.

Ed White	C. E. DeWeese	Duncan Houchin	Stanley Sexton	Albert Hunt
1st Tenor	Lead & Mgr.	2nd Tenor	Bass	Pianist

The Sacred Five of Bowling Green. Because of the many changes in personnel over the years, even people who have sung with the group find it hard to remember who the original members were. *Photo courtesy of C.E. Deweese.*

suitable sponsors could be obtained. They were picked up quickly, however, by local branches of National Stores and National Farm Stores. On August 30, 1948, WKCT distributed handbills announcing that "as a result of the huge amount of mail received requesting a daily program by this unusual organization," the Sacred Five would begin the following Monday to broadcast live shows daily at 6:00 A.M. weekdays and at 9:00 A.M. on Sundays. "I was never late a single time," Deweese told me. "We'd drink a cup of coffee at the station, then eat breakfast when we got home."

This outstanding group remained intact until about 1949, at which time Deweese announced his decision to begin teaching music on a full-time basis for the Vaughan Company, a position he held until 1958 when he joined the faculty of the Florida Bible Institute in Lakeland, Florida. Stanley Sexton moved to Louisville and sang with the Kentucky Harmoneers, hailed as one of Kentucky's all-time great groups. Ed White and Duncan Houchens became the nucleus of a new group formed that same year known as the Southern Harmony Boys.

The quartet involvements of Reual and Flossie Thomas of the Seventy Six community in Clinton County covered essentially the same time span as that of the Sacred Five. And, like the latter, the Thomases' groups won regional and national acclaim in the process. This duo of public school teachers grew up singing the shape-notes at church. Shortly after their marriage in the mid-1930s, they formed the Crusaders Quartet with the assistance of Leslie Andrew and Marvin York. Flossie sang alto and Reual the lead. Andrew played guitar and sang baritone, while York sang bass.

When John Lair moved his barn dance program from Cincinnati to Renfro Valley in November 1939,[6] Reual and Flossie volunteered the singing services of the Crusaders to Lair free of charge. They did this, claimed Morris Gaskin, because of the broad coverage the group would get over WLW in Cincinnati, the station that carried the Renfro Valley broadcasts during the early years of World War II.

Gaskin replaced Marvin York in 1940, following a stint with the short-lived Harmony Quartet (1939 only) of Russell County. At that time, the Thomases were in Lexington, teaching school and singing daily over WLAP in Lexington. On Saturday nights, they sang with the Crusaders at the Renfro Valley Barn Dance and then again on the Sunday Morning Gathering. Gaskin voluntarily left the group in the early 1940s after realizing that, in his own words, he "wasn't far enough advanced vocally to carry the load." He enrolled in a Stamps-Baxter normal school, studying voice under W.W. Combs. The Crusaders replaced Gaskin, and later Andrew as well, with Clay and Jerry Colson and continued singing at Renfro Valley. The group (with a name change to the Seventy Six Quartet) was subsequently heard over WHAS, Louisville, when that CBS affiliate began carrying the Renfro Valley broadcasts by virtue of a General Foods Corporation sponsorship.

Flossie dropped out of the Seventy Six Quartet in 1950. Personnel at that time included Reual, lead; Edward Snell of Somerset, first tenor; Leslie Andrew, baritone; and Morris Gaskin, who had been with other singing groups in the interim, was once again singing bass. Gaskin's wife, June, was their pianist. At first it appeared that General Foods would sponsor the Seventy Six Quartet on a fifteen-minute, six-days-a-week program to be aired over the CBS network. The deal fell through, however, when Gaskin was called back into the military as a reservist. General Foods refused to accept his intended replacement as bass singer. This action signaled the death of the

Seventy Six Quartet and ended the Thomases' public singing careers. Reual died on Easter Sunday 1958, and Flossie was killed in a car accident four years later.

Among the 1930s all-male groups that had women pianists were the Campground, Little Barren, and Sunshine quartets. Of the three, the Campground ensemble was first to organize, in 1935. All of the personnel in this group were members of the Campground Methodist Church, a small rural church located about three miles west of Bonnieville. That church's reputation for quality shape-note singing, which continues to the present, was especially strong in the 1920s and 1930s. During that time, the future members of the Campground Quartet were growing to maturity. Cecil Clausen, first tenor; Ralph Clausen, second tenor; Marvin Dodson, lead; and Lee Caswell, bass, made up the ensemble. Because of their mastery of the shape-notes, the four exhibited a remarkable talent for singing four-part harmony without musical accompaniment.

The Campground Quartet was invited to sing at the USO Club in Elizabethtown on December 13, 1940, for an appreciative audience of army personnel from nearby Ft. Knox. They were recorded during the concert that evening, and four 78 rpm records were pressed to commemorate the event. Among the songs recorded was "Home on the Range."[7] When asked why it was chosen to go along with seven religious songs, Lee Caswell explained that "it was President Roosevelt's favorite song and we wanted to do it as a patriotic gesture." The group disbanded a year later, in 1941, when Dodson moved to Frankfort and Caswell, along with one of the Clausens, entered the army.

The Little Barren Quartet was organized in 1937 by Leon Thompson, Richard Thompson, Luard Lyle, and Stanley Curry, all members of the Little Barren Separate Baptist Church in southern Green County. Edwin Brown, a later member of the group, commented that "the original members went from one singing engagement to another in churches in the area by traveling on foot most of the time. Walking along on muddy roads or riding horseback to get to singings was common back then."

Although the Little Barren group remained intact for forty-three years until 1979, there were surprisingly few personnel changes. Lyle sang for thirty-nine of those years, Richard Thompson for thirty-six, and Curry for twenty-nine. Leon Thompson sang first tenor during the entire life of the group. Four pianists—Debbie Compton, Loman Rayburn, Marlene Houk, and Kay Ralston—played for the quartet. The Little Barren singers sang at more than 1,400 funerals after they began to keep tally. For over thirty years, they had a standing request from the Cowherd-Parrott Funeral Home in Greensburg to sing at all funerals conducted there, unless the family of the deceased requested otherwise.

The roster of the Sunshine Quartet, made up of various Allen County residents between 1938 and 1948, like that of the Sacred Five, reads like a cast of celebrities. Indeed, one member did go on to achieve national prominence in gospel music circles. The Sunshine Quartet was organized with "chubby-fingered" Lazarus Thomas as pianist and lead singer; Palmer Wheeler, who made important early records with the Vaughan Quartet in 1928 for RCA Victor, first tenor; Ernest Johnson, second tenor; and Vesper Jones, bass. This group disbanded about 1940, but the name Sunshine Quartet was retained and used by Garnet Cassaday, lead; Erlis Austin, formerly with the Bowling Green Quartet, first tenor; Joe Howell, second tenor; and Vesper Jones's brother, James, as bass. Catherine Austin, Erlis's daughter, played piano. This group sang every Sunday morning for fifteen minutes over WLBJ in Bowling Green, sponsored by York and Massey of Scottsville.

The group was reorganized again in 1942. Catherine Austin was still the group's pianist and Erlis continued as first tenor. Newcomers Jonas Britt and Anthony Hood held down the second tenor and bass slots, and Lazarus Thomas returned to the group as its baritone singer. The final configuration of Sunshine Quartet personnel in 1948 included Vesper Jones, lead; Erlis Austin, first tenor; Azzie Oaks, second tenor; J.D. Oaks, bass; and Mabel Oaks, pianist.

Noticeably absent following the 1942 regrouping of the Sunshine Quartet was the name of Jimmy Jones, who had left the group to serve a stint in the army. Upon release from the military, Jones went on to carve out a lasting niche in professional gospel music circles. He joined Odis Echols and the Melody Boys in Hot Springs, Arkansas, in 1944. Seven years later, in 1951, Jones became a member of the Rangers Quartet, operating out of Dallas. He remained with that group until 1954, at which time he organized his own group, the Deep South Quartet, which included his brother, Brownie Jones. The Deep South Quartet was featured on the Jimmy Dean TV show in Washington, D.C., during much of the three years that the ensemble remained intact. Jones left the quartet in 1957 and moved to Atlanta, where he became affiliated with the LeFevres, and remained there until 1968. For approximately ten of those years, the LeFevres were seen by national audiences on the syndicated television show "Gospel Singing Caravan." After his stint with the LeFevres, Jimmy Jones established his own publishing company in Atlanta and ran it until

The Sunshine Quartet from Allen County, c. 1942. The group was made up of various Allen County residents and performed from 1938 to 1948. *Photo courtesy of E.D. Austin.*

1974. He sang with the Atlanta-based Good News Singers into the early 1980s, then formed a group called Jimmy Jones and the Heralds, an outfit that still sings on weekends.

Previous to their affiliation with the Sunshine Quartet, Erlis Austin and Jonas Britt had both been members of the Allen County Quartet, an all-male group. Austin and Britt sang the second tenor and baritone parts respectively. With them were Ernest Marion, bass; Dewey French, first tenor, and Bill Piper, pianist. French also performed a popular routine during concerts by drawing a fiddle bow across a handsaw to produce easily recognizable tunes.

The Dixie Four was another all-male quartet of the 1930s. In keeping with what was still commonplace elsewhere in the South, the only musical instrument employed by the group was a guitar played by one of the singers. Organized in 1937, members of the Dixie Four included Mack Withers, soprano; Ernest Ward, baritone; Ivis Roy, first tenor and guitarist; and Elbert Smith, bass. This Russell County ensemble sang together until the outbreak of World War II, performing mainly for local and regional audiences. Some of the group's personnel, however, continued prominently in gospel music both during and after the War. Ivis Roy declined an offer in 1942 to sing professionally with an entirely different Dixie Four operating out of Indianapolis.

Representative all-male a cappella groups from the 1930s include the Columbian, Templeman, and Vaughan Kentucky quartets. The first of these three was organized in Russell County in the winter of 1929, making its first public appearance in 1930. Personnel included Silas W. Grider, first tenor; D.W. Wilkerson, second tenor; Malcolm Withers, baritone; and Albert Wilkerson, father of D.W., bass. Their ages ranged from fourteen to forty-three years. In a letter to me, Mrs. Wilkerson observed, "They had no way to travel except horseback, wagon or on foot. And even though they lived within 14 miles of each other, they practiced only when weather and convenience permitted."

"J.R. Grider, a Baptist preacher, and father of the first tenor singer," she continued, "took the quartet to sing for him in churches where he preached occasionally. When they sang in churches very far away, they'd have to hire their transportation, or sometimes the pastors of churches that invited them to sing would come get them or send a car and driver. They sang in Russell, Casey, Taylor, Adair, Wayne and Pulaski counties in churches and conventions. They were also invited to Cincinnati, and while there sang over Radio Station

Above: The Allen County Quartet. As part of their performances, Dewey French would produce recognizable tunes by drawing a fiddle bow across a handsaw. *Photo courtesy of E.D. Austin.* Below: The Templeman Quartet in 1946. Even though the group was formed in Hart County, all of the original members were from Edmonson County. *Photo courtesy of Guy Templeman.*

WLW." All in all, a remarkable record for a group that remained intact for only two years!

The Templeman Quartet of Hart County originated in 1934 in the Horse Cave-Munfordville area, but all of its male members were natives of Edmonson County and the products of singing schools there. Moreover, all of them taught shape-note schools for much of their adult lives. Guy Templeman sang first tenor for the group; Marvin Dennison, second tenor; Charlie Sturgeon, soprano lead; and Hollis Templeman, bass. They sang a cappella until Wesley Tucker of Scottsville joined them as pianist in 1940. He was still with the group in 1946, the year that the Templeman Quartet began singing live on WLBJ in Bowling Green.

The original Templeman four, accompanied by their second pianist, Betty Peebles, sang live over radio stations WTCO and WTKY in Campbellsville and Glasgow until the mid-1950s. About that time, Hollis Templeman stepped aside as bass singer and was replaced by Amos Waddle. The latter, claimed Audie Dennison on the basis of firsthand information, changed his name to Waddell (with stress on the second syllable) because "Waddle don't sound too good over the air." J.T. Light, singer and music teacher from Glasgow, said of the Templeman Quartet, "They were the best amateur group I ever heard sing." Such a plaudit notwithstanding, the group never issued any disc recordings. The year of their demise (1958) was still a bit early for the recording rage that was soon to grip local amateur groups. Scattered home recordings of their radio programs do exist, however.

Four other Edmonson County fellows joined forces in 1933 and sang a cappella for a year without a group name. They were Denny Stewart, Emmons Kinser, C.E. Deweese, and Billy Carrier. Deweese and Carrier formed another quartet about 1935 with Jesse Gilbert and Herman Luttrell. The latter group subsequently decided to attend one of Vaughan's normal schools. They left Lawrenceburg at the end of the session bearing the prestigious name Vaughan Kentucky Quartet and were commissioned to peddle Vaughan's songbooks at singings and singing conventions across Kentucky and adjacent states. The Vaughan Kentucky Quartet remained intact until 1938, when Deweese, Carrier, and Luttrell moved to Knoxville where they were joined by Stacy Abner to form the Vaughan Four. This new foursome had a daily radio broadcast over a Knoxville station and did well in that geographical area as Vaughan's representatives. Deweese left the group in 1939, however, following rumors that an unnamed member was "running around with other women." Deweese returned to Kentucky and soon united with the Sacred Five, whose members lived mostly in Bowling Green. Billy Carrier went from the Vaughan Four to become an original member of the Sewanee River Boys, a professional group based in Cincinnati at the time.[8]

The 1930s closed with a remarkably large number of local singing groups that had made it successfully through the throes of the Great Depression. Up to that point, congregations and quartets had been largely unaware of the large impact that shape-note music was having on other people in the South. But some of the singers had a sense of belonging to a larger stream of gospel music, thanks to the music publishing companies' newsletters, which told of music events and happenings in other states. Also, shape-note teachers, who taught music to local congregations and sold them songbooks that were printed by already legendary publishing companies, provided some information about singing activities elsewhere. Even these teachers themselves, however, had no local network that served to bind them together. Each of them worked for music companies that had strong, often bitter rivalries. Competition among some of the teachers for teaching appointments and book sales further served to keep them apart. And while it is true that touring professional quartets such as the Vaughan and Stamps groups began to enter the area by the mid- to late 1920s, performances by such groups would not become common across south central Kentucky until the late 1930s. Only then was shape-note singing seen by local people in a broad perspective.

Virtually all of the groups that originated prior to World War I, and especially before 1930, are still surrounded with a certain mystique that present-day groups cannot lay claim to. According to area residents who have lived long enough to hear the best vocalists and ensembles of both eras, later ensembles seldom measure up to the vocal and hamonic quality of the early quartets. Romanticism of the past certainly accounts for a sizable portion of this claim. Yet, the fact that most early singers had been pronounced experts both by shape-note music teachers and by peer judgment lends credibility to claims of excellence for those pioneer foursomes.

Quartets enjoyed increased popularity throughout the 1930s, but singing by church choirs also remained very much in vogue. Both types of ensembles stayed close to home during that decade, however, as the Great Depression lay heavy on the land. Singers and non-singers were of necessity homebodies. It is true that there were a few automobiles by then, but unimproved roads, especially during winter months, made travel to distant points virtually impossible. Those people who could and did travel in cars still talk about the inordinate numbers of flat tires they fixed, especially during the early 1930s.

One group had six flats en route to a singing engagement eight miles away. The church remained the center of social life in the community, and the focal event in many churches was a regularly scheduled gospel singing, usually monthly, but sometimes weekly.

To this point, small group singing ensembles were largely reflections of shape-note music schools. Indeed, many of the singers doubled as music teachers. Changes in gospel music were just around the corner, however. Sweeping changes in sounds, performance, and commercialization would take this type music away from its singing school roots.

4

THE TRANSITION YEARS

The onset of the 1940s brought slightly improved economic conditions to south central Kentucky. Better roads were being built and this meant newer cars and pick-up trucks, at least until the advent of World War II brought the manufacture of civilian vehicles to a sudden halt. Counties began the long, laborious process of consolidating rural schools and providing bus service for students who had until then walked up to two miles each way to and from school. Churches retained strict adherence to biblical teachings and they still treasured good congregational singing—quality singing that was to lose its luster by the late 1940s for a membership that was by then becoming increasingly mobile and consumer conscious. Even people who remained loyal to their home churches during the post-war years became passive consumers of gospel music by turning the singing over to visiting quartets with their electrically powered public address systems, fancy clothing, and flashy showmanship. Numerous local quartets that originated in the 1940s moved into this remarkably strong gospel music current that increasingly dominated the gospel music scene.

Not all of the amateur quartets formed in the 1940s changed their images in response to the influence of the visiting quartets. Some of them preferred to operate within the parameters staked out by earlier ensembles, especially in the matter of singing without musical accompaniment. There were at least twelve groups formed during this decade in south central Kentucky that chose to use neither guitar nor piano. Instead, they preferred to demonstrate that, by virtue of shape-note training, it was still possible for the human voice to provide all

NOEL VINCENT, ELRIE LINDSEY, HOYT WEBB, ELZIE LINDSEY, JOHNNIE LIND
SAM ALGOOD, Announcer

The Lindseyville Quartet in the late 1940s. They performed live over WKCT in Bowling Green in 1949 and were regulars on Rev. L.D. Robinson's preaching program during the 1950s. *Photo courtesy of Johnnie Lindsey.*

the music needed to sing a song properly. The Embry Quartet of Brooklyn in Butler County used only a pitch pipe for keying songs between 1946 and 1959. Four Pulaski County groups, namely the Ansel Quartet (1948-63), Nancy Bunch (1943-52), Old Country Church Quartet (1948-51), and the Woodstock Quartet (1945-58) also performed without accompaniment. Other groups that sang a cappella during the 1940s included the Elmore Quartet of Glasgow (1947-49); the Old Timers of Edmonson County (1945-48); the Jamestown Quartet (1948-53); the Scrap Iron Quartet of Munfordville (1947-49); the Riddle Quartet of Bow in Cumberland County (1942-52); the Lindseyville Quartet of north Edmonson; and the York Quartet of Albany.

The Lindseyville and York Quartets are representative of singers and singing patterns in the forties. The Lindseyville Quartet was organized in 1943 and was comprised of two brothers, Johnnie M. and Elrie Lindsey, who sang bass and baritone, Claude Skaggs as lead, and Noel Vincent on the first tenor part. A third Lindsey brother, Elzie, formerly of the Holly Springs Quartet, began singing lead for the group in 1944 when Skaggs left. Hoyt Webb joined the ensemble as bass singer in 1945, following his return from the army. He sang bass, Vincent became their full-time guitarist, Elrie Lindsey switched to first tenor, and Johnnie sang baritone. Beginning in 1949, they performed live every Saturday afternoon over station WKCT in Bowling Green, at a time when one microphone was standard equipment. In the early 1950s, the Lindseyville Quartet was also heard over WGGC in Glasgow, which is now WPRX. They performed as part of Rev. L.D. Robinson's preaching program.

Robinson asked the group to have some recordings made at his expense for him to use when they could not be present. These recordings "played from the inside out, that is, the needle played from the inside of the disc outward," recalled Johnnie Lindsey. Lacking the faith that they could make it as professionals, the boys from Lindseyville declined an offer to travel with the John Daniel Quartet as opening act. They continued to sing at local functions and, with the same personnel still intact, disbanded in 1965.

The York Quartet was formed in 1947 by Marvin York and three teenage boys from the Albany area. York sang bass, George Butler sang lead, Johnny Howard was the first tenor, and Harlin Farmer, the second tenor. The York Quartet comprised these same four singers until it was dissolved in 1949. Johnny Howard recalled, "Most of the singing we did was at the funerals of servicemen whose bodies had been returned home after the War. There was one after another after another."

Early in the group's career, they were invited by John Lair to come to Renfro Valley to perform at the National Singing Convention in 1947. Howard's recollection of the event illustrates typical audience support of unknown amateur quartets:

WLW and WHAS were both carrying the Convention. And there were two thousand people inside and five thousand people outside that day listening through speakers. A large group of singers from everywhere. But the number one quartet in the nation at that time was the Sunshine Boys. They were the featured quartet.

Well, it fell our lot to sing right after them. And we'd already been told there were to be no encores. So the Sunshine Boys sang their song and got a big hand. Then we came out and did our number and just brought the house down. And they wouldn't hush. We went backstage. And they finally motioned us to come out. We had to come out and sing another chorus. And I think that we were the only ones that had an encore that day.

Part of the reception that we got that day was because Marvin was so uptight hoping that we could handle this appearance before all that crowd, singing together into one microphone. You have to get pretty close. And Marvin was on the opposite end of the group from me. And he had my arm in his grip and was about to break it! And I reached across the other guys and got Marvin by the tie and pulled his face right down into the mike when he was singing a bass note. See, he didn't realize that he was about to squeeze my arm off!

But there was a good lesson from that because us young guys all got the big head something terrible that week. Well, the very next week we were at Sgt. York's home church in Tennessee. He was a distant relative of Marvin's and I knew him personally. We still had a big head. Well, we got up to sing our song and did a good job and the crowd was appreciative. And then a little trio—two girls and a boy—got up with an old strum guitar and did their number and brought the house down. And that put us back on our heels pretty good. So, it's not how good you are; it's where you are when you're singing.[1]

At least five other all-male groups that originated in the 1940s chose to use only a guitar for accompaniment. These were the New Hope Quartet of Logan County; the Cumberland Mountain Boys of Russell County; the Smith Brothers Quartet of Quality in Butler County; the Bethany Quartet of Somerset; and the Bethelridge Junior Quartet. The sound produced by these groups was still southern four-part harmony, however, rather than country. Such groups chose to use the guitar because numerous churches where they sang did not have pianoes. Most of those that did, it is said, failed to keep them tuned. It was simpler to take along a guitar, tuned and ready, as a device for keying the songs and accompaning the vocalists.

The Cumberland Mountain Boys (1942-47) included widely her-alded Mack Withers as soprano; equally renowned Ivis Roy as first tenor; Joe Setser as bass; and Clifton Carroll as baritone and guitarist for the group. Their quick fame won bookings for them all over Ohio, Indiana, and Michigan. In one instance the Cumberland Mountain Boys sang in Canada. They called Cincinnati home, although Roy continued to reside in Russell County throughout his affiliation with the group. He maintained ties with the others by commuting every weekend from his home near Font Hill to the Queen City via the Short Way Bus Lines to Somerset, and Greyhound on to Cincinnati—a trip of four and one-half hours. At the conclusion of each Sunday evening singing engagement, most of which were within three hours of the Cincinnati bus terminal, the other singers rushed Ivis back to

The Cumberland Mountain Boys sang not only in Kentucky, but also in Ohio, Indiana, Michigan, and even Canada. *Photo courtesy of Ivis Roy.*

the station in time for him to board the midnight bus bound for Somerset. Roy's wife, Thelma, met her travel-weary husband at Font Hill at daybreak, took him home, fed him a hearty breakfast, and then watched him leave for the barn to harness the mules in preparation for a full day's work on the farm.

Both the Smith Brothers ensemble (1946-72), which comprised Raymond, Donnie, Dewey, and Ralph, who was also guitarist, and the Bethelridge Junior Quartet (1948-53) began when the members were young boys. The latter foursome (described more fully in a later chapter) was composed of two brothers—Lewis Randolph and Ronald Haste—and two of their uncles, Virgil and Harold Haste. A third uncle, Drude Haste, played guitar for the boys, whose ages ranged from six to ten years. The youngsters' main claim to fame then was the number of times they sang at Renfro Valley and, consequently, over national radio broadcasts. After a twenty-year hiatus, the group reformed as the Happy Travelers in 1971, with virtually no changes in personnel. Thanks to a lifetime of singing and to their progenitors, who drilled music into their heads, these fellows produce what is perhaps the most finely tuned four-part harmony ever heard in the Lake Cumberland area, past or present.

Another group of singers from the eastern part of the region is the Bethany Quartet. This Somerset-based foursome was organized in 1946 with Esau Huff as soprano; Cordell Eldridge, first tenor; Robert Whitaker, second tenor; and Lee Harper, bass. Edward Whitaker was their guitarist. They sang over WCPT in Corbin in 1946. The second set of personnel included Esau Huff and Robert Whitaker in their familiar roles, with Ray and Elva Phelps, husband and wife, singing the bass and alto parts. Edward Whitaker was still guitarist. The latter personnel were featured on WSFC in Somerset from 1947 to 1952.

In 1957, most members of the Bethany Quartet moved to Indianapolis, where they continued to sing under the group's old name. Huff, who by then was a Baptist minister, stepped aside in favor of Blind Bill Stanley, who played the piano as well. The Whitakers were no longer with the group, having been replaced by Stanley as musician and a tenor singer from Monticello.

The Indiana contingency of the Bethany Quartet issued an LP album under the title "Time Has Made a Change," bearing the imprint of the Cincinnati-based Rite Records Productions. The group placed their own photograph on the front of the album, but the cover contains an old picture of the Bethany Quartet posed in front of the WSFC microphone in Somerset, which makes a strong statement about the group's roots and of the members' desire to cling to their southern origins.

Two of the top local ensembles organized in the 1940s were all-male groups. These were the Crusaders and the Kentucky Crusaders. The former group was originally composed of men from Allen and Warren counties, including Garnet Cassaday, Harold McCleary, William Buchanan, Wilmot Carter, and H.G. Sledge, pianist. The Crusaders were featured on WKCT in Bowling Green during the late 1940s and early 1950s and garnered a rather large following of fans in the process. And while most of the original members left the group to form the Kentucky Crusaders in 1948, another set of singers assumed the name Crusaders and continued to sing under that banner until 1958.

The Kentucky Crusaders was an Allen County ensemble that sang all over Kentucky and Tennessee, as well as in three adjacent states, between the years 1948 and 1959. Original members included Harold McCleary, Wilmot McCleary, Garnet Cassaday, and William

Above: The Bethany Quartet from Somerset was organized in 1946 and sang in Kentucky until 1957, when most of the members moved to Indianapolis. *Photo courtesy of Ray and Elva Phelps.* Below: The Crusaders in 1950. Most of the original members left the group in 1948 to form the Kentucky Crusaders, and a new cast of Crusaders took their place and performed until 1958. *Photo courtesy of Garnet Cassaday.*

Above: The Southern Harmony Boys, c. 1950. In 1983 they changed their name from "Boys" to "Quartet," when Hazel Eaton Bryson joined the group as alto. *Photo courtesy of Ed White.* Below: The Cumberland River Boys in 1949. The group originated in Cincinnati in 1941 when three Russell County natives teamed up with a Corbin man. *Photo courtesy of Curtis Wilson.*

Buchanan, with the well-known Lazarus Thomas as their pianist. This group issued numerous 78 rpm recordings, the last of which was "Every Day Will Be Sunday Bye and Bye."

Groups with male singers and female pianists included, from the western part of the region, the Burton Memorial Quartet (1943-48) and the Southern Harmony Boys, both of Bowling Green, and the Patterson Quartet (1940-41) of Franklin. The Lake Cumberland area boasted of five women pianists in the 1940s, including those who played for the Cumberland River Boys, Sunny Valley Boys, and the Dixie Melody Boys, all from Russell County; the East Somerset Quartet (1946-50); and the Highway Quartet (1949-51) from Clinton County.

The Southern Harmony Boys appeared on the gospel music scene in 1949, and the group remained intact without a change in personnel (except for a brief period when Keith Gabehart substituted for Ed White) until 1971 when M.B. Fleming had a stroke and had to stop singing. The original members again joined forces in 1977 and sang until Duncan Houchens left the group in 1980. That legendary quartet included Ed White, one of the finest first tenors to be identified with south central Kentucky. The lead part was sung by Frank Weaver, who had played country music with the Allen County Ramblers prior to his military service during World War II. Duncan Houchens, who was described by Garnet Cassaday as having the best second tenor voice he ever heard, sang baritone; M.B. Fleming of Gallatin, Tennessee, who was also renowned for his vocal ability, sang bass for the group; and Fleming's wife, Mae, who studied piano under Everett J. Butrum, was pianist. Brodus Tabor, formerly of the Melody Makers, joined the group when Houchens retired. The group changed their name from "Boys" to "Quartet" in 1983 when Hazel Eaton Bryson, alto, replaced the ailing Ed White to become the group's first female vocalist.[2]

The Cumberland River Boys originated in Cincinnati in 1941 when three Russell County natives (Armes Smith, lead; Lawrence Wilson, first tenor; and Morris Gaskin, bass) combined talents with Clifton Carrol, a Corbin native who sang baritone and played guitar for the group. That particular configuration was short-lived, however, as Smith and Gaskin were inducted into the army. For an entire year before their dissolution, the group was featured live each Sunday evening over WCPO in Cincinnati.

A second set of personnel came together in 1946 to form a Cumberland River Boys ensemble, this time in Russell County. Smith and Gaskin were charter members again, along with Hubert Wilson, baritone; Delmain Powell, first tenor; and June Gaskin, Morris's wife, as the group's pianist. They sang for six months over a Danville radio station, then for a year over WTCO in Campbellsville. In June 1948, they were on the program at a Stamps all-night singing in Dallas.

That same year, the Cumberland River Boys did a series of fifteen-minute radio broadcasts for Buhner Feed Company over station WAVE in Louisville every Saturday morning. The program was syndicated and was carried on a network of twelve Kentucky radio stations. This particular set of Cumberland River personnel disbanded when the Buhner contract expired.

The Cumberland River Boys continued until 1958, but by then only one familiar name, that of Armes Smith, was still included in the group. Other members at various times in the 1950s included Hartsell Hodges, Curtis Wilson, Faldeen "Flukie" McKinley, Keith Gabehart, Brodus Tabor, and Elgin Altheiser. Pianists included Albert Hunt of Morgantown and Wesley Tucker of Scottsville.

The Sunny Valley Boys came into existence in 1947, drawing upon some of the later members of the Cumberland River Boys, namely Flukie McKinley and Curtis Wilson. Walden Rexroat, Ermil Wilson, and Zelvia McKinley, pianist, were the other charter members. At the suggestion of Frank Spencer, a music teacher from Nancy, they took the name of his earlier quartet. The personnel remained intact until 1949, at which time Curtis Wilson left to join the Cumberland River Boys. The Sunny Valley name was revived again in 1956 with Wilson taking the lead in reactivating the group. This set of personnel remained intact for only a short time, however, and the name Sunny Valley Boys was laid to rest permanently.

The fluidity of personnel in the Cumberland River Boys and the Sunny Valley Boys, as well as the Crusaders and Kentucky Crusaders, illustrates how easily a singer or musician slipped out of one group to join another. It was not uncommon in those days for a singer to be with as many as six different ensembles in a lifetime. Dit Madison, now with the Hopewell Quartet in Edmonson County, claims to have sung with a total of twelve groups.

The Dixie Melody Boys offered no exception to this rule. From the time of the group's inception in 1948 until its demise in 1968, at least one dozen singers and musicians performed with the group at one time or another. The original Dixie Melody Boys included Ivis Roy as first tenor, Gover Rexroat as baritone, Mack Withers on the lead, and Morris Gaskin as bass singer. June Gaskin, Morris's wife, was pianist for the group. These singers issued two 78 rpm recordings bearing the Acme label and containing the songs "Just a Closer Walk with Thee," "Death Will Never Knock on Heaven's Door," "I Am Thine Forever," and "You've Got to Have That Old-Time Religion." By 1950, Oscar Robertson had replaced Gaskin as bass singer; Leonard Sears sang the baritone; Withers and Roy were in their familiar spots as lead and tenor, respectively; and Elva Sears, Leonard's wife, was pianist.

The high-pitched harmony of the Dixie Melody Boys won for them the state gospel singing competition in 1951, an event sponsored by the Kentucky Farm Bureau. From 1952 to 1957 they sang over WAIN in Columbia, a radio station that was by then well-known in gospel music circles. Other people who sang with the Dixie Melody Boys at one time or another included Lucian Ware, now high tenor with the Crossroads Quartet; Walden Rexroat; Bernard Setser; and Doug Roy. Betty Smith and Roger Popplewell enjoyed periods of service as pianists for this renowned group.

Women performers sang in a surprisingly large number of ensembles in the 1940s. They had been performing in limited numbers all along, despite opposition from those who believed that an all-male group could produce the finest quality harmony. Some people with whom I talked felt that the presence of a woman, whether as singer or pianist, precluded longer road trips by the group, especially if she was not the spouse of one of the singers.

Included among the 1940s groups that benefited from the presence of female soprano and/or alto vocalists were the Walker's Chapel Quartet of Allen County; the Happy Valley Quartet and John G. Salmon Quartet from Glasgow; the Butler County News Quartet; the Mills Quartet from Clinton County; the Hart County Quartet; the Janes, Grace Union, Beaumont, and Antioch quartets, all from Metcalfe County; the Berea and Gamaliel quartets of Monroe County; the Whittaker and Edwards quartets from Pulaski County; the New Friendship and Gospel Harmoneers quartets of Russell County; the Friendly Five, Hudson-Thomas, Plano, and Spiritual Five quartets from Warren County; and the Rector's Flat Church Quartet of Wayne County. All of these were very fine ensembles, it is said, and deserve to be described at some length. I have chosen, however, to feature only the Grace Union Quartet and the Melody Makers, which in one or more ways are typical of the other ensembles.

Original members of the Grace Union Quartet included Mary Hurt, alto; Sherman Hurt, Mary's husband, bass; Ollie England, tenor; and Henry Froedge, who sang lead and played guitar for the group. The quartet was organized in the late 1940s, taking the name of their home church, the Grace Union Baptist Church. All personnel

Known as "The Blind Troubador" since his early country music days, Troy Basil leads the Cave City–based Gospel Troubadors in a poignant rendering of "Send the Same Angel for My Mama." *Photo by the author.*

could sing the shape-notes, as they had studied music under Archie Hume. From the onset, theirs was one of the most popular singing groups in all of south central Kentucky, a reputation this seasoned ensemble retained until it was disbanded about 1974. John Lair (not the Lair associated with Renfro Valley) had replaced Froedge when the latter moved to Indiana, and Elma Lair, John's wife, became the group's first pianist. At the death of Mr. Lair, young Wayne Sexton sang the lead part and played bass guitar for the next twelve years. Others who played or sang with the Grace Union Quartet include Clifton Steele (formerly of the Steele Twins country music act), Lester Dillon, Barbara Hurt, and Troy Basil, "The Blind Troubador," who, since 1960, has headed up his own very fine country gospel group called the Gospel Troubadors.

The charter cast of the Grace Union Quartet sang live over WAIN in Columbia for an hour each Sunday beginning in 1951. Their theme song for the twenty-six years they were on the air was "Just a Little Talk with Jesus." They consistently received fifty to sixty fan letters each week, many of which carried requests for the song "Tree of Life." These requests were all acknowledged over the air between

The Grace Union Quartet was organized in the late 1940s. The original members sang the shape-notes they learned from Archie Hume. *Photo courtesy of Mary Hurt.*

songs and sips of coffee. Mary Hurt recalled that the group always took a large thermos of Maxwell House coffee with them each week. "We would talk about our Maxwell House coffee on the radio," she said. "And the FCC called in and said we couldn't call the name of the coffee. We could say 'coffee' but not 'Maxwell House.' Well, we got a bunch of letters that we just tied up and sent to New York to the company," she went on. "They wrote back and said, 'We'll be your sponsor for two years.'"

The group choose to terminate its tenure with WAIN after the station's broadcasting format was altered in the mid-1970s, leaving no room for live shows. Rather than provide the pre-recorded tapes requested by the station management, the Grace Union outfit ended the longest continuous gospel broadcast affiliation ever in south central Kentucky.

The Grace Union group traveled extensively, singing in one or more places each weekend. The Hurts' son, Jack, who now has his own group called the Spirituals, recalled their hectic schedule in the 1950s and 1960s: "We would get up at 6:00 on Sunday morning, get dressed, and head for Columbia to the radio station. They would sing there every Sunday morning. They would then leave there and drive maybe fifty or sixty miles to an appointment that afternoon or that night. . . . I can remember one time in my life, but I can't tell you the places they went, but they made five different singings in one day."

This historic group began the process of retirement in 1973, because of Sherman's failing health. By 1975, it was all over. Sherman lived an additional fourteen years but was never well again. Mary still resides in Edmonton.

Equally as famous as the Grace Union ensemble and just as long-tenured were the Melody Makers of Bowling Green. The group was organized in 1946 with Clara Helen Reynolds, alto; Glen Conner, tenor; T.Y. Tabor, bass; Brodus Tabor, baritone; and Wesley Tucker at the piano. They immediately won a position of prominence among the region's gospel singers by virtue of their very fine four-part harmony. And while the group's personnel changed from time to time over the next thirty-three years, the quality of their sound remained constant. Many knowledgeable locals rank the Melody Makers among the top groups ever produced in south central Kentucky.

Frank Weaver, who replaced Conner, joined the Melody Makers about 1948, then left the group in 1949 to become a charter member of the Southern Harmony Boys. Ralph Conner, lead, and Bronville Tabor, tenor, had joined the group by 1955. By then, Clara Helen Reynolds had left the group. Subsequent additions included Curtis Wilson, Bobby Bullock, and Bobby Simpson, all noted singers before and after their stints with the Melody Makers. Wilson declined an opportunity to join the Stamps Quartet, a professional group operating out of Dallas, although Bullock did sing with the touring Frost Brothers in the early 1970s, and Bobby Simpson sang with the Ambassadors of Nashville in 1973-74.

The five all-female groups that originated in the mid- to late 1940s are remembered for their strong emphasis on vocal control and tight harmony. Two of these ensembles were from Allen County, that bastion of quality gospel singing. The other three groups that originated in 1948 were from Casey, Clinton, and Taylor counties. The first of the two Allen County groups was the Holland All-Stars, an ensemble that likely began in late 1944, following a singing school taught by Perkin Meador. Thelma Wade Gibbs sang the alto part, Chlorine Wade Wood sang tenor, Lula Gray sang soprano, and Mildred Hudson sang the bass. Their pianist was Pauline Hinton. Unlike the other well-traveled female groups of that decade, the All-Stars sang close to home and generally in connection with singing engagements that also involved the choir from their home church. The larger group typically traveled to appointments on truck beds or in buses chartered for the occasion.

Above: The Melody Makers, c. 1947. Many rank them among the top groups ever organized in south central Kentucky because of their superior four-part harmony. *Photo courtesy of Brodus Tabor.* Below: The Holland All-Stars in the mid-1940s. They sang close to home—Allen County—and usually at singing engagements that included the choir from their home church. *Photo courtesy of Thelma Wade Gibbs.*

The Reeder Trio, formed in the mid-1940s, was made up of twins Mary and Margaret Reeder, and their cousin Ruth Ann Pope (center). Their pianist is Everett Butrum. *Photo courtesy of Mary Reeder Britt.*

The other all-female ensemble formed in Allen County in the mid-1940s was the Reeder Trio from the Midway community near the Simpson County line. The group comprised twins Mary and Margaret Reeder, and Ruth Ann Pope, a cousin. The twins were taught music by their mother, who, like their singer father, expected them to someday be gospel singers. "We sang because singing was all we knew," Margaret commented. "We grew up on it, and we sang because we enjoyed it."

The Reeder Trio went to Madison, Tennessee, on more than one occasion around 1950 to study music under Everett J. Butrum. A former pianist for the John Daniel Quartet and Odis Echols and the Melody Boys, among others, Butrum became pianist for the Reeder Trio. The Reeders won honorable mention on one of Ted Mack's talent search shows, held in Louisville. Had not Butrum been disqualified on the grounds that he was a professional pianist, the girls feel that they would have placed first. As it was, they had to sing with a substitute pianist chosen on the spot who was unable to keep precise pace with their singing.

The Reeder Trio performed widely in Kentucky, Tennessee, and, on occasion, in Indiana. Their most vivid recollection involving a singing engagement is of a 1953 appearance on stage at Ryman Auditorium in Nashville as opening act for the Oak Ridge Boys. "And we sang their song!" Mary recalled. "We sang, 'I Want to Go There,' and that was their song at the time. They didn't know we were going to sing it, but Everett Jewell made us do it. They followed us right up and sang it again, but they didn't seem the least upset with us," Mary went on. "They came backstage and told us if we'd had a little movement about us, we'd be the hottest thing on the stage! [Laughter]"

The Reeder girls got some of their songs from shape-note hymnals, thanks to their friend J.C. Haliburton, well-known Tennessee music teacher, who often made the actual song selections for the trio. Other songs in their repertoire came from recordings issued by professional groups and from sheet music that was becoming increasingly important by the early 1950s. They called it quits in 1956, when both Mary and Margaret were married at age eighteen. Their husbands, Depp Britt and Gene Oakes, were members of the Scottsvilleaires at the time. The Scottsvilleaires continued on after the weddings, and, in addition, the twins and their new husbands formed the Scottsville Echoes. Both groups still sing on occasion. Ruth Ann Pope (Law) continued to sing with area groups, and Sue Borders Holder, who replaced Butrum at the Reeders' piano, now plays and sings with her family group, the Holders, from Westmoreland/Scottsville.

The Haste Sisters of Bethelridge (discussed in chapter 9) and the Peanut Quartet, like the Holland All-Stars, were largely unheralded outside their home county and immediately adjacent ones. Hazel Farmer, one of the Peanuts, was destined for a singing career with two of her aunts in a country group known as the Farmer Sisters. They were regulars on John Lair's Renfro Valley broadcasts during the late 1940s and 1950s.

In addition to Hazel, the Peanut Quartet included Joy and Rosemary Pierce and Wanda Pittman. This foursome sang only those songs selected for them out of shape-note books by Hazel's grandparents, State Senator and Mrs. Claude Farmer. The Peanuts performed at monthly singings along the Kentucky-Tennessee border, as well as county fairs and Senator Farmer's political rallies. They were in heavy demand as a funeral quartet until disbanding in 1954.

The fifth and final all-women's group to be organized in the late 1940s was the Sunshine Girls from Campbellsville, a trio that had its beginnings in 1948 at the First Church of God in East Campbellsville. The group comprised Imogene Eastridge (Muncie), who sang alto and played the piano; Mildred Pike (Walker), bass; and Frances Eastridge, who sang the vocal lead. In 1949 the Sunshine Girls became a regular feature over WTCO in Campbellsville. At that time, Mary Frances Wilson (Neeley) was their pianist. The group was also featured on the Renfro Valley radio broadcasts.

The Sunshine Girls had early encouragement from Rev. John G. Salmon, pastor of St. Mark's Methodist Church in their home town and founder of the Kentucky State Singing Convention. He taught them to sing the shape-notes and to use shape-note songbooks during their concerts. They began to buy sheet music by the early 1950s, however, and looked to that market as the source of their songs thereafter. They left WTCO in 1953, when Frances Eastridge moved to Louisville. At that time, their pianist was Barbara Moore; Eastridge was tenor; Muncie was alto; and Maurice Eastridge (Wethington), Muncie's sister, sang the lead. Mary Frances Neeley replaced Eastridge at the tenor position. It was Muncie, Wethington, and Neeley who carried the vocal load until the group virtually disbanded in 1977 due to Muncie's failing health. They had at least four pianists (Rebecca Gabehart, Keith Gabehart, Mildred Ann Graham, and Garry Polston) during that period. The Sunshine Girls sang mainly at revivals and funerals after 1977. Their last public appearance was at a group reunion in 1987, an event that had been urged by their many fans. On that occasion they sang only "the old songs we used to sing," according to Imogene Muncie, who died in early 1989.

Over the years, the Sunshine Girls' style of singing remained consistent. They used both "broken" or "jumpy" songs, as the group called them, along with harmony songs during their concerts. Broken songs permitted each voice to take the lead on certain verses, while harmony songs called for greater vocal synthesis. Their fans' favorite songs included, "When Fair Heaven I See," "Help Me Lord to Stand," "Riding the Range for Jesus," and "Looking for a City."

High-quality acts like the ones described made it easy for touring professional quartets to find a friendly atmosphere for their appearances in south central Kentucky during the mid- to late 1940s. Singer Brodus Tabor observed that "quartet music, especially professional, was new to the area, and it began to catch on. People had heard class singing and congregational singing for years and years. This was something different." The process by which professional and local amateur quartets replaced shape-note singing in south central Kentucky was complete within a decade. Not only did the amateur quartet movement kill off its competition, it left in its wake a trail of hard feelings and torn allegiances that have yet to be totally mended.

In his article "Gospel Music Goes Uptown," Charles K. Wolfe cites *Billboard*, the leading trade publication for the commercial music industry, to demonstrate that it was not until about 1953 that gospel music was viewed as a professional genre. This increasingly popular music had been thoroughly commercialized for some time, however, by Vaughan, Stamps-Baxter, and other music publishers that had sent teachers and company-sponsored quartets into the field to publicize and sell company songbooks.[3]

Generally speaking, local singers and congregations were not aware of the friction that developed in the late 1930s and early 1940s between the publishing houses and the independent professional quartets like the Statesmen and the Blackwood Brothers who, by then, were realizing royalties from radio and record contracts and commodity endorsements. By the end of the 1940s, some of the big-name singing groups began buying out the songbook publishers. They sought ownership of the publishing houses, both as a means of carving heavier financial inroads into the gospel music industry and as a means of saving face at local county singing conventions across the South where they were often embarrassed at having to sit through congregational shape-note singing without being able to take part in sight-reading the music.[4]

The rift that occurred between the quartets and proponents of congregational and class singing lives on in the hearts and minds of some local singers. Ernest McKinley, long-time president of the still-active Russell County Singing Convention, pulled no punches in his indictment of quartet music and its participants. "It has ruined congregational singing," he asserted. "Just as soon as a quartet group is formed, they expect to be paid for singing," he went on. "And instead of coming to local singing conventions, the quartets will go wherever they can get an offering. I sing in a quartet and I love a quartet, but I think they have sung people to death. The churches have had just about all the singing that they care about," McKinley concluded.

His comments help to explain why he organized "a singing" for me in June 1988. That interesting event was staged at Coffey's Chapel Methodist Church, McKinley's home church. Featured that day were a half dozen song leaders who led the congregation in singing the notes and then the words to each of the songs. The leaders, most of whom are or were affiliated with quartets, included McKinley and Woodrow Wilson of Russell County, Johnny Janes and Hartsell Hodges of Adair, and Clarence Bertram, one-time minister at Coffey's Chapel but now a pastor in Taylor County. Two quartets were also present for the event, one of which was the Coffey's Chapel ensemble, and the other being Bertram's family group. The unequal balance between song leaders and quartets present that day clearly demonstrated how local singing conventions were carried out at one time and made a statement as to how such singing events should still be conducted. I came away from Coffey's Chapel that day fully aware that the rift between quartet and congregational singing that largely began in the 1940s and extended well into the 1950s and beyond has yet to be put to rest entirely. Such an achievement will take yet another generation.

5
THE BEGINNINGS OF
A NEW ERA

The period from 1950 to 1990 is one in which gospel music groups in south central Kentucky were spawned in abundance. There were all-male groups, all-female groups, mixed groups, and groups whose singers were of one sex with musicians of the opposite sex. Gender distinctions were generally of no consequence to these gospel music performers but such groupings help to describe them. The 1950s and 1960s were particularily productive years for gospel music, both in terms of new groups organized in the study area and in the overall advancement of gospel music around the country. When the 1950s began, eighty-seven gospel singing groups from previous decades were still active. Twenty years later, at the close of the 1960s, there were 142 active groups, representing a net increase of fifty-five. There were 204 new groups created during the twenty-year era, but a majority of them lasted for only a few years. The bulk of activity in both formation and cessation took place in the 1960s, due largely to changing sounds and performance styles in gospel music brought about because of the influence of rock and roll music and a changing technology.

In the 1950s, new sounds in gospel music began to emerge. No longer was the sound of this music produced by a small body of singers using only a guitar or piano for accompaniment. Marked changes in sounds and technology during the period of 1950 through 1969 were largely because of gospel music radio and television broadcasts, the introduction and widespread acceptance of 45 rpm recordings,[1] song sheets, and, to a lesser extent, rock and roll music. While the heavy percussion sound in local gospel music would not appear until the 1970s, electrically amplified equipment was introduced in the early 1960s. In all these matters, the amateurs attempted to emulate the professionals such as the Lefevres, the Happy Goodman Family, and the Rambos.[2] Professional gospel groups loomed large among the forces of change at work on local amateur quartets and trios in south central Kentucky and elsewhere across the South and Midwest by the early 1950s.

The influence of the professional groups began in the mid-1920s when quartets representing the Vaughan and Stamps-Baxter music companies began to make infrequent appearances here. By the mid-1930s, the Cycling Rangers (later called the Texas Rangers, then just the Rangers), who parked their "T-Models" at the edge of town and rode to the sites of singings on bicycles, were making appearances in the Bowling Green-Scottsville area.[3] By the late 1930s, and especially in the 1940s, the local scene was fertile ground for other big names. Odis Echols and the Melody Boys, the Statesmen, the Chuck Wagon Gang, the Blackwood Brothers, and the Oak Ridge Boys all came into southern Kentucky in their flashy automobiles and expensive, elegantly tailored suits. Garnet Cassaday vividly recalled those visits and how excited the local fans and singers were to have the early groups in the area. "We followed the big visiting quartets around from night to night," he reminisced. "We thought they was out of this world."

In their desire to emulate the touring pros, most of the locals were dressing alike and using public address systems during singing events; some even did a bit of clowning on stage, especially at non-church functions. Pianists, too, sometimes put on a show at the keyboard. In so doing, these musicians were following after the flamboyant keyboard patterns established by Albert Williams and Everett J. Butrum of the John Daniel Quartet, Hovie Lister, pianist for Conner Hall's Homeline Harmony Quartet, Dwight Brock of the Stamps Quartet, and the Blackwoods' Jack Marshall.

At least two local quartets active in the 1920s adopted the practice of wearing matching suits in efforts to look like the professionals; these were the Bowling Green Quartet and the Columbian Quartet of Russell County, noted for its blue serge suits. In the 1930s, other local singers adopted the dress-alike practice, and by the late 1940s virtually every area group that sang frequently away from home base chose to wear matching outfits. Kemble Johnson of Bowling Green and member of the TKI Boys in the 1950s, explains the choice to do so on the grounds that "looking good was part of the show. You had to look your best as well as sing your best."

"We were patterning after the Blackwood Brothers and the States-men," Frank Weaver commented. "The Southern Harmony Boys started to dress alike as soon as we organized in 1949," he recalled. "Dark blue suits with pin stripes. We've used everything since then! And still do. Not many do it now, but I still think it looks good," Weaver continued. "You're identified when you go out. If people see two or more members dressed alike, they know that you're members of the same group."

Lonnie Cockriel "always thought the practice was kind of silly" and still does. He recalled the tinge of resentment he felt in the late 1950s when he joined his first group and was told that he had to purchase a black wool suit to match those of the other three members.

As with every other facet of singing gospel music, the dress-alike fad is not without its humorous moments. Curtis Wilson of Columbia, who could vie with anyone in the region for the distinction of having sung with the most groups across the years, recalled an event in which his new suit was accidentally donned by another singer:

We stayed all night with C.C. Stout over in Macon County, Tennessee, and was getting ready to go to church and sing the next morning. As you can see, I'm not too tall. I'm 5'8". Well, Mr. Stout was a good 6'5". As the old saying goes, "I was built for comfort and he was built for speed."

We got ready to get dressed. We'd just got new matching suits. And he had a new suit, too, the same color. And I hadn't put mine on. I was just fixing to get dressed.

Well, Mr. Stout goes in there and gets dressed. And he came back out and he yelled, "Mama, how come you to get this suit so small?"

She says, "Why, it's not small." Says, "It's your size."

And he came through the living room, and those pants were about half way to his knees! And [heavy laughter] he says, "Mama, come and look at these pant legs." Said, "They're almost to my knees!"

He'd went in there and got *my* pants. Said, "Look here, too. They're too big around. Said, "They lap around my waist."

Most area trios and quartets no longer attempt to dress alike; singers figure that the practice is not worth the effort and cost involved. Likely, however, they would be amenable in the future to pressures of conformity in the matter of dress or, for that matter, other areas that might affect their style, performance, and appearance. Donnie Parker, formerly with the Servants and Joyways, articulates the trendy nature of some area groups, especially those with aspirations of becoming touring professionals:

Used to be, you know, everybody had to have a suit alike, a tie alike, a puff [handkerchief] in their little shirt, in their little coat, and drive a bus. That was their main ambition. Man, everybody had to have that. The heck with anything else.

At one time we [Servants] bought four bright red sharkskin suits. And they looked tough, really. Up on a stage with the lights on, they really looked tough, because we were trying to go professional. That's what we wanted to do.

And if you're to sing with the guys, the big guys, you're going to look like 'em and act like 'em and do like 'em. Really, that's just the way it is. So we tried that and we made it, but now it's all changed. We don't even have a suit that's alike. We dress in anything we feel like dressing in. And you see, just like in country music, some of those guys dress very sloppy, and they don't look nice to me; to me they don't. Even in rock, you know, they're really way out. I always thought an entertainer should be a person that would be in front of somebody and look decent, especially in gospel.

The use of public address systems was even more rare than dressing alike during the pre–World War II years of gospel music in south central Kentucky. Not only was electricity not available in all schools and churches where singings were held, but most of the church congregations would not have approved of the use of electrical amplification systems in the sanctuary, indeed would have viewed their presence in the altar area as a hindrance to worship. Hobart Haste of the Bethelridge Quartet commented that his group "did not use a PA system for years and years; we just reared back and belted it out." Similarly, Johnny Howard, with the York Quartet in the 1940s, recalled that his Clinton County ensemble did not employ an amplification system. "It was just all volume singing," Howard said. "Even now, I have trouble keeping my voice under control," he continued. "When I try to lower my tenor voice, it squeaks."

Erlis D. Austin, who sang with the Scottsvilleaires and other groups, felt that microphones were unnecessary, especially in rural churches with relatively small sanctuaries. And Doyle Rexroat of the Twilight Singers felt that "PA systems were not needed in earlier times because of the high ceilings in the old churches. Voices carried well in them. But anymore, church ceilings are low and absorb sounds," he went on. "If you don't have a PA system, many times it sounds like your voice is coming right back in your face." Doyle's wife, Reva, justified the use of microphones these days on the grounds that "they conserve your voice, and you can balance the different voices so that one doesn't drown out the others." Kemble Johnson commented that the first tenor and bass voices "have to strain pretty hard to hit those high and low notes." Amplification systems thus allow singers to create a sound that harmonizes with the other singers in the quartet, while protecting their own voices from over-work and strain. Bobby Sears of Somerset echoed the notion that singers will burn out in a short time without the use of amplification. "The loss of voice is a sure mark of an old-time singer," he com-mented, noting that his grandfather's voice was weak from years of "belting out the words."

Public address systems had first been introduced to local singers by visiting professional quartets who began exhibiting them in the early 1940s as an added means of entertaining church congregations and other public gatherings. Opinions of early area singers differ rather sharply over the question as to why they personally began to use amplification systems in the first place. Some agree with the above comments that it was to prevent excessive strain on the sing-ers' voices. Others sheepishly admit that they were slavishly copying the big-time groups for the sake of being in style and in step with the times. Unquestionably, there is truth in support of both positions.

During the early years of amplification, singing groups had one large microphone that they shared during concerts. Everett Butrum recalled that it was 1940 when the John Daniel Quartet purchased the then-popular one-mike Bogen system. Jack Hurt, leader of the pres-ent-day Spirituals, recalled the one-mike, one-speaker system used during the 1950s by the Grace Union Quartet:

They'd pick up their equipment and they're gone. Didn't have high-priced sound equipment. Mom and Dad carried it on the back end of a '56 Chevrolet.

It was a box that stood about twenty-four inches high and about twelve inches wide, and it separated. And there was a little fifty-watt amplifier inside of it with two cords that went from it to the speakers that you would put in the windows on each side of the church. And then you'd run one cord from the amplifier up to the mike. It stood up right in the center of everybody and everybody'd gather around that one mike. And they used an old flat top guitar.

And it took them about two minutes to pack that stuff up and take it out and set it in the back end of their car, versus today when a lot of the groups pull up in a van or a bus and they unload anywhere from $3,000 to $9,000 worth of sound equipment to take inside.

J.T. Light, leader of the Happy Aires of Glasgow, recalled seeing a public address system in 1948 for the first time. It was a one-mike system that belonged to the Gospel Five of Bowling Green. Not long after that, Light purchased one for the Happy Aires. "But nowdays amplification is overdone a lot," Light commented. "I'm not down on PA systems, but I just don't feel like the music should be so loud that you can't hear the singers."

As if cued by Light's concluding remarks, Libby McWhorter Mullinix of Albany, who is still remembered for her excellent soprano/alto singing with the McWhorter Trio and the Clear Chapel Trio in the 1960s, commented, "In this day and time, the PA system covers up a group's weaknesses." Her sentiments were echoed by numerous singers and fans alike, who generally feel that some gospel groups of the 1970s and 1980s used amplified instruments and other acoustical devices at the expense of good vocal harmony. Such groups traveled from one singing engagement to another in varying modes of transportation "dragging their p.a. systems behind them [in small trailers]," to quote from a feature story written by Joan Melloan of the Hart County-based Gospel Voices.[4] In spite of the aggravations involved with transporting sophisticated public address systems, the groups that use such equipment insist that their ensembles best serve the gospel music needs of modern-day Christians.

Perhaps in reference to the excessive use of amplification by some later groups, Erlis D. Austin claimed that "interest in quartet music was at its strongest in the 1940s, '50s, and into the '60s. It began to go down in the mid-1960s." Public interest in and attendance at gospel music events did decline sharply in the 1960s but for a multitude of reasons, not just because of the decibel factor brought about by more amplification.

In spite of the growing dependence on PA systems and electrical equipment, some of the a cappella groups whose personnel knew music fundamentals were still around in 1950 to greet the new era. Their style of delivery continued in importance between 1950 and 1969, as seven new a cappella groups sprang up in the 1950s, and two more in the 1960s. Most groups that typically used musical accompaniment sang at least one song without benefit of piano or guitar during each gospel music concert. This tradition continues today. Songs sung by talented a cappella groups do not suffer from lack of accompaniment, most people say. The sounds of harmony produced by these trained singers warm the hearts of listeners.

Among the a cappella groups that originated in the 1950s were the Casey County Quartet; the Happy Hitters of Lindseyville; the

Happy Four and the Pathfinders of Casey in Butler County; the Flat Lick Quartet of Shopville; the Lake Cumberland Quartet from Pulaski County; and the Johnson Family of Morgantown. The two a cappella groups formed in the 1960s were the Union Light Quartet of north Edmonson and the Brooklyn Quartet from Butler County.

The Union Light group was organized in 1961 by Georgie, Elsie, and Floyd Childress, along with Oren and Irene Priddy. They sang in churches, at singing conventions, and at funerals throughout their home area for about ten years. The group disbanded in 1972 when Oren Priddy dropped dead at church while singing. They regrouped a few years later, with the Childress family providing all the singers. Presently, the Union Light Quartet is composed of brothers Floyd and Georgie, Georgie's daughter, Elsie, and Elsie's teenage daughter, Andrea. All four know and faithfully employ the shape-notes, and continue to sing from new shape-note hymnals purchased twice annually. They eschew all fanfare, singing only at sister religious institutions in their immediate area and at funerals.

Perhaps influenced by the presence of female rock and roll acts, six female ensembles were formed in the 1950s, and eight additional ones in the 1960s. Three of these groups had male pianists. The very first group organized in that significant era of local gospel music history was the Stuart Sisters Trio, remembered for some of the tightest harmony ever heard in these parts. Sandra, Lana, and Norah Lee Stuart were all born in the 1940s in Portland, Michigan, to Kentucky-born parents. The Stuart family moved from Michigan to Springfield, Tennessee, in 1948, then to Bowling Green, Kentucky, in 1953. The girls began singing formally as a trio in 1952, with their father, Noble, playing piano and selecting and arranging their songs. Noble, a product of area music schools and years of quartet and congregational singing, knew music of all kinds from the inside out. His wife, Ima Mae, described Noble as a taskmaster. "When the girls practiced," she commented, "I left the house. He was a perfectionist. And he made them as near perfect as you could make three scatterbrained kids."

Noble defended the way he had dealt with the girls, then explained, "When we got a new song, we learned it exactly as it was written. Then we changed it the way we wanted to in order to make it fit their style." One of his teaching tactics was to have the three girls lie on the floor on their backs with their heads together. They sang in that position. Lana took the lead, Sandra the alto, and Norah Lee sang the baritone part an octave high. Everett J. Butrum claimed that the latter had a perfect ear for the fifth part—the harmony baritone.

The Stuart Sisters Trio. They won first place in the talent search conducted by the National Quartet Convention in 1960. *Photo courtesy of Noble Stuart.*

The Stuart Sisters Trio won first place over twenty-seven other groups in the talent search conducted in 1960 by the National Quartet Convention. They sang "Searching for You" at that event. The trio performed every weekend somewhere in Alabama, Arkansas, Georgia, Illinois, Indiana, Kentucky, or Tennessee from that point in their career until they disbanded in 1965 when Lana married Maurice Miller. Norah Lee continued in gospel music, joining forces for four years with Bobby Bullock (tenor), Terry Thornton (baritone), and Dave Hooker (piano) to form the Majestics, an ensemble that was described by Leonard Sears, Somerset singer and one-time State Convention president, as "the best mixed trio ever in the state of Kentucky." Norah Lee then sang for a brief period in 1966 with the Chuck Wagon Gang, and since 1980 has been a member of the Carol Lee Singers, the premier Nashville vocal backup group, which works regularly with the house band on the Grand Ole Opry. She is married to Duane Allen of the Oak Ridge Boys.

The other female groups to be organized during this twenty-year period included, in the 1950s, the Tonettes of Alvaton; the McWhorter Trio of Albany; the Kessinger Trio of Aberdeen; the Reederettes of Midway in Allen County; and the Melody Trio of Monticello. Groups that originated in the 1960s were the Three B's of Salem in Russell County; the Gospelettes (later the Trinity Trio) from Columbia; the Wooten Sisters of Eubank; the Gosser Sisters of Nancy; the Guffey Sisters of Wayne County; and the Gloryettes of Glasgow.

The McWhorter Trio was one of the finest quality female groups to come out of south central Kentucky, then and now. This family ensemble was formed in 1954 by Dorothy McWhorter (alto) and her daughters, Libby (soprano) and June (tenor). They sang to the accompaniment of Libby's accordian. June's husband, Larry Spears, replaced Dorothy in 1961. June and Larry went on to later fame as members of the semi-professional Rhythm Masters of Cincinnati. The McWhorter Trio remained intact until 1971, although the multitalented Libby also sang with the Albany-based Clear Fork Trio from 1962 to 1966.

Two additional all-female groups were formed in the 1960s that, like the Stuart Sisters Trio, had male pianists. The first of these was the Sunshine Girls from Scottsville, of which Margaret Keen Martin, who now sings with the Singing Martins, was a member. Gordon Meador, who has for many years been in the recording studio business in and around Nashville, was their pianist. The second group was the Friendly Four of Morgantown, comprising four talented singers who were accompanied at the piano by Doyle Lee. They disbanded about 1968 when one of the members left to get married. The others continued to sing as a group under the name Trebleaires before quitting entirely in 1969.

Excluding the three ensembles that had male pianists, the other "girl groups" (to employ the term used to describe female rock and roll groups such as the Teddy Bears, the Shondells, and the Chord-ettes) were equally recognized and heralded locally for their very fine tight harmony and performance styles. Most of them fancied up their acts a bit by using runs on the piano keys, choral backups for soloists, and other stylistic devices to demonstrate their command of the music. None of these girl acts are active at present, but the Guffey Sisters, the McWhorter Trio, the Stuart Sisters, and the Tonettes (along with the Friendly Four and Doyle) regrouped and sang again for their many fans at the Kentucky State Singing Convention's Heritage Sunday on October 15, 1989.

The large number of female ensembles created during the 1950s and 1960s should not be too surprising, given the large number of female rock and roll groups just before and after 1960. Also, the gospel music world was more liberal at that time than in the pre-1950 era. What had essentially been a male-dominated music genre now made more space and provision for women singers—in spite of scattered, unorganized but continuing resentment against the presence of one or more women singers in gospel music ensembles. And while the majority of groups of the 1950-69 era did include women in their ranks, there were other ensembles that did not. Most of the groups that had no women singers can offer reasons for their absence, some of which are totally valid; others are rather flimsily constructed.

The all-male quartets formed during this era may be grouped according to whether they used a guitar or a piano for accompaniment. The performance styles and vocal sounds of both categories were remarkably similar, thus indicating that those who used guitars only preferred the simplicity of the sound, the ease with which they could be transported, and the assurance of having a tuned instrument upon arrival at their destination.

Included among the new male groups of the 1950s that used only a guitar—at least at first—were the Happy Four from Breeding; the Renfrow Brothers Quartet of Brooklyn; and the Gospel Travelers of Columbia. The latter group was formed in 1950 when Paul Curry (first tenor), Lester Curry (baritone), Charlie Brockman (bass), and Gene Conover (lead vocalist and guitarist) came together as a four-some in Paul Curry's upholstery shop where they met weekly to sing. The Gospel Travelers were a smashing success from the onset, sing-ing over radio WAIN in Columbia, and on Channel 13 TV in Bowling Green. Problems arose within the group, however, and they disbanded in 1959.

Paul Curry set about immediately to organize a new group, this one to be called the Melody Aires. Curry continued to sing the tenor part; Elbert Burton, whose wife had suggested the group's name, sang lead; Houston Jenkins of Metcalfe County took the bass part; and Charlie Brockman switched to baritone. Burton's daughter, Thelma, was their pianist for a few years; her brother, Bob, was the guitarist. Thelma was replaced after six years by Steve Stepp of Russell Springs, who eventually turned the job as pianist over to Johnnie Johnson. Following a brief stint by Johnson, Darrell Moore, a youthful Elizabethtown school teacher, assumed the role as pianist and lead singer in 1978.

This fine gospel group has been and continues to be one of the most popular groups in south central Kentucky and across the Upper South. While retaining the status of amateur singers, they have performed all over Tennessee, Kentucky, Ohio, Indiana, and Illinois. At one time, they fulfilled 300 to 350 singing engagements each year but were forced by weary bodies to slow down a bit. Much of their success can be attributed to the members' benevolent spirits and their belief that they are doing their Lord's work. Money is, consequently, not a real factor to be reckoned with. All of them have full-time jobs. "I'd go back to a church five hundred miles away that gave us only fifty dollars," Curry observed, "just as quick as I would fifty miles to a church that gave us five hundred dollars."

In all, thirteen members of the Melody Aires have been called into the pulpit ministry, thus indicating something of the dedication and devotion that they have exhibited across the years. Personnel in 1989 included Curry and Jenkins, who have been together in the group all along. Other members included Moore, Chris Noll (baritone), and Larry Tarter on the bass guitar. Darrell Moore, still in his thirties, was struck down by serious illness in mid-1989. The group canceled all existing engagements, awaiting his return. He died in May 1990, with his position still unfilled.

Like other male singers with whom I have spoken about the lack of women in their quartet, Curry feels that a woman singer with a heavily traveled quartet provides people with an excuse to gossip. In his own words:

That's really why we have not used women members. It's not because of what might happen within the group. It would be too easy for people to start a tale on that woman, and they will do just that. And a scar like that hurts. If a husband was a member of the group, it would be fine to have his wife also; or a brother and sister, or a daddy and his daughter. It would be different then.

We've never had a member to act out of line. We've always cautioned

The Melody Aires in 1987. As of 1990, thirteen members of the group had been called to the pulpit ministry, indicating the dedication and devotion of the members.

each other about that, to always be careful. Personally, I think a woman's voice harmonizes better with three men, than four men together. But we've never considered a woman for the reason I talked about. You have to watch what you're doing and do your best to live the life you sing about. But it's not easy. A lot of good groups have gone down because of that one thing.

Curry then illustrated the need to be careful with the following humorous anecdote:

We was over in Albany. Huge crowd at a Baptist Church. And I knowed these people, a lot of people in that church. Well, there was this man and this woman on the front seat.

Well, the preacher told us to come down in front of the pulpit, and he told everybody else to stand. He said, "If there's anybody in this church that means anything to you, go to them and tell them." Of course, there was a big stir with people hugging necks and shaking hands, and a lot of them came up and shook our hands. After it was all over, everybody went back to their seats and set down. This lady on the front bench had never moved, but her husband came and shook hands with all our group.

About the time everybody got set down, she came and right around my neck she went. And kissed me! Oh, I was embarrassed. Right on the lips! And I just stuck my arms straight out and done like this [waves both hands up and down repeatedly]. I didn't want the people to think that I was hugging her or anything. So I just dangled my hands. After she got through kissing on me, she went back and set down by her husband. He didn't say a word.

Numerous other excellent all-male groups were formed in the 1950s and 1960s. They include the Southern Aires from Columbia; the Bonnieville Quartet; the Gospel Echoes of Franklin-Bowling Green-Scottsville; the Clintonaires of Albany; the Crossroads Quartet of Russell Springs; the Brooks Brothers of Casey in Butler County; the Forest Park Quartet, Travel Masters, Messengers, Kinsmen, and Faithful Aires, all of Bowling Green; the Thomas Trio/Quartet of Scottsville; the Gospel Melody Quartet, whose members were drawn from various area counties; the Servants of Campbellsville; and the Midway and Commanders quartets from Midway in Edmonson County.

All of these male groups were accorded immeasurable plaudits by both their fans and other area singing groups for demonstrating one or more of the qualities necessary to have a long and successful singing life. Namely, they were either very good singers, had a lot of performance pizazz, or knew the Lord they were singing about. Most possessed all three characteristics. The names of three groups are most prominent, however, when quality groups are singled out. They are the Crossroads Quartet, the Thomas Trio/Quartet, and the Servants. Like the Kinsmen and the Commanders (formerly the Midway Quartet), all three of these ensembles declined offers to turn professional. Actually, the Servants, under the capable leadership of Ernie Wise and Charles Witty (their resident song composer), did tour the East Coast, South, and Midwest as semiprofessionals on numerous occasions. They sold copies of their thirteen albums and tapes as they journeyed from place to place.

The Servants were accorded national recognition in 1985 when Witty's song "I Went to Jesus" climbed to number fourteen on the gospel charts. Of the three groups, only the Crossroads Quartet is active at the present time. That fine ensemble consists of S.D. McGaha (baritone); his son, Vernie (lead and piano); Lucian Ware (first tenor); Randy Wooldridge (bass); and Randy Ware (drums, since 1983). Wooldridge was the last singer to join the group, in 1976. The others were there at the start in 1960.

The Servants from Campbellsville toured the East Coast, South, and Midwest as a semiprofessional group and made thirteen albums.

During the period from 1950 to 1969, approximately nineteen additional quartets were formed of all-male singers with female pianists; more than sixty new mixed groups sprang up that used only a piano for accompaniment; twenty new mixed groups used only a guitar; ten mixed groups used both guitar and piano; one mixed ensemble, the Clear Chapel Trio of Albany, used a piano and an accordian; and one outfit formed late in the period, the Liberty-based Williams Family, was bluegrass in style.

Among the groups comprising male singers and a female pianist were the widely heralded Scottsvilleaires, Melody Masters, Tone Masters, Happy Rhythm Boys, Gospel Five, Dixie Airs, Gospel Tones, Travelers (Albany), Sons of Faith and Orena, Crusaders (Lewisburg), Joymakers, Jubilaires, Gospel Harmony Boys, and Christianaires (Fountain Run/Lafayette). All of these ensembles were high quality acts, according to informed reports, and the recordings I have heard of some of them bear out such claims of excellence.

The Crusaders from Lewisburg were widely acclaimed for their close four-part harmony. *Photo courtesy of Tom Webb.*

Many of these groups sang over one or more radio stations during their lifespans, and some performed on television. Most of them issued two or three LP albums, and some produced cassette tapes during the latter stages of their active years. The Joymakers, a semi-professional group under the guidance of Buddy Lowe of Greensburg, have twelve albums (some of which had concurrent issues of tapes) and seven more recent cassette tapes to their credit. Possessors of a quality sound in gospel music, the Joymakers have sung in virtually every southern and midwestern state. "We go anyplace," Lowe said, "just as long as we can get there and back in a long weekend." Like the Christianaires, Crusaders, and Scottsvilleaires, the Joymakers were still active at the beginning of the 1990s. Worthy of mention here also is Haywood Swift's Gospel Five of Franklin, whose roster of personnel reads like an all-star cast of area gospel singers. This widely known group had a weekly thirty-minute program over radio WFKN in Franklin, which ran uninterrupted for nine years in the late 1950s and 1960s. The following list of songs used on a Gospel Five program

in 1964 illustrates the content of one of those broadcasts and indicates something of the popularity of certain songs of that era:
"Getting Ready," "Without Him," "Happy in Knowing," "Life Begins
at Calvary," "When He Blessed My Soul," "My Soul Shall Live On,"
"Sweeter Each Day," and "I'm Too Near My Heavenly Home." All of
these songs except the third, fourth, and sixth are still sung by some
area groups.

Among the sixty-plus mixed-gender groups formed from 1950 to
1969, those that sang to the accompaniment of a piano only were
the Scottsville Echoes, an ensemble that declined offers to turn professional; the Union Aires of Tracy; the Waddell Quartet of Hart
County; Buddy Coursey's star-studded Kentucky Harmoneers of
Lewisburg; the Godby Quartet of Science Hill, described by a fellow
Pulaski County singer as "absolutely superb"; the talented Bertram
Quartet of southern Wayne County; the Templeman Family of Munfordville; and the Holder Trio/Quartet of Scottsville and Westmore-
land, a family-based singing group that was still around to welcome
the 1990s.

Among the other mixed groups of that era that were accompanied
by piano were the Southern Melody Quartet of Franklin with its well-
known cast of singers (Haywood Swift, Hazel Eaton Hire, Frank
Weaver, Edwin Dye, and Shirley Downey, pianist); the Whitter Fam-
ily, the Lake Cumberland Quartet, and the Fellowship Quartet, all of
Pulaski County; the Melody Singers of Lamb; the Messengers and the
Joyful Four of Butler County; the Happy Aires of Glasgow (made
famous in southern Kentucky and northern Tennessee by continuous
radio play of their recording "When the Sun Sets Over Jordan"); the
Harmony Echoes, the ever-popular Lyles, the Friendly Five, and the
Christianaires, all of Scottsville/Allen County; the Austin Aires; the
Singing Stuarts; and the still-active Turner Family of Bowling Green.

The Joyful Four of Morgantown is typical of the groups listed, as it
was one of the fine singing ensembles that brought much credit to
gospel music circles during the 1960s. This group began as the Joyful
Five in 1965 in the Brooklyn community of Butler County. Personnel
for both groups were the same for a brief period, even after the name
change occurred in 1968. Early members included Eulema Lindsey
Keith (lead), Ralph Wilson (tenor), Sue Lindsey Felty (alto), and Roy
Felty (bass). Their pianist was Oral Snodgrass, who was blind from
birth. When the Joyful Four disbanded in 1982, Snodgrass was still
playing the piano, but sang baritone as well. It is said that his vocal
rendering of "Most of All I Want to See Jesus" brought tears to the
eyes of believers and nonbelievers alike. Eulema was singing alto in

Above: The Scottsvilleaires were still actively performing in 1990. *Photo courtesy of Depp and Mary Britt.* Below: Buddy Coursey's star-studded Kentucky Harmoneers of Lewisburg. *Photo courtesy of Edwin Dye.*

The Gospel Five of Franklin sang for radio, steamboat, church, and school audiences for almost twenty years beginning in 1950. *Photo courtesy of Edna Swift.*

1982. The Lindsey brothers, Don and Doug, were with the group at that time, singing the lead and bass parts. In the group's later years, they added Larry Johnson as drummer and Phillip Rose as bass guitarist.

The Joyful Four were widely acclaimed during the group's lifetime but perhaps enjoyed their greatest fame from 1972 to 1976. It was then that they, along with another of Butler County's superior groups, the Travelers (headed up by the Fleners), co-hosted a monthly singing at the Butler County High School gym. It was during that period, too, that they made frequent trips into Tennessee, Indiana, and Illinois, singing for their fans there. Their reputation earned for them the front spot on a 1975 program with the Kingsmen at a Nashville singing event.

Mixed-gender ensembles of the period that used both guitar and piano from the very first included the always-popular, semi-country Temple Trio from Glasgow. The singers included Tommy Bellamy, one-time country musician who had toured the nation with Uncle Henry and the Kentucky Mountaineers; Bellamy's talented daughter, Tommie Kay, who turned down offers in Nashville to turn professional soloist; and Stanley Greer, who played piano professionally for the Sego Brothers and Naomi at one point in the early 1970s. The Temple Trio, formed in 1960, finally disbanded in early 1989, still singing to packed church sanctuaries and auditoriums. Tommy Bellamy now sings with the indefatigable Frank Weaver and the Southern Harmony Quartet of Bowling Green.

Groups from this period that used only guitar accompaniment included the Southern Harmony Quartet of Yosemite; the Egypt Hollow Quartet and the Lowhorn-Davis Trio from the Cumberland River area; the Baker Family of Cincinnati/Somerset; the Egypt, Feese, and Sunshine quartets of Adair County; and the Cedar Springs Quartet of eastern Russell County. In all, there were twelve known guitar-only groups from what is presently referred to as the Lake Cumberland area, and at least ten of these were Chuck Wagon Gang sound-alikes. The LP albums and tapes issued by these groups reveal that all of them did a fine job of reproducing the singing style made famous by the Gang. Little wonder that they copied the sound of this Texas-based group, however, as David Parker "Dad" Carter, founder of the Chuck Wagon Gang, was their neighbor from Milltown in Adair County.

Glen Roy of Nancy, Doyle Rexroat of the Cedar Springs ensemble, and others from the area, explained that Carter was a kind of hero to them. Not only had he founded the famous Gang, he had made it a point to return for annual concerts to the land of his birth. Roy recalled that in 1946, the Chuck Wagon Gang gave a concert in Columbia and netted $2,200 for their efforts, an unheard of amount to the local singers. Rexroat also noted, "Back in the 1950s and early 1960s they were still about the only professional group that ever performed in this area. And everybody liked their type of singing and copied after them." Their sound is produced by two strong female voices (alto and soprano), a male lead that often shifts to the melody part, and a deep, resonant bass voice. Properly emulated, the Chuck Wagon sound is soft, melodic, and beautiful. Rexroat described it as "not country but somewhere between the old singing convention sound and southern four-part harmony. A guitar is better than a piano for this type singing."[5]

All ten of the Lake Cumberland groups under consideration excelled at duplicating the Gang's sound, and some of them continue in this same tradition today. The Bakers, under the leadership of Donald and Wanda Baker of Somerset, still incorporate some of the older songs into their performances. And the Cedar Springs Quartet, now active under the name Twilight Singers, sang "O, Come Angel

Above: The Happy Aires from Glasgow are still remembered for their rendering of "When the Sun Sets over Jordan." *Photo courtesy of J.T. Light.* Below: The Sunshine Quartet of Columbia was heavily influenced by the sound of the Chuck Wagon Gang, whose founder was from Adair County. *Photo courtesy of Earl Feese.*

Band," one of the Chuck Wagon favorites, at the 1989 Kentucky State Singing Convention. Finally, the Egypt Quartet still employs this time-honored sound and style in all its songs, even when some of the compositions used are of recent vintage. While Mary Feese Cooley of this group did not mention the Chuck Wagon Gang in her August 1986 letter to me, her historical sketch of the Egypt Quartet is classic insofar as details surrounding group personnel are concerned. The letter reveals the importance she placed on identifying the group's singers and musicians, their periods of service, and their reasons for leaving the group:

In 1960, Earl Feese, his wife, Verna Feese, their daughter Mary and her husband Calvin Cooley decided to call their singing group the Egypt Quartet because we all lived in a little farm community called Egypt. Kay Bault played piano for the singers but Kay went to a Tennessee college in 1961 and Calvin Piercy joined the group to play guitar. In 1962, because of a heart condition suffered by Verna Feese, Hattie Denton would sing alto part of the time. Verna had open heart surgery just before Christmas 1962 and for awhile Hattie sang all the alto. Verna recovered enough to rejoin us again in the spring of 1963 but began to feel worse and had to quit again. Hattie decided to get married. She and her husband were moving to Indiana so she quit too in the fall of 1963.

Earl wanted to spend more time with Verna who was steadily getting worse so he quit also. Russell Holmes and his daughter Joyce [formerly of the Harmony Makers] then sang the tenor and alto. After about a year, Joyce decided that she needed to spend more time on school work and Russell quit when Joyce did. At about this same time, the soprano for the Southern Gospel Quartet [of Yosemite in Casey County] got married and moved away. Avery Carmon and Rebecca Williams of that quartet joined us to sing tenor and alto. In the summer of 1965, Calvin Piercy had decided the quartet was too time consuming and he wanted weekends free. We had done a radio program every Sunday since October of 1962, except in sickness or death in the family.[6] Billy Kassum had played guitar for years then joined us as musician and also sang from time to time with the quartet in the background. In 1966, Rebecca became ill and Callie Smith sang alto until 1969 when she moved away. Heloise Neat then joined us as alto. And in 1969 our younger daughter, Doris Jean Cooley, became bass guitar player for us. In 1971, Mr. Carmon began to have his throat hurt when he sang and he was then 70 years old and the traveling was hard on him. Mr. Albert Norris sang tenor until Heloise quit in 1973.

We could not find an alto but we did find a husband and wife who would sing tenor and alto. So Mr. Norris said o. k. and Robert and Katie McKinney sang tenor and alto. And Robert played guitar along with Billy and Jean. Early on in 1973 Jean got busy looking for a husband and Billy wanted to spend more time with his family. They both quit. Earl rejoined us and Jean sang alto for about six months. Heloise rejoined us in November of 1977. On August 19, 1986, we have Mary Cooley, soprano, Calvin Cooley, bass, Earl Feese, tenor, Heloise Neat, alto. Mary Cooley, guitar.

/s/ Mary Cooley

Some of the groups described in this chapter were by-products of the singing school era, as numerous singers had been schooled in music fundamentals. Other singers affiliated with trios and quartets knew that close harmony was the key to a good sound in gospel music, but by the end of the 1960s some of the newer performers were not as able as others to control their voices and manipulate the music to their needs. More than ever, the local ensembles, whose total numbers were now legion, were attempting to emulate the sounds and styles of the professional gospel groups. And they were not always successful. Some of the singers who had been around gospel music for awhile began to comment on the lack of harmony exhibited by some of these groups. Hartsell Hodges, easygoing quartet singer from Columbia, offered the following astute commentary on the declining quality of gospel music:

Too many people got involved in singing gospel music. Brought the situation to a peak with too many quartets, trios, and duos. Everybody got involved. Everywhere you went, there were all these groups. People finally just got worn out. We brought the people up, raised their standards of singing [by means of singing schools]. Well, the wrong people got involved in music and lowered our standards of singing. Too many of the groups couldn't give the public the quality of music that they had come to expect. People knew what a good sound was; we had taught them the importance of knowing the scales and so on. They knew if a person was singing off key, or singing the wrong part. Too many of the groups were singing without knowing their parts, or maybe they were all singing the same part—singing in unison. Well, just imagine how that sounded to people who had been to a singing school and knew something about music.

Many of the groups that originated in the 1960s knew very little about the fundamentals of music. This problem was compounded by the abundance of new ensembles formed during that decade for, as one person commented, "They just grew up like grass. Everywhere you went, there was a new gospel group." The lack of musical knowledge by the newcomers, however, was only one factor contributing to what was viewed as a decline in gospel music in the 1960s. Another divisive issue was what was first called "gospel boogie," and then "rhythm gospel." Some local amateur singing groups employed a vocal sound in the early 1960s that lived in the shadow of boogie yet portended the unorthodox tempo of rock and roll. And because of the song lyrics that personalized Jesus, many area singers began performing what one person called "Jesus-is-my-boyfriend music." By way of illustration, a quartet at the 1964 Kentucky State Singing Convention sang, "I'm In Love with Jesus, and He's in Love with Me." If a divergence in personal gospel music tastes was being registered on lesser matters in the 1960s, the rift would only widen in the coming years.

6

PRESENT TIMES

The year 1970 marks the beginning of the modern era in gospel music in south central Kentucky. One cannot date it from the 1960s even though some area groups issued LP albums early in that decade. These albums were a sure indication of changing times; however, the sounds of the singers and their musical accompaniment on those early albums were not unlike the older sounds of gospel music.

Even though rock and roll music had been around since the mid-1950s and had influenced the singing styles of some of the local gospel groups, the sound of a full set of drums was unheard of in gospel music until Jake Hess and the Imperials introduced them at mid-year in 1965 during a month-long series of gospel concerts for Kentucky's rural electric cooperatives. Later that fall, the Imperials used drums at an all-night singing in Birmingham, only to have a third of the audience walk out on them. Leaders of two other prominent quartets there that evening rushed up to Hess, exclaiming, "Now you've ruined yourself! You can't come back here anymore." Hess laughingly told me recently that both groups added drums to their own acts within five to six months. It seems humorous in retrospect, but the Imperials shook the gospel music world that year and created tension among gospel groups and their followers that has yet to be totally resolved.[1]

Changes occurred on the local level, but the transformation in the sounds created by gospel groups in south central Kentucky did not occur overnight. The Veterans, a Grayson County quartet from Leitchfield headed by Larry Mudd, was the first known Kentucky group to introduce the sound of drums, but that did not occur until

1968. Then in mid-1971 Buddy Lowe's Greensburg-based Joymakers employed a full set of drums. Following Lowe's lead, a few other ensembles in south central Kentucky, including the Edmonton Quartet and the Cook Family of Bonnieville, began using drums and other accoustical devices. Numerous groups tried their hands at drums in the 1980s.

Most area singing groups of the 1970s, some even in the 1980s, preferred to adhere to their comfortable, more traditional way of performing gospel music. Such was certainly the case with the eight known a cappella groups formed between 1972 and 1987. Six of them were from Edmonson County, that traditional stronghold of shape-note singing, while one of the others was formed in neighboring Hart County, and still another in distant Pulaski County.[2] Most of these singers are now between thirty-five and fifty years old, thus revealing the continued vigor of the singing school tradition, especially in the Mammoth Cave region. The Madison Brothers Quartet of Browns-ville nicely illustrates the rich singing heritage that most of these a cappella ensembles enjoy.

There are eight Madison brothers and all of them sing. The tenor singer, Joel, is a big fellow. At a 1986 outdoor singing on the court-house grounds in Brownsville, the emcee for the event introduced the Madison Brothers by commenting that the eight brothers had argued among themselves before singing that day as to which ones would go on stage. "It was decided," he announced, "to let the little ones sing today." The crowd erupted in laughter, for there on stage stood Joel, dwarfing the others. Joel, Anthony, David, and John teamed up to sing "I'll Have a New Life," "O, What a Savior," "Child, Child" (a song of recent popular vintage), "The Sweetest Song I Know," and "Hide Me, Blest Rock of Ages."[3]

All of the Madison brothers are members of the Poplar Springs Baptist Church, where they grew to maturity in their Christian faith. Throughout their childhood, their father, who was a strong proponent of four-part southern harmony, led the boys daily in singing the notes and words to numerous shape-note songs. He had the entire Madison family singing publicly by 1955. Their father is gone now, but his strong musical influence lives on in and through his sons.

The forty all-male groups formed in south central Kentucky since 1970 outnumbered their all-female counterparts by three to one.[4] The ratio of male to female singing groups across south central Kentucky has remained fairly constant since about 1950, although the women, because of a sudden increase in their participation around 1960, gained some ground. Of all the single-sex groups formed

The Madison Brothers of Brownsville, shown here in 1989, give credit to their father, who was a proponent of four-part southern harmony and led them daily in singing the shape-note songs when they were children. *Photo by the author.*

within the past twenty years, only four in the women's category have stopped singing actively, while thirty of the male ensembles fell from the active list. Both gender groups could be subdivided, perhaps to no real advantage, on the basis of musical accompaniment employed during concerts. There were those ensembles that used pianos or guitars only; those that liked the sound of a bass guitar along with the piano; or a piano and rhythm guitar together. Some groups went still farther by employing a piano, bass guitar, and lead guitar.

The real issue at hand is not one of gender. It is the extent to which all singing groups responded to the heavier accoustical rock beat that began in the 1970s to influence the sounds of gospel music here and elsewhere in the South and Midwest. Many singers and listeners back then felt that a lone piano or guitar would hardly suffice if amateur groups hoped to compete for audiences with the ever-increasing numbers of touring professionals who were exposing people to the sounds of drums and other forms of rock music. Consequently, some local groups were fairly quick to introduce drums into their performances.

While most area groups have never used drums in their acts, most of them moved in the direction of using more electrically amplified instruments. Thus, while the bass guitar and rhythm guitar had been around for years to a minimal extent, they appeared with much greater frequency in the late 1960s and early 1970s. These instruments provided an accoustical beat without competing with the pianist and vocalists for center stage, and their use was a mild form of compromise with the new, upbeat sounds associated with rock music. The electric bass is presently used by approximately half of all the local singing groups. Add to the electric bass and piano (now often replaced by the electric keyboard) an electrically amplified lead or rhythm guitar, and a group has a background sound that is a few decibels above a lone piano or guitar but stops short of the full band sound produced by the oft-criticized drums. Because there are so many sounds associated with modern-day gospel music, it is understandable why some groups still prefer "the old way," while the up-tempo groups "do it the way modern Christians prefer." Even the contemporary-sounding groups have yet to widely accept pre-recorded music tapes as back-ups for singers, however.

Among the relatively small number of local single-sex groups formed between 1970 and 1989 that used only a piano, at least at the onset, were the Barren River Boys and the Gospel Aires of Glasgow, the Bertram Sisters of Wayne County, the Chapel Aires and New Freedom Singers of Auburn, the Chordsmen of Bowling Green, the Crusaders from Somerset, the Good News Trio of Clinton County, the Harmoneers of Lewisburg, the Keith Sisters of Science Hill/ Eubank, the King's Daughters of Columbia, the Kentuckians, the Sword and Shield, and the Wolfe Family of Scottsville, the Rock of Ages and the Spirits of Russell Springs, the Sunshine Singers of Burkesville, the Templeman Sisters of Munfordville, and the Campbellsville-based Tributes.

All of these groups were or are staffed by fine vocalists and pianists. On the basis of the albums they issued, along with the oral testimonies by those persons who knew them best, "top-notch" is an appropriate word to describe most of these groups. By way of illustration, Rick Cooper, himself a member of both the widely heralded Spirits and the Tributes, said of the Chordsmen, "They were about the best group to ever sing in this entire region." The same sorts of

The Harmoneers from Logan County comprise the Addison sisters, shown here at a performance in Bowling Green in 1987. *Photo by the author.*

accolades have been heaped on the Kentuckians and the Harmoneers, two outfits that are still active. The Kentuckians is an all-male, old-time southern harmony quartet that, since its birth in 1980, has enjoyed the services of deep bass Corbin Napier on one end of the vocal spectrum and the high tenor voice of Buell Gibbs on the other. Both fellows are seasoned veterans of the gospel music circuit, having previously sung for the Thomas Quartet, among others.

The Harmoneers of north Logan is an extremely popular, multi-talented ensemble comprising the four Addison Sisters, Hester (Coursey) Johnson, Mary Allen, Violet Simmons, and Coleen DeArmond. Young Jeff Costellow was pianist for the Harmoneers until his untimely death in early 1990. The group's name is a shortened version of the Kentucky Harmoneers of Lewisburg, a well-remembered outfit that Hester and her husband, Buddy Coursey, who is now deceased, formed many years ago.

The last group from the piano-only category to be described here is the Sword and Shield, an all-male ensemble comprising two sets of Allen County–Scottsville High School students between the years 1970 and 1974. Original members included Martin Jones, nephew of professional singers Jimmy and Vesper Jones, Robert Ogles, Kerry Garmon, David Oakes, and Joe Wade, pianist. Depp Britt, Jr., joined the group in 1973 and sang with them until graduation from high school that year. Young Britt auditioned at Opryland and won a role in the musical *I Hear America Singing*. Later, both he and his brother, William, performed in another Opryland musical, *Showboat*. In 1980, at the formation of the Opryland Quartet, Depp was asked to sing the lead part. He later switched to tenor, the vocal position he filled at the time the quartet changed its name to the Cumberland Boys. William, too, is one of the Cumberland Boys, a ranking professional gospel group that watched its song "Hallelujah Heavenly Horn" soar to the number eight spot of the gospel charts in September 1988. Depp Britt, Jr., often writes words and music to the songs performed by the Cumberland Boys. The group has a booking agent who charges a set fee for their big gospel concerts but the Britt brothers still insist that the Cumberland Boys sing at churches and schools for freewill offerings only.

Among the twenty-five or more additional single-sex groups of the last two decades were or are the Brotherhood Quartet of Milltown, the Brothers and the Counsellor's of Somerset, the Challengers of north Logan, the Commonwealth and the Lake City quartets of Columbia, the Dusty Road Boys, the Good News Edition, and the Watchmen, all of Bowling Green, and the Burkesville-based trio with the unique name Of One Accord. Of these groups, eight were still active in 1990, producing a professional-like sound when they perform. Only the Brotherhood and Commonwealth quartets have called it quits, although the former may still be active in the Indianapolis area.

The Brotherhood's story is most interesting and involves a year-long stint as a professional ensemble. Garry Polston, the group's founder, recounted a bit of autobiography and a brief history of the Brotherhood Quartet:

Mom and Dad and my twin brother and I started singing together there in Jabez. I suppose we sang at five hundred funerals all over Russell and Pulaski counties. We didn't get paid for singing. Many times I have seen Dad go to the store to buy gas and tell the storekeeper to "put it on the books." He bought gas many times on credit, yet the congregation where we sang would just say, "thank you."

The Brotherhood Quartet. Garry Polston (center) and pianist Bobby Lee (lower left) are prolific song writers and original members of the quartet. *Photo courtesy of Garry Polston.*

After one year's college at Somerset, I went to sing with the Servants in Campbellsville. I had heard them sing in concerts with professional groups and thought they were fantastic. I still do. I sang for about six years [1971-77] with the Servants as their lead singer. The first trip I ever took with them was to Delaware on their bus. I'd never sung any farther away than Indiana.

I left them about 1977 to do some preaching and to organize my own quartet, the Brotherhood. It ranged between semi-professional and professional. We worked so hard at having professionalism on stage and with our harmony, but we were never known well enough to have the big promoters work for us. We all held down full-time jobs, thus were not able to travel like the professionals except Fridays through Sundays. But you get to the point of professionalism that the local churches hear you and think that they can't afford you. They see you drive up in a big greyhound bus and they know they're expensive to operate. So the Brotherhood was in that bind, finding that we had to travel a long way to sing. But the only time that was difficult to stay booked was in the winter time—December and January.

After a year, I went into full-time evangelism under the title Brotherhood Ministries, and the group worked with me that year in my revivals on weekends. The second year, I took the quartet with me full-time. I paid everybody a salary of $150 a week, plus eats, when we were on the road. I also paid for the suits we wore, and if we stayed in a motel, I paid for that. I paid myself $175 weekly, which was not very much. We did 275 dates that year [1983], which is running your tail off.

Garry Polston, who was honored by being asked to preach James Sego's funeral, and his strong supporting cast of Brotherhood personnel, including Larry Polston, took their ensemble to a top national ranking in gospel music. They placed fifth in a large field of competitors at the 1985 National Quartet Convention in Nashville. Much of the credit for the group's success goes to pianist Bobby Lee, who, like Polston himself, is a prolific song writer. Lee, a native of Liberty, first played piano for the Rock of Ages and the Notesmen of Russell Springs, then the Tributes of Campbellsville. He traveled extensively with the professional Celestials of Nashville in 1980 before returning to Kentucky to assist Polston in organizing the Brotherhood Ministries.

Polston sold the Brotherhood Quartet franchise in 1986 to his cousin, Barry Polston, who lives in Indianapolis. Garry's decision to quit singing was due to his impending ordination as a minister in the United Methodist Church, and because, in his own words, "singing was killing me." Polston explained by recalling, "We'd often leave here at noon Saturday on the bus and go sing in another state; get back at four o'clock in the morning. Sleep two to three hours, get up and shower and go preach; come back, get on the bus and leave again. Get home late Sunday night or early the next morning."

As stated earlier, mixed-gender singing groups comprised the bulk of gospel groups organized during the past twenty years, thus continuing the tradition that began in the 1950s. Numerous mixed groups that originated after 1970 will be described here because of their interesting histories, personalities involved, or the specific sounds for which they were known. Sometimes, all three factors come into play as the various but viable threads that held the groups together are unraveled.

Top quality mixed ensembles of this recent era that used only the piano as accompaniment include the Seekers of Bowling Green, a group noted for the piano artistry of Larry Overton. Richard Tinsley's Canaanland Quartet, in spite of fairly frequent personnel changes, produces a rarely matched, traditional four-part harmony sound. The Journeymen and Jan of Franklin have one of the better modern-day sounds in the region, as does Jeff Sneed's Glory Bound, a Glasgow-based group that originated in 1983. The Glory Road Singers of Greensburg, whose singing style offers a hint of country, deliver powerful and memorable interpretations of such songs as "There Is a River," "I Came on Business for the King," and "On Zion's Hill."

The Harmony Echoes of Bowling Green, in spite of several changes in personnel in recent times, have an inviting warmness to accompany their polished harmony. On their calling cards are inscribed the words "It's so peaceful in the arms of the Lord." Other top-notch piano-only ensembles of recent years are the Liberty Quartet of Glasgow, whose personnel included former members of the Canaanland Quartet; the New Covenant Singers, headed up by Richard Edwards, prominent gospel music promoter in the Lake Cumberland area; the Tarter Trio of Nancy; the Walnut Grove Singers (a female ensemble) from Clinton County; the multimembered Skaggs Family Singers of Chalybeate Springs, known for their soft, harmonious song interpretations; the newly formed Southern Harmonaires of Bowling Green, a traditional southern harmony ensemble headed up by brothers Michael and Clayton Lindsey, who have known gospel music all their lives; and the Butler County–based Travelers.

The Travelers, mentioned earlier in connection with the Joyful Four of Morgantown, began as the Messengers, then became the Flener Boys and, finally, the Travelers. This very talented ensemble from the Green River country is among the finest traditional four-part harmony groups currently singing in the area and may very well rank with the best ever to sing in south central Kentucky.

As mentioned earlier, electric bass guitars were adopted by most groups that originated in the 1970s and 1980s. At least thirty-eight ensembles of that period used only the piano and bass guitar. Among them were a host of fine groups, including Roger Leigh's Believers of Liberty, a contemporary-style gospel group organized in 1980 with Clydia King at the piano and Doby Coppage on bass guitar. Other groups that had a delivery style similar to the Believers both before and after 1980 were Anne Rose's Ambassadors of Russellville; Heaven Sent, Followers of the Son, and the Messengers, all of Scottsville; the Sextons of Hart County; Rex Allen Patterson's Good News Singers of Glasgow; and the Gloryland Express of Burkesville. Even

Above: The Travelers from Morgantown, shown here in 1989, began as the Messengers, then became the Flener Boys. *Photo by the author.* Below: Like many other singing groups, the Believers from Liberty advertise their ministry on the side of their trailer. *Photo courtesy of Roger Leigh.*

Above: Anne Rose's Ambassadors of Russellville was a heavily booked group in the western portion of the study area during the early 1980s. *Photo courtesy of Anne Rose.* Below: The Jubilee Singers at a Christmas party in 1988. *Photo by the author.*

some of the group names of this era signify changing times in gospel music circles.

Contrasted with the more contemporary sounds of the above outfits, the traditional sounding groups that were proponents of the combination of piano and bass guitar, at least when they were first created, included the Strode Family of Lamb in western Monroe County; Alvin York's Steps of Faith of Franklin, a quality group that enjoyed the piano and vocal artistry of former Reeder Trio member Ruth Ann Law; the Southern Harmony Quartet of Bowling Green; the Heartland Singers of Elizabethtown, whose singers and musicians were natives of south central Kentucky and had earlier participated in a host of gospel groups in the area; the Gospel Aires and Gospel Jordonaires of Glasgow; and the Cockriel Family of Bowling Green.

The Cockriel Family is heralded as one of the best singing groups active in southern Kentucky at the present time. The Cockriels include Lonnie, Toby, and Mark Cockriel, along with "Big Jim" Tucker on the vocal lead and bass guitar. Toby, the daughter of regionally famous tenor singer Ed White, sang alto and played piano for the group until 1989. In 1989, she relinquished the piano to Debbie Allen but still sings alto for this family group, which occasionally features her own song compositions.

Area groups formed during the past twenty years that first used a piano and either a rhythm or flat top guitar include the Tonemasters of Scottsville; the Thompsons of Metcalfe County; the House of Prayer Singers of Casey County; Bill and Margaret Jones's Gospel Crusaders from Glasgow; the Gospel Servants of Horse Cave; the Harvest Singers of Edmonton, a group that is led by guitarist Stanley Syra and exhibits an old-time singing convention sound much like that of the Chuck Wagon Gang; and, finally, the Jubilee Singers of Lamb, a group largely derived from the earlier Strode Family Quartet. Known for the soft, close harmony produced by Wayne Strode, his sister Eva, her husband Joe Spear, and Rodney Burgess, the Jubilee Singers have earned a lasting niche in the area's gospel music scene. They have been accompanied by Shirley Williams at the piano since late 1987. Prior to that time, their pianist was Judy Burgess, who now sings alto/lead part of the time. The Jubilee's quiet, dignified interpretations of "Look What I've Traded for a Mansion," "Old Ship of Zion," and "When I'm in the Lowest Valley" are pleasing to all ears.

Numerous other groups that originated in the 1970s and 1980s use some combination of piano, guitar, rhythm guitar, banjo, mandolin, or sound tracks. Some of these outfits are bluegrass, some

The Gospel Jordanaires of Glasgow reveal something of the appeal that gospel music holds for younger generations of singers. *Photo by the author.*

country; others have retained the traditional four-part southern harmony style, and three or four groups produce varying sounds that fall within the parameters of what is loosely termed contemporary gospel—a musical genre that typically features solo parts sung to the accompaniment of "pop style" music. Finally, there are numerous ensembles—a surprising number indeed—that either do or did use drums and other accoustical instruments at one time to produce what is referred to in gospel music circles as the full band sound.

Four groups are described here as representative of the types of gospel sounds that are produced by the various combinations of musical instruments listed above. Roy Allen and the Gospel Carriers illustrate the bluegrass genre, while the career of Lee Norris, an individual performer, provides an insight into the field of country gospel. The Twilight Singers of Russell Springs serve as a prototype of the recent groups that sing traditional four-part southern harmony to the accompaniment of guitars. Finally, the Spirituals of Edmonton nicely epitomize the contemporary full band sound.

Close vocal and instrumental harmony was the key to the tremendous success enjoyed by Roy Allen and the Gospel Carriers of

Raymond Crenshaw and Norma Jean Rogers of the Hallelujah Gloryland Singers talk gospel music with Earl Cooley of the Egypt Quartet on July 4, 1986. *Photo by the author.*

Campbellsville during their relatively short life span, from 1981 to 1988. Their soft, mellow, winsome vocal interpretations of the song lyrics earned invitations for the Gospel Carriers to sing all over Kentucky, as well as Indiana, Ohio, Virginia, Tennessee, and Georgia. This was one amateur bluegrass outfit that ranked with the best the professionals had to offer.

Roy Allen played both lead and rhythm guitar, and sang tenor and lead, depending on the song. His brother, Lewis, played the electric bass guitar and sang the bass part. Lewis's son, Lee, played rhythm guitar and sang lead, while Shelby Hurt played the mandolin and sang baritone. The latter left the group in 1983 and was replaced by Roy Allen's son, Mark. Most all of these fellows had been members of the Pitman Valley Boys, another bluegrass band from Campbellsville, at one time or another. And while they all played string instruments for the Gospel Carriers, the fiddle and banjo were missing.

Roy Allen commented, "We weren't really bluegrass, but everyone took us for bluegrass because of our music instruments. Actually, we thought of ourselves as southern gospel [four-part harmony]. " The fact that Roy and his nephew, Lee, wrote virtually every song in the group's repertoire likely accounts for their distinctive vocal style. Most of their compositions featured Roy's naturally high, melodious tenor voice.

High tenor Lee Norris, the epitome of an old-time country musician and singer, has devoted all his musical talents to the Lord he sings about. Norris was born in the Kettle community of southern Cumberland County, an area long known for its secular and religious music traditions. More than thirty years ago, he began singing gospel music with other members of the Norris family. Later in life, he teamed up with blind Troy Basil of Barren County to organize the Gospel Troubadors, a country ensemble that Basil and other family members have continued to this day. The banjo-picking Norris remained with the Troubadors for sixteen years and then organized his own group called Lee Norris and the Bilbrey Family in 1977. His singing daughter, Nelda, had married into the musically inclined Bilbrey family. Lee performed with his daughter and in-laws for a decade or so, producing some of the best old-time country gospel heard in these parts. Their voices were strongly flavored, as they often employed the traditional nasal sound. When Norris stepped aside about 1985, the others continued on as the Bilbrey Family, still producing a quality country sound under the group name of the Full Gospel Singers.

Lee Norris teamed up in 1986 with Cathy and Darrell Milam in a group called the Jesus Mission Singers. Both of these country ensembles were present at the singing held July 4, 1986, at the Metcalfe Lake and Park, north of Edmonton. Betty J. ("B.J.") Crenshaw, who had until 1985 been a member of the Singing Crenshaws of Edmonton and was now a member of the Hallelujah Gloryland Singers, was guest vocalist with both the Jesus Mission Singers and the Full Gospel Singers that day. Her sister, Norma Jean Rogers, also of the Hallelujah group, played the tambourine for them. Lee Norris did the high vocal part for the Full Gospel Singers on "Scarlet Purple Robe." The Jesus Mission Singers and Hallelujah Gloryland Singers banded together in 1987 to form an evangelistic team known as the Jesus Mission Hallelujah Gloryland Singers. As for Lee Norris, he lives in his trailer home in Eighty Eight and still sings on occasion but is no longer as active in country gospel music as he once was.

The Twilight Singers of Russell Springs had their beginnings in the Cedar Springs Quartet, a Chuck Wagon Gang sound-alike, in the early 1960s. The singing group consisted of the Rexroat brothers, Doyle and Lyle, Reva, Doyle's wife-to-be, and Bonnie Roy. They remained together as a foursome until 1973, at which time their

Although Roy Allen's Gospel Carriers of Campbellsville used only guitars and a mandolin, they were often thought of as a bluegrass gospel ensemble. *Photo courtesy of the Gospel Carriers.*

travel schedule became burdensome, and friction developed between Reva and Lyle's wife, Della, over the alto slot. Reva decided it best to leave the group in favor of Della, but her leaving caused Doyle also to resign from the group. The two of them remained inactive for five years. Reva says of her departure, "I regretted not singing but I didn't begrudge Della the opportunity to sing."

Lyle and Della, along with Bonnie Roy and Bernell Turner, formed the Joy Bell Singers (1973-85), a quality group that enjoyed the services of talented musicians Joseph Hainey on the electric guitar, Dale Lawson on the bass, and Donald Lawson on the steel guitar. Lyle himself played rhythm guitar and sang lead, a vocal part for which he is widely acclaimed.

In 1979, Don Beasley, formerly with the bluegrass Melody Trio (1974-78), asked Doyle and Reva to come to his home and sing one evening. After two or three sessions, the three decided to form a new group that would be neither bluegrass nor Chuck Wagon in sound.[6]

The resulting Twilight Singers, a trio, produced "a strictly southern harmony sound" to the accompaniment of Beasley's guitar. They were joined occasionally in 1985 by Boyd Rexroat, the eleven-year-old son of Doyle and Reva, who sang the lead part. That same year, another of the Rexroat's sons, Brad, seventeen, began playing bass guitar, and Dana Garner introduced the piano into the group's sound. Dana left the Twilight Singers in 1987. She was not replaced by another pianist; instead the guitar-playing Lawson brothers, formerly of the by then defunct Joy Bell Singers, joined the group. Since that year, the Twilight Singers' musicians have been Dale Lawson as lead guitarist, Donnie Lawson on the steel, Don Beasley playing rhythm guitar, and Brad Rexroat on the bass. Lyle Rexroat also became a member of the Twilight Singers in 1987, resuming the vocal lead slot he had held with the Cedar Springs and Joy Bell ensembles.

The Twilight Singers have a full band by some standards, although they do not employ drums. The term "full band" is strictly reserved for groups that use drums to accompany an up-tempo group sound. And as might be expected, most true full band religious ensembles across the South, like their traditional sounding counterparts, refer to their music as "southern gospel." They are quite comfortable with the term, although a host of critics remain insistent that such groups do not sing southern gospel music, charging that the accoustical music instruments employed by these contemporary groups are too loud to merit the label. "How can a group produce southern four-part harmony when the instrumentalists typically override the voices of the singers?" they ask. These same critics charge that the stage antics and loud music exhibited by the nouveau southern gospel groups override the importance of the words.

My purpose is neither to take sides in the ongoing debate nor to arbitrate the issue. Suffice it to say that at least sixty local gospel outfits have tried drums since they were first introduced in the early 1970s. Some discontinued using this heavy accoustical instrument almost immediately, largely because of their inability to incorporate the new sound into their performances, and also because of a measurable degree of public disapproval. In spite of criticism against the practice, other groups continued to use drums because of the encouragement they received from fans and sympathizers. Numerous letters on the subject to the editor of the Munfordville-based newsletter *Gospel Reaching Out* were carried during the early months of 1980. Some people defended the practice of using drums, citing biblical passages as supporting evidence; others attacked the use of drums on the grounds that it is not possible to worship in their presence. Battle lines were still drawn at the beginning of the 1990s, but perhaps not as rigidly as they once were.

At present there are eighteen to twenty local groups that use drums on a regular basis. Most of them, such as the Conquerers of Edmonton,[7] the Thrasher Family of Summer Shade,[8] and the Guiding Light of Columbia, maintain a low-profile percussion beat to accompany the vocalists.[9] Other contemporary gospel groups build their performance repertoires around their percussion sections, turning up the voltage a bit when the drummer and associates take the lead between verses.

Among the high-voltage ensembles are the Spirituals of Edmonton, consisting largely of young singers and musicians, some of whom came out of the older four-part harmony school. The Spirituals as a group came into being in the early 1970s as a traditional-sounding sextet consisting of newlyweds Jack and Patty Hurt and Jack's uncle, Jack Shive, along with three of Shive's children. It was not long, however, until the Spirituals consisted only of the three named individuals. Shive sang lead and played the piano. In the mid-1970s, Jack and Patty's five-year-old daughter, Marla, began singing one to two songs at each of the group's public singing events. She enjoyed the attention of performing in public and continually begged for a bigger chunk of the act. Thus it was that drums entered the picture. "We bought her a little set of drums that she played for six to eight months," Patty recalled. When the Spirituals' bass guitarist quit the group, Marla chose the bass over drums. Almost immediately she began to sing the "high part," while continuing to play the bass guitar. Then, with Shive's departure in 1984, Marla assumed the lead vocal part and Teresa Fields, twenty, was brought in as pianist. Teresa sang the soprano part as well.

About that same time, a host of musicians were added to the group and the sound of the present-day Spirituals was born. Seventeen-year-old Kevin Gibson began playing the bass guitar; Keith Gibson, sixteen, was still lead guitarist; Kelly Moss, sixteen, became group drummer; Joe Acree, twenty, began singing bass. The other vocalists were Marla on the lead, and Jack and Patty (called Mom and Dad by the group), who held down the bass and alto parts. Their other daughter, Melissa, sixteen, was the group's sound technician at the mixing board. Some changes in personnel have occurred since that time, but the Spirituals appear to have only profited as a result of the changes. Kelly Moss (now married to Melissa) plays the bass guitar and sings lead; Marla is the tenor. Lane Garmon joined the Spirituals as drummer in August 1987.

The full band sound of the Spirituals and the guitar-wielding Moss emulating a rock-artist on the vocal lead helped the group earn the number six spot in amateur competition at the 1989 National Quartet Convention. And not only does the ensemble do a superior job with full band gospel music, some of the members write songs as well. The group issued a cassette tape in 1989 containing nine songs written by Patty, Jack, Marla, Kelly, Keith, and Teresa. They sing actively in south central Kentucky, but scheduling flexibility affords them ample opportunity to sing elsewhere in the state as well as in Tennessee and Alabama, where they have a host of friends and supporters.

Gospel music in south central Kentucky was at a crossroads in the early to mid-1970s when the more traditional-sounding Spirituals were in their infancy. Not only were drums and other accoustical instruments taking gospel music far from its traditional moorings, these rock-inspired tools of the trade were strongly assisted by increased "innovative arrangements of songs . . . and a growth out of the established mold which at one time was the standard pattern for gospel music," wrote Johnny Melloan, editor of *Gospel Reaching Out.* Melloan's editorial continued in its attack on "the old idea of a gospel group consisting of four singers and a piano player." Six months later and still defending the "new gospel music," Melloan wrote, "If gospel music is to reach its maximum potential, it must be an honest music. And if it is to be an honest music, we must be willing to honestly recognize problems. A problem which has arisen concerns the form that gospel music should take. There seems to be a reluctance on the part of many to accept the new sounds which are emerging in gospel music."

The new sounds to which Melloan, himself a gospel musician, referred were subsequently made explicit in his column for July 1974. His comments were in response to a note that a gospel music fan had dropped into the suggestion box at the recent anniversary singing of Hart County's Gospel Music Association. The author of the note urged the Association to ban all contemporary-sounding songs and "bring back the old-time spirit-filled songs." Melloan defended every gospel music group's right to choose the songs they sing on the grounds that their choices appeal to group members for one or more personal reasons. He defined "contemporary songs" as "music that makes use of new ideas and new sounds," then defended contemporary music in these words: "Just because a song is new does not make it bad. After all, 'I'll Have a New Life' was once a new song. And the convention style which it typifies was a radical change from the

The Spirituals, known for their upbeat tempo, at the Cumberland Valley Singing in Burkesville in 1989. *Photo by the author.*

average church music of that period. It is probable that today's contemporary songs will be the old spirit-filled songs of 1994. There is a contemporary audience that needs to hear gospel music just as there is an old-time audience. Nobody has to like every style of gospel music. And nobody has the right to throw out any style of songs from gospel music as a whole."

Unquestionably speaking for a host of others as well as himself, former State Singing Convention President Rick Cooper articulated a totally opposite view of the contemporary sounds in gospel music during a 1987 interview. "There are some gospel songs that I won't sing because I know who wrote them," he commented. "And I'm sure that there would be others that I wouldn't sing if I knew the persons who wrote them." Cooper, who considers himself a member of the younger generation of singers, paused to ponder his next words. "Christian rock is hypocritical," he mused. "You don't mix muddy water and milk together and then drink it. Basically, the rock 'n' roll sound in gospel music causes gospel music to lose its distinction." Vernie McGaha, a high school music teacher and member of the Crossroads Quartet, agreed with Cooper but in a less critical vein. "When we speak of the contemporary sound in gospel music," he said, "we are referring to a sound that is based more on music than the song lyrics."

Most of the contemporary groups to which Melloan and Cooper

referred have vanished from the gospel music scene; others survived and remained vigorous in 1990. Likewise, most of the more traditional-sounding ensembles spawned in the past twenty years have also disappeared. In order to understand what happened to these groups, a look at their birth-death statistics for the period from 1970 to 1989 is in order. There were 380 known new groups representing all types of gospel music formed in south central Kentucky during these two decades; 281, or 74 percent, of them have since disbanded. That figure is not totally staggering, however, as 73 percent of all groups originating between 1950 and 1969 have likewise quit singing. The truly revealing statistic has to do with individual group longevity since 1950. Gospel groups formed during the 1950s averaged 10.2 years of active service; sister ensembles born in the 1960s lasted 6.8 years on the average; those formed in the 1970s remained together 5.0 years, while the average life of the groups organized in the 1980s was only 2.6 years. Another revealing count indicates that of all the gospel groups originating in the 1950s, only two of them disbanded during their first year of active service; there were four such one-year groups in the 1960s (three of which came after 1968), and eleven in the 1970s. But the decade of the 1980s witnessed the cessation of thirty-one groups within their first twelve to eighteen months of public singing.

The explanation for the tremendously large death rate in the 1980s is not to be found in the musical accompaniment employed by these unsuccessful groups, nor is it to be looked for in the themes, metaphors, and messages contained in their songs. "Contemporary" is not the issue, for there are too many fine current groups—groups that were born in prior decades as well as in the 1980s—that have a contemporary sound, large fan followings, and bright futures.[10] So it is, too, with currently active "traditional" groups that were born before and during the 1980s—quality ensembles that employ and thrive on the old-time four-part southern harmony sound produced with minimal musical accompaniment.[11]

Successful groups, whether traditional or contemporary, can attribute their longevity to commitment; close harmony; mellow, sweet sounding vocal tones; precise timing and overall polish; clear articulation of words; and knowledge of music sufficient for adapting media-disseminated songs to fit group needs. Very few present-day groups boast of all these qualities, but most can claim three or four. The groups that were short-lived generally lacked these qualities. One quote from a singer in a group that lasted less than two years says much. As I listened to this group perform at a singing event in the western part of the study area, I had difficulty connecting the singers with their individual vocal parts. Later I asked one of them, "What part do you sing? "

"Oh, I don't sing a part," he responded, "I just sing."

I am aware that the lack of vocal quality does not explain the demise of each of the thirty-one groups. A few of them, perhaps as many as eight, dissolved for bonafide reasons, sickness, death and divorce being at or near the top. However, the bulk of the short-term ensembles of the 1980s, perhaps like a few others in previous decades, did have trouble producing a sound capable of attracting and holding an audience. At work also in these group failures was the lack of total commitment necessary to mold a singing ensemble and hold it together, a condition that quite naturally resulted in a lack of invitations to sing in area churches. Also, with few to no invitations to perform outside their home churches, such groups experienced difficulty in obtaining funding necessary for the purchase of PA systems and trailers or vans in which to transport them.

At the beginning of 1990, there were approximately 230 amateur bluegrass, country, contemporary, and traditional four-part harmony gospel music groups currently active, i.e., singing at least four times a year by invitation, in south central Kentucky. Some ensembles rarely receive invitations to sing; others are booked weeks in advance. Regardless of how gospel music followers feel about these diversified forms of gospel music and the quality of the individual groups, these fans fully expect to hear two or more of the four sounds performed at local nonchurch singing events. And people are quite content to sit and listen to the wide range of sounds produced by these gospel groups. Although all gospel music enthusiasts lean toward one musical form or the other, they are seldom vociferous these days when it comes to taking sides publicly. They feel, and I concur, that their favorite type of gospel music will still be around when they personally come to the banks of the River and are called upon to cross over.

In the meantime, the practitioners of the four different sounds in gospel music will continue to share the same stage at a given event, often in area churches as well as school auditoriums and fairgrounds. It thus seems appropriate at this time to take a close look at some typical singing events and, equally important, at the composite anatomy of the singing groups that have mastered the secrets of remaining alive and vigorous in the competitive world of gospel music. These topics claim the focus of the next two chapters.

7

WALKING STRAIGHTER
AND NARROWER

We have considered gospel music groups in terms of vocal styles and musical accompaniment and have identified certain ensembles and singers by name. No attempt has been made, however, to look at individual singers in terms of their reasons for singing or to illuminate the nature of their relationship with other persons in the group. Certain factors may cause a singer (the term is used in this chapter to denote musicians also) to stay with the same group for a number of years or, for that matter, to leave one group and affiliate with another. And, as with individuals, issues may be at work sufficient to cause the entire ensemble to disband, perhaps never to sing again. These and other important interpersonal matters that deal both with individual singers and with the group as a whole will be considered in the following pages.

Virtually all of these singers are born-again Christians. They have had an experience of salvation and will share it with others at every opportunity. Rarely do groups consist of individuals who do not know the Lord about whom they sing. One's particular church affiliation is seldom of any consequence, as groups often have two or more Protestant denominations represented among their personnel. To carry the denominational analogy to the group level, it is not at all uncommon for an all non-Baptist gospel ensemble to sing in one of the fundamentally conservative Baptist churches that, most likely, does not invite members of other denominations to partake of the Lord's Supper with them. As stated earlier, gospel music is the greatest ecumenical force operating today in south central Kentucky. These singers know both as individuals and as groups that they will be welcome without reservation when they enter another denomination's place of worship.

Today's gospel singers are no longer dwellers of rural areas only. Such was never the case entirely, but pre–World War II singers by and large were country people. The rural roots of this music helps to explain why country churches are still its major supporters. Probably more than one half of all singers in south central Kentucky now reside in the area's county seat towns; at least that is where they pursue their occupations, making no pretense at farming other than perhaps cultivating a vegetable garden.

Doyle Rexroat of the Twilight Singers does work at a forty-acre truck gardening operation, while Reva, his wife and a member of the Twilights as well, works at a factory in Somerset, about thirty miles away. Reva's world revolves around "fast time" and "slow time." The Rexroats live in the Central Time Zone, while Somerset is located in the Eastern Time Zone. Reva leaves home at 4:45 A.M. each morning, or 5:45 fast time. She is accustomed to this routine to the extent that she actually thinks of herself as "living on fast time," and the clock in the kitchen reflects this. Thus, when she arrives home in the afternoon at "four o'clock," according to the clock, it is actually only three to her husband and sons, who have spent the day on slow time. The time factor becomes more of an issue when their group sings on Sunday evenings at churches located in the slow time zone, gets home around midnight, and Reva has to be on the road again bound for work in less than four hours.

The Rexroat's son Brad, who plays bass guitar and trumpet for the group, is a carpenter; another son, Boyd, an occasional singer with the Twilight Singers, is in high school. Doyle's brother Lyle, lead vocalist, is manager of an auto parts store, and Don Beasley, group tenor, is a truck driver. Guitarists Donnie and Dale Lawson are both Somerset factory employees.

Norma and Morris Butler of the Burkesville-based Seminary Trio are also factory workers, and their singing colleague Gary Cash is a banker-turned-preacher. The Brothers Quartet of Somerset provides an interesting array of occupations. Tim Eaton, lead vocalist and rhythm guitarist, is a school administrator; Jim Rogers, tenor singer and pianist, is employed as an insurance agent; baritone Charles Randall works for the State Highway Department; Coy Wilson, who sings bass with the group, is self-employed; Dave Hall, lead guitarist, is a used car salesman; and bass guitarist David Hadley owns and operates a country store. Across the region, the Templeman Sisters of Munfordville also provide an interesting employment profile. Karen

The Templeman Sisters from Munfordville come from a distinguished line of gospel singers. *Photo courtesy of Karen Templeman Warren.*

Templeman Warren, the group's tenor, was a truck driver before taking her present position as a secretary; Cathy Gardner, lead singer and pianist, is a teacher; Mary Jo Gaddie, alto, works as a warranty clerk at a local automobile dealership; and Rebecca Sidebottom, who sings low alto, is employed as a bookkeeper at a sawmill.

All of these ensembles accept only weekend bookings. Some of them, along with a few other area amateur singing groups, could likely make it on the professional circuit. They do not view themselves as candidates for that life, however, preferring instead the peace and security afforded by close ties with their families and friends and a secure job in the workplace. This brief listing of occupations nicely illustrates the diversified backgounds these singers bring to the gospel music scene. Their on-the-job colleagues do not always share their love for this music, however, nor understand the devotion that is necessary in order to make it as a gospel singer. Occasionally, colleagues at work poke fun at these dedicated singers and "that

Gospel Music is at center stage for the Seminary Trio of Burkesville, shown here performing in 1989. *Photo by the author.*

happy Jesus stuff." The other side of the picture is one that has understanding fellow workers willingly stepping in to take up the slack when the gospel performer in their midst must leave work early to begin a long road trip to a scheduled singing event miles away. With scoffing peers, long grueling road trips, out-of-pocket personal expenses, and a host of other factors that could easily deter the weak, one might question why these singers stick it out as members of a gospel music ensemble.

There are at least three aspects of the answer to this question. First, most of them sing as a service to their Lord; their goal is to help spread the divine message of repentance and deliverance to their listeners. Second, they sing for the personal satisfaction and the sheer enjoyment of doing so. Their jobs, once mastered, are essentially routine. Singing provides them with an outlet through which they can channel creative, artistic expression. Their often tedious occupations stand in stark contrast to their weekend roles as neatly attired, professional looking singers who often serve not only as performing artists but as polished speakers during the course of the song program. I know a fellow who works five days a week as an automobile mechanic with very little contact with the public, who blossoms on weekends as an extroverted gospel music emcee, cracking jokes and giving spiritual testimony throughout the course of the singing event. A third reason for singing in a gospel group is to fulfill a need to commune with like-minded talent. Being spiritually inclined, these performers receive a blessing while doing the thing they love very much—singing. This spirit-filled activity, then, becomes their principal form of artistic expression and entertainment. Norma Butler admitted, "This is the highlight of our life."

J.T. Light of Glasgow experienced mental anguish when he had to give up music for health reasons after thirty-six years. "What's it like," I asked, "to have to stop singing after all those years?" "It's like misery," he responded, almost at the point of tears. "Gospel singing was my life. After leading the life of traveling with the Happy Aires and others like I did, the walls [of my house] are closing in on me."

Willis Shores, former member of the Gospel Five, among others, commented with enthusiasm about his one-time involvement with gospel music: "I just had an air of exuberance while singing. Playing golf would have bored me to tears. I'd of rather watched paint dry than play golf. I felt like I was fulfilling a calling by singing. I just flat out enjoyed it!"

The question as to whether or not they are really "singing the gospel"—i.e., preaching through song—is a point of considerable disagreement among the singers themselves. There are two clearly defined sides of the issue, and both points of view appear to be grounded in biblical interpretation. J.T. Light articulated the strong conviction held by a host of singers who insist that the gospel must be proclaimed by a minister who has received a divine calling into the pulpit ministry. "In no way was I singing the gospel," Light insisted. "The gospel must be preached." [1]

Dixine Proffitt of the Tracy community, who sang with the Happy Five and other groups until 1970, was equally insistent that the gospel must be proclaimed from the pulpit. Her singing husband, Arlen, defended the other point of view. With a nervous chuckle, he countered with the words, "Well, I'd have to say a small 'yes' to the question." Charles Lee Carver, former singer with the Carver Family, the Happy Five and the Gospel Echoes, sat listening to the Proffitts. In an attempt to bridge their differences, Carver observed, "They's a whole lot of gospel in the songs."

Morris Gaskin of Russell Springs supported Carver's position. "It all depends on the song—the literature of the song," he said, and then continued by explaining that the gospel is "the good news about the death, burial, and resurrection of Jesus and its effect on the individual. If you sing a song that bears that message, you are singing the gospel. But now if something in a song doesn't pertain to that, it's just a bunch of words to fill up space." Toby Cockriel of Bowling Green agreed, saying, "As long as songs are based on the Bible, then we are singing the gospel." Her husband, Lonnie, added quickly, "I've heard a lot of preachers say that singing is not gospel proclamation. And, admittedly, I've never had a voice from on high to say, 'Lonnie, you've got to sing.' But it is possible for a person to be saved while we're singing. For that reason, I believe that we are singing the gospel." On a similar positive note, in 1988, the pastor of Lick Branch Cumberland Presbyterian Church in Barren County opened that church's gospel singing event featuring the Crossroads Quartet with a prayer in which he asked the Lord to "bless the singers who are about to proclaim the Word in song." Likewise, the pastor of Glen Lily Baptist Church in Bowling Green, praised the Southern Harmony Quartet for "preaching the gospel in song." Haskell McCubbins of the Munfordville-based McCubbins Family was emphatic about the matter. "Any born-again Christian is capable of spreading the gospel, whether by singing or standing behind the pulpit," he asserted.

It is unlikely that there will ever be full agreement among these singers regarding the question of singing the gospel. All of them do agree on one thing, however. That point of accord was expressed by Rick Cooper of Liberty. "If my attitude is right when I sing," Cooper commented, "then I bring glory to God. If not, I might as well be throwing rocks."

Spiritual matters such as being called into a song ministry or whether it is possible to sing the gospel do not typically enter into the picture when the individuals who make up a gospel group come together to rehearse songs. Some gather at church or at a home of one of the members once weekly for this purpose; others meet twice monthly; some meet seldom, if ever. Rehearsals are times when the singers run through their old songs, as necessary, occasionally learn new numbers, and simply bask in the friendship and warmth of their friends or family members. After the initial greetings are said and the light chatter is over (Mike Durrett of the Durrett Family calls it "mass confusion"), the group proceeds with the purpose at hand.

For those who use only the piano and bass, very little preliminary activity is necessary before moving directly into rehearsal. Some groups make a big to-do of the gathering, however, and even set up a

PA system, replete with all the accoustical instruments. I have witnessed such a practice session held by the Spirituals and can agree
with the description provided by Gennie Basham of Bowling Green,
who, with her manager-husband, headed up a group called Gennie
and the Redemptions: "At a typical rehearsal we get out all of our
equipment and set it up. Roger does the sound checks—checks everybody's mikes out; gets all the instruments and everything ready. And
then we have a vocal test that everybody does. I'll start lead, then the
tenor will see if her mike's set. Then the baritone will see if his mike's
set, and if it's level. Then we get all the guitars and everything tuned
to the piano in 440 standard, because the harp player is always in 440.
Then, we all take off and start singing. We do three or four warm-ups,
then we ask if there's anything that anybody has on their mind in the
way of a new song."

    Lonnie Cockriel admitted that his group, perhaps typical of many
of the older, heavily booked groups, do not practice very often. But the
New Freedom Singers of Auburn are likely typical of most newer
singing groups by having weekly rehearsals. Nick Stamps, baritone
vocalist for this classy, youthful outfit provided the following account of their weekly get-together:

The main purpose of our meeting is to prepare for a gospel singing by
practicing the songs which we will sing. Sometimes I feel as though we
practice for the fun of it, but we also practice to receive a blessing from the
Lord by praising Him. We meet to practice every Thursday night at 6:30
P.M. We usually end up getting there from 6 to 7 P.M. Some of us are early
and some are late, like Melvin! We begin by just talking about each
other's week and how it has gone. Then we get down to business by going
through our date book to see when our next singings are going to be and
where. The next thing that we do is to start the practice with a prayer. We
just thank God that we are together and ask for His guidance in all our
endeavors. We do this because He brought us together, and He is what we
are singing about. We sing southern gospel music, and love every minute
of it.

    After prayer, we get down to the nitty-gritty and start singing. We've
always started with the song "Feelin' Fine" every time we have practiced.
It is sort of our pep song; gets us started in the right mood and keeps us
going through the practice. Next, we practice every song that we currently sing everywhere we go. We sing them once and then go over them
with a fine-tooth comb to see if there is any place we need to work on or to
change. It is usually Melvin Chambers, a little dude with a high-pitched
voice, or Mark Belcher, the big guy, who does the changing around. Jeff

White, Darlene Little, and I also make some suggestions about the songs. Keith Jones just says, "Do whatever makes you happy. It don't matter with me." Melvin and Mark usually have the disagreements because one is just as stubborn as the other. Keith and I just sit back and watch them fuss, and we laugh and make fun of them. After disagreements are ironed out, we agree to do the song a certain way and go on with the practice.

We like to have fun with each other. If we are not having a productive practice, it is usually because we are trying to think of ways to play tricks on each other. I always try to goose Mark when he is not looking, or during one of his solos when he is singing real high. He is so jumpy that if he had hold of anything he would probably break it. We all pick at Melvin and make jokes about him being so short.

The next part of practice is when we start to sing new songs that we have heard of, or that are recommended or requested by people. This is when we all gather around the piano and sight read the music while Jeff is playing. Then we ask which one of us would like to sing the solo part of the song. That decided, we begin to practice on the song. We may practice on a song for weeks before we try to sing it on the road. By the time all of that is done, we're starting to wear down and decide to call it quits for the night.

For most singing groups, such sessions often last about four hours, especially when new songs are being incorporated into their performance repertoire. The decision as to the frequency with which new songs are incorporated is different for each group. Garry Polston tried to work up a new song every two or three weeks for incorporation into the Brotherhood's repertoire in order to keep their concerts from getting stale. "People out there hear that song only when you sing it for them," Polston commented, "but when you sing that same song three times on a weekend, week after week after week, the song ceases to be exciting to you." Vernie McGaha gave the same line of reasoning in defense of the Crossroads' constantly changing repertoire:

We hear groups that are singing the same songs they did fifteen years ago. For us, personally, we change songs in order to stay fresh, interested, and enthusiastic about what we are doing. We have to have new material. It's a challenge on the road for us to see if we can get through it; to see if people like it. Sometimes, if we sing a song once and it's a dud, we'll never sing it again although we may have spent fifteen hours preparing it. And we may spend ten hours working on a new song but never sing it outside. We'll decide, "Hey, this doesn't fit us; it doesn't work for us; it doesn't sound like us." After twenty-seven years, if we were still singing the same songs, I'd be bored stiff. And I would be ineffective in trying to present it to someone else.

Most present-day gospel singers are not trained in the fundamentals of music, thus are unable to sing a song as it is written, nor can they rearrange it to suit their personal taste and performance style. And while a few groups do have at least one member who can adapt a song from sheet music, most groups get their songs and sounds from recordings issued by current professional ensembles. One singer explained to a church audience the process by which her group gets most of its new songs. "I call the local radio station and pester them to death to play certain songs," she laughingly admitted, "then I'll record them on my tape recorder, and try to teach them to the others here."

Like her group, most of today's ensembles obtain songs from recordings. As such, they are copying sounds, not notes. Many singers, however, do have excellent ears for music. Frank Weaver commented that if a choice had to be made between a singer who knows music theory and a person with a good ear for music, "pick the singer with the ear. You can teach him." Indeed, some present-day local ensembles are blessed by having a vocalist or pianist who can listen to commercial recordings and hear all four parts. They also are able to interpret the various sounds for the other singers, perhaps changing the arrangement a bit to suit group needs. On the other hand are those groups that sound just like their singing neighbors down the road. Both ensembles are simply imitating—sometimes splendidly, sometimes poorly—the sounds and styles of professional groups. It is little wonder that singers from seven local quartets were present in August 1987, at Rocky Hill Baptist Church, when the Spencers from Shiloh, Ohio, sang their then popular "Praying" and "I'm Climbing Up the Rough Side of the Mountain." These local singers were there to hear and see firsthand how their role models did it.

My field notes written at that event indicate that I felt the Spencers to be fairly polished, possessing all the necessary professional mannerisms but not overly showy. At the same time, I wrote that they were only one or two cuts, if that much, above some of the better local groups. Why, then, do the locals try to emulate the touring professionals? The answer is simple. Professional groups such as the Spencers, the Primitive Quartet, the Singing Cooks, the Kingsmen, and the Cathedrals provide the locals with words and music to songs that are proven winners by virtue of the heavy play their recordings receive over area radio stations. The consuming

The Freedom Singers of Fountain Run prefer the full band sound provided by the use of drums. *Photo by the author.*

audience—that is, those persons who both listen to radio broadcasts and attend singings that feature area groups—have come to expect the locals to know and sing these same songs. An excellent case in point is the song "I Want Us to Be Together in Heaven." From the time it was first introduced in 1987 through mid-summer 1989, at least 90 percent of the local groups incorporated the song into their repertoires. Invariably, if a group failed to sing this emotion-filled song, someone in the audience asked for it.

Repertoire sizes vary from one group to another. It appears, however, that the better, long-lived ensembles have in excess of one hundred performance-ready songs to draw upon. Buell Gibbs of Scottsville pointed to a specific occasion when a large repertoire was really something for which he was thankful. The Thomas Trio had gone to Indianapolis to take part in an all-night singing. But they were the only group to show up. "We had to sing until two o'clock in the morning," Gibbs recalled, "but we never had to repeat the same song."

Large repertoires filled with a balance of songs with a variety of tempos—slow, medium, and fast—as well as songs that address a wide range of themes, are essential to successful singing events. Groups that hope to address the needs of different audience types should have at least one person among them able to quickly grasp and interpret audience reaction and response to the lyrics and tempo of the music. The better singing groups are thus able to create an air of reverence and an attitude of worship at religious singing events. Concomitantly, a group's ability and willingness to shift gears on the spot—to know what type of song to sing next—is a major requisite for fulfilling audience expectations and being invited back to sing again year after year.

There are times when those persons who invite a group to sing are not in touch with the group's needs or aware of the sorts of things that are, for the most part, inexcusable from the group's point of view. For example, some groups reported that singing events for which they were booked were canceled without their being notified until they arrived on the premises. In another vein, groups often feel slighted when their appearance is not publicized in the media, or when an adequate amount of time for their part on the scheduled program is not protected by the arranger(s). The groups feel that many churches are guilty of using too much time featuring their own pianist(s), soloist(s), and singing ensemble(s) during the midpoint break in the singing event.

Another point of concern, one that was seldom articulated by the singers because it is a touchy subject, is the attitude sometimes exhibited by pastors and congregations that a singing group is doing the Lord's work and thus is not in real need of financial support. After all, the presumed reasoning goes, these singers all have jobs. At the break in the program, an often small "love offering" is taken to give to the singers as an expression of appreciation for their coming. The love offering refers to the amount of money donated by the audience for distribution among the singers and musicians. One group reported going to a "well-to-do" church in a distant city where over three hundred people were present in the audience. The total offering for the singers was $34.83.

A woman singer recently commented to me, "We tell people that we'll come for a love offering. Well, let me tell you, when some of them take up a love offering for us, we mostly get love [and not money]." Her group has since stopped singing entirely. A male singer recalled the numerous times when host church members slapped him on the shoulder and said, " 'God bless you, brother, we sure did enjoy that good singing.' But, you know," he went on, "that don't put gas in a car."

The bulk of the singing groups use these offerings to cover travel expenses, including payments on PA systems and the trailers or vans used in transporting equipment and singers. A member of the Madison Family of Smiths Grove/Bowling Green reported that only twice in five years (1983-87) did they purchase a meal with a portion of the offering. Most groups do, however, use offerings to pay for food on the road. Anything left over typically goes toward outstanding debts on equipment, vehicles, and clothing for the singers. One singer put the matter of monetary receipts in perspective. "Whatever you get is never enough to cover all of your expenses. You just do the rest out of your own pockets because you enjoy what you are doing." Some of these performers may express a mild complaint against the lack of financial support from the public, but they continue to climb into their vans or step into their buses the very next weekend, filled with excitement and eager anticipation of singing once again.

Rather than taking a chance on receiving a slim offering for the singers when the plates are passed among the persons present, some churches are beginning to pay these groups a set fee that has already been budgeted. Most groups look for ways other than offerings or fees to help defray costs involved in mounting and maintaining a successful gospel song ministry. Many of them issue commercially produced sound recordings to sell at their scheduled singing events. The majority of these issues eventually sell out and some groups may even ask for a second pressing. Sometimes a group can ill afford to bear the costs involved in tape or album production. Loryn Atwell of Atwell Recording Studio in Lafayette, Tennessee,[2] said that quite a few gospel outfits have yet to pay him for services rendered, likely because they were unable to sell their recordings. In such cases, group vanity may be at fault when a lesser known ensemble issues a commercial recording, especially when they do so for the simple reason that other singing groups around them are making and selling tapes and albums. I wished later that I had asked the former wife of a member of the Mt. Lebanon Quartet to verbalize why she had listed the title and date of issuance of the group's album in the family Bible in the section labeled "Important Events."

There is a growing fad among some groups these days to exhibit more than tapes and albums on tables in the lobby or vestibule where they are singing. Ballpoint pens, T-shirts, two-inch metal buttons, banners, and the like, bearing the group's name and imprinted messages, are there for sale also. The messages include slogans, sayings, and biblical quotations such as "Pray for America," "I'm Gonna Live for Jesus," "Born Again," "I Believe," and "I Love Gospel Music."

A few of the gospel groups are operated like businesses. They keep ledgers on every church they go to, indicating the number of people there, amount of the offering, amount earned from sales, the amount spent on gasoline, meals, and lodging. Also, once the group has received an invitation to sing at a distant location, the group's manager gets on the telephone and calls personal acquaintances in that area. "Hey, we're going to be near you on the third Sunday of April. Would you like to have us sing for you again?" asks the energetic manager, who hopes to schedule a Saturday night, Sunday morning, and Sunday afternoon singing. That way, three separate congregations help bear the costs of the trip.

"What do singers do to pass off time on a road trip?" I asked Debbie Reece, pianist for the Gospelaires of Glasgow for eight years. She enumerated four things: people play tapes recently issued by other local groups, practice on the group's new songs, talk about all sorts of things ranging from the spiritual to the humorous that took place at recent singings, and try to decide where to eat next. Virtually all others queried about time spent on the road also mentioned pranking among the singers. Sometimes such pranking is downright cruel, such as the time that an all-male group from Columbia slipped numerous laxative tablets to their bass singer, pretending to give him chewing gum. Another form of pranking takes the form of daring maneuvers at the wheel. Curtis Wilson told of such a stunt he pulled while the others in the van were asleep: "We were over at Elizabethtown at the loop, getting off the Interstate. Coming in from Indiana. I looked back and seen that everybody was resting but me. I was driving. There was one fellow lying in the floor; had him a pillow down there. And two were stretched out on the bunks on each side. And when I came up that cloverleaf, I was looking through the mirror. And I just thought, 'Well everybody is resting but me.' And I pulled over just a little and gave the steering wheel a quick cut, and rolled one of the boys off the bunk on top of the one that was lying on the floor. And he was astraddle him! They thought we'd wrecked!"

Singers and musicians at home and on the road must be very careful to maintain a professional distance between themselves and persons of the opposite sex. Anything at all out of the ordinary is likely to be misinterpreted by the public at large, and rumors are started that have little or no substance in fact. If for no other reason than this, as Debbie Reece astutely observed, "People in gospel music have to walk the 'straight and narrow' straighter and narrower." The rumor mill is often cranked up when fans and followers are overly friendly with the singers and, in the words of C.E. Deweese, "push themselves a little too far." Garry Polston also spoke to this point: "The problem with sex comes with young men who are on the road with their fans. Fans give trouble. I'd be stupid if I didn't admit that there are times when opportunities arise. Some people see you in a three-piece suit; you an entertainer. You have to love your fans; let them know that you appreciate their buying your records and coming to your concerts. At the same time, you can get too close to your fans. You have to keep a distance."

In a few instances, fans and singers did let down their guards. Subsequent embarrassment to the singing group as a whole resulted, sometimes to the point that the ensemble disbanded. More often than not, however, both guilty parties were members of the same singing group. My files contain instances of these situations and subsequent repercussions that are explainable in basic human terms. These singers spend a large amount of time together practicing, traveling to singing sites sitting side by side, eating together, and singing together during concerts. Innocent flirtations have eventually culminated in marriage breakups and, consequently, in group dissolutions. I shall not soon forget the response that a woman provided when, looking at a photograph of her husband's quartet, I asked her why the female pianist's face was scratched out. "Hmph," the woman retorted, "I didn't like her. That thing was interested in anybody that wore pants, and only men wore pants back then." The implication was quite clear.

Less serious insofar as the future of the whole ensemble is concerned are those instances when a jealous spouse forces a husband or wife to quit a group. Innocent flirtations may be at fault here in some cases, but vivid imaginations and/or feelings of being neglected must also share the blame, claim singers close to these situations. In such instances, the individual singer typically leaves the group, but there is little or no residual embarrassment involved for the group as a whole.

Groups dissolve and/or members leave for reasons other than extramarital relationships within the group. Other reasons include personal pressures; the need to spend more time with one's family; lack of devotion to the cause; intergroup conflict and tension over such matters as leadership, song selection, allocation of vocal parts, and control of the sound system; bad health; retirement; and relocation. Don Parker illustrated the demands made on one's personal time:

People leave because there's too much pressure put on them. You leave on Friday and come back on Monday at 6:30 or 7 o'clock in the morning, just in time for your jobs. You're just getting back in from off the road and don't have time to change clothes; just run in.

We had a Volkswagen station wagon, can you believe that! We traveled in that thing, I'm talking about 2,500 miles on the weekends, and then come in. Me jump out of that thing and run into the A & P Store and go to work. Too much pressure.

And finances! You never make your expense money on these trips. Pay for them out of your own pocket.

On the matter of family neglect, Curtis Wilson commented that groups often split up over family commitments by some of the group members. "Singers are willing to sacrifice for a period of time," he said, "but when family conditions and patterns of life changes, they often find it necessary to drop out of the group. Or, maybe a member feels he is holding the group back. Maybe can't afford the expense." Wilson went on to say that when as many as two members quit, "you just get disgusted and will lay the whole thing down for awhile."

Of interest here are the emotions that these individual singers and musicians experience when they feel compelled to leave a group for family or personal reasons after years of faithful and dedicated service. Debbie Reece, who left the Gospelaires for family reasons, provides a keen insight along these lines:

I felt like I got a divorce when I left the Gospelaires. My friends had told me what it was like to get a divorce. But it hurt me so bad when I left the Gospelaires that it took a whole year before I could go hear them sing again. That was the worst pain I ever had. I left them because my husband and I needed to be together more. I recall one month when we filled sixteen engagements, including a trip to Indianapolis. And my husband couldn't go with us much of the time.

When I first tried to quit, I couldn't get the words out. So I played for them for another month. Then, when I finally got up enough nerve to tell them, I couldn't do it in person. I had to call up Ernest [Dickson] and tell him over the telephone. Then I cried all the rest of that day.

J.T. Light, speaking the minds of numerous leaders of gospel music groups, insisted that lack of dedication is the biggest factor in causing a member to quit singing. "You know, there's an awful lot of people that are good singers, and they would love to sing if they could just sing when they wanted to," he said, somewhat critically. "But it just doesn't work that way," he went on. "If you are in a gospel group and it is in demand, you'd better well believe that the group comes first."

Jealousy and conflict within the group are major reasons why individuals quit singing and why entire ensembles dissolve, never to sing again. Johnny Howard observed that gospel music "has more jealous people in it than anything I've ever been involved with." Such has always been the case, according to numerous persons who were queried about the matter. Ivis Roy of Russell Springs shared an example that stands at the top of the list. "When Joe Setser sang with this group up in Ohio—he really had a low voice, about two steps lower than anybody else," Roy explained. "Well, this other fellow was jealous of him, so when they'd come to the bass part, this other singer would step back there and turn Joe's mike down. Jealous of him!"

A visit in the Glasgow home of Bill and Margaret Jones, competent manager and singer, respectively, for the Gospel Crusaders, verified claims I had heard of current intergroup rivalry. The Joneses had just returned from a singing conducted by the Kentuckians of Scottsville at the Lick Branch Cumberland Presbyterian Church in eastern Barren County. Few local groups were booked elsewhere on that cold November evening; still only Bill and Margaret and Richard Tinsley of the Canaanland Quartet were present to hear the Kentuckians, an ensemble from an adjacent county. Bill, Margaret, and I talked of jealousy and rivalries that evening. Although unspoken by either of them, it was apparent that the Joneses attributed the absence of other area performing groups that evening to envy of the Kentuckians. After all, the presumed reasoning ran, "one of our in-county groups could and should be singing at Lick Branch tonight."

Another instance of jealousy occurred recently in Bowling Green, causing the group to split up. At the time of the dissolution, the ensemble consisted of Tommy Blakeman, leader of the group, with Les Story and Delphine Scott singing soprano, and Tammy Jones singing alto. (All names are pseudonyms.) Desiring to vary the format of their singing events, Tommy asked Les, Les's wife (who was presently not singing with the group), and his own singing wife, Patty, to form a trio. Since Story's wife was an alto, she was invited to sing that part with the trio. They sang together as a threesome and were quite good.

Tammy, the regular alto vocalist, became jealous of Mrs. Story and announced her decision to quit the group entirely. Her cousin Delphine left the group, too, on the basis that the two of them had always sung together. "I wouldn't feel right without her," Delphine said. The two cousins left, and Story's wife then took Tammy's part on a regular basis. Pianist Marya Grinstead continued on in her regular position as group musician.

The rest of the story is not one of jealousy, but it does illustrate the fluidity of personnel in these singing ensembles. It was not very long until both Mr. and Mrs. Story decided to leave the group. At that point, Marya assumed a vocal slot while continuing to play the piano, and outsider Helen Woods was brought in to fill out the complement of singers. In recent months, the Storys returned for reasons still unknown to me, replacing Marya and Helen as group vocalists. Helen, now without a singing affiliation for the first time in many, many years, harbors no resentment for what took place. She only commented, "Well, the Storys did say when they left the group that they *might* want to come back sometime."

A final instance of group breakup illustrates what happens when more than one person attempts to lead a group. Without being specific as to group identity, suffice it to say that intergroup tension culminated in the dissolution of a parent group, the formation of an entirely new group, and the continuance of the parent group with a new set of singers. The parent group was good, one of the very best in the region, always heavily booked. One of its members was described by another singer as having been quiet and somewhat introverted until becoming a member of the parent group in the mid- to late 1980s. At that point, presumably because of involvement in the group, this individual underwent a total personality change—positive attitude, winsome personality, always smiling. Aggressive leadership characteristics were soon manifested by this singer when the group was together. After two or so years with the parent group, this singer reputedly made moves to take over the reins of group leadership. A meeting of all members, except the old leader, was called, and plans were announced to form a new outfit. And a new group, quite good, came into being.

The leader of the old parent group scrambled around and came up with new personnel in a matter of a few weeks. The new configuration of singers, as might be expected, is virtually on a par with the older parent group.

Interestingly enough, when the old parent group was dismantled, I received a letter from the leader of the splinter group telling me that details of the breakup would be shared with me at the first opportunity. And the leader of the parent group sought me out soon afterward to tell me of his regrets about the breakup. His words were, "I don't know how you'll handle this in your book, but I'm really sorry about what happened." He proceeded to praise the ones who walked out on him by saying, "That last group I had together as a quartet was both my favorite and my best." At the point of tears, he concluded, "I just wanted you to know how I feel about them." Now that the break and formation of the two new groups are in the past, it appears that all parties concerned have put that unpleasant episode behind them.

The problem of replacing members is difficult to address, as many variables enter into the picture. Christian commitment, performance record with past groups, dedication to the cause of gospel music, ability to get along with others while traveling many miles under cramped conditions, willingness to give as well as take, and conformity to established social norms are all essential if a singer hopes to be chosen and then to make it as a new member of a small ensemble of gospel musicians. Not only must newcomers be able to sing and to switch vocal parts on certain songs, they must be able to harmonize with the other voices in the group. But the question remains: how does a group go about finding a suitable replacement for a missing member? One way is to advertise in appropriate places, perhaps in the local newspaper or in throwaway weekly advertisement bulletins available in public places. A typical ad appeared in the June 1981 issue of *Gospel Reaching Out*: "WANTED. The Stewards of the King are needing an alto singer for the group. Any Christian girl that's interested may call . . . by June 15."

The process of advertising works for individuals looking for a singing group as well. A note was taped in the window at Louise's Bible Bookstore, Glasgow, in July 1986, bearing the message: "Female vocalist (alto/soprano) looking for a group to sing with. Call Barb."

Word of mouth is a popular method of contacting individuals interested in filling a vacant singing slot. A friend tells a friend about the opening. However, "the most disturbing thing about this method," says Curtis Wilson, "is when your friends recommend someone to you but that person doesn't work out. That's embarrassing all the way around." Direct contact with an active singer personally known to the group in need is another method sometimes employed in replacing someone. Strained relations typically occur under such circumstances, however, as the reluctant donor group feels offended and often becomes jealous and resentful. The best and most often used method of filling an empty slot is to look to the gospel groups that have dissolved recently. "You think to yourself," Don Parker says, "hey, that person just might want to sing with us." A personal contact is then made by means of a visit or telephone call, and an invitation is issued to "come join us at our next rehearsal. Let's see how things work out."

Things eventually do work out quite satisfactorily for most singers and groups. Gospel music is very much a part of their everyday lives and a considerable amount of their spare time in one way or another focuses on their involvement with this music. And while the lyrics to the songs carry a religious message, gospel singing itself is still very much a human endeavor. As with any other activity, the practitioners of this music genre are very human. They are not always able to live up to the standards about which they sing and people have come to expect of them. But gospel music is a continuing force even in the midst of adversity. Gospel ensembles may suffer embarrassment when individuals exhibit human failings and go astray. Such groups may even be forced to change personnel or to dissolve completely for one reason or another, but gospel music goes on. Singers come and go, but the music tradition they represent is bigger than all these singers combined. It goes on—and on.

8

SINGING THE GLORY DOWN

The focus of this chapter is on performance aspects at gospel music events and on the lyric content of the songs used in this connection.[1] While gospel singings are conducted in a myriad of places, churches are the most common staging grounds. Whether located in rural areas or in the county seat towns, host churches are typically more informal than their "uptown" neighbors, such as the First Baptist, First United Methodist, and similar other churches located in larger towns and cities, which are known for tightly programmed, formal religious services. Denominational affiliation in and of itself is not really a consideration in the matter of gospel music, as the host churches collectively represent virtually every evangelical Protestant denomination. Most of them have relatively small memberships and fewer persons still who regularly attend Sunday School and Sunday morning "preaching services."

In October 1987, I attended a Sunday evening singing at a small General Baptist Church in Bowling Green that had only nine persons present for Sunday School that morning, and fourteen for morning preaching service. But the singing Cockriel Family attracted an audience of twenty-two that evening. The increased attendance for the gospel singing indicates something of the importance that local church congregations place on these events.

The attendance figure for the singing at this church was considerably smaller than the number of people who typically turn out to hear and observe the performance of their favorite gospel groups. Ordinarily there are between sixty and eighty-five persons present at these singings. The audience consists primarily of married couples, often with small children, along with older people. Family members and fans of the singers are usually on hand as well. Conspicuously absent at 90 percent of these events are teenagers and young singles. Church singings are typically scheduled at night, once monthly. In such instances, they replace the regular preaching service.

Because of their sacred context, funerals represent another type of event to which gospel singers may be invited as participants in eulogizing the deceased. The two or three numbers rendered by the singers may include the deceased's favorite religious song, or they may be compositions that are deemed appropriate to commemorate the "home-going" of the departed. Frequently heard at these solemn occasions are songs like "Where We'll Never Grow Old," "Beautiful Isle of Somewhere," "O, Come Angel Band," and "At the Crossing." Some singers clearly want their own funerals to feature gospel music, the one compelling thing to which they dedicated their earthly lives. Taylor Chapman of Lewisburg, an old-time shape-note teacher and singer, died in 1987. Shortly before his passing, Chapman asked Tom Webb, friend, neighbor, and fellow singer, to organize a choir comprising people in the community who knew how to sing the shape-notes. "I want the choir to sing at my funeral for at least thirty minutes," he instructed Webb, "and I want you to call out the song number from the book just like you would at a singing convention." Webb agreed.

"Number eighty-four; number eighty-four ," Webb called out to the funeral choir, and they began singing "There's a Light at the River for Me." That done, Webb announced, "Number eighty-six; let's sing number eighty-six, 'I Will Meet You in the Morning.'" The choir continued through seven additional songs. It was not until some of the singers broke down and wept while the group sang "He'll Hold to My Hand as Over Life's River I Go," that the choir ceased to honor their beloved brother in this emotion-charged manner.

Woodrow Wilson of the Jabez community, located on the other side of the region from Lewisburg, shares Chapman's love for gospel music. He, too, wants a lot of singing at his funeral: "When I die, I want people to sing and sing. And I don't want no quiet singing. I want them to sing and enjoy themselves, for I've gone home when I leave here. I don't want no sadness. I want them to sing with good loud singing, and if they want to shout, let them go to it!"

In addition to funerals, singings are also scheduled at church homecomings, revival services, all-night sings,[2] and Watch Night services on New Year's Eve.[3] Homecomings are religious events at which regular worship services are conducted during the morning, followed by lunch, which is now typically spread on tables in the church basement, and then singing in the afternoon featuring one or two invited quartets. Revivals are evangelizing events held annually at most churches in the region. They typically last seven to ten nights, unlike their earlier counterparts, which were convened every day and every night for "as long as the Spirit led." Revivals are structured to allow time for a visiting quartet to sing about four songs at each service. Testimonials by one or more of the singers as to the efficacy of prayer and/or the saving power of Jesus are in order and fully expected by the congregation.

Both the Kentucky State Singing Convention, convened annually in different locations, and the Ohio Valley Singing Convention, held annually at Cave City, attract numerous singing ensembles to each of their two sessions. Group spokespersons are asked to take only enough time to announce the title of their next song. Testimonials are strictly forbidden. To violate protocol would be to infringe on the other quartets waiting their turn to sing much later on the program when the audience has dwindled away to a faithful few. This rule of silence notwithstanding, an occasional singer, usually the group leader, will break into testimony, during which the audience may be asked to "Clap if you love Jesus," "Let's give Jesus a big hand," or "Stand up if you've been saved." Some people in the audience appreciate this form of evangelism, while others deplore such tactics, which are referred to by one local gospel musician as "gospel aerobics."

Regionwide public events of this nature provide a forum for much intergroup fellowship in the foyer and in restrooms. Singers typically know each other but have not had an opportunity to chat at leisure for some time. It is not at all unusual for them to support each other to the extent possible, even while performing. A singer from one group may fill in for a member absent from another group. Bass players are especially noteworthy in this regard, as they have played for as many as four groups during the course of an evening. If jealousy is present in such instances, the audience is not made aware of it.

The Kentucky State Convention, the Ohio Valley Convention, and the half-dozen still-active county conventions in south central Kentucky are not religious events per se. They do begin and end on a note of prayer, however, and, occasionally, a brief testimony may be given during the song service. By and large, however, such singings are secular events, held in public locations such as school auditoriums. They simply feature religious music. Perhaps it was the secular nature of the 1988 Kentucky State Convention that prompted David Allgood of the Veterans Quartet to break the singing routine at midpoint. He ran up to Ronnie Williams, president of the convention, lifted the microphone from his hands and yelled into it, "What I'd like to do right here is to take time for Old Ron. I want you to give him a big 'un. Don't do it 'til I say so, but when I say so, tell him how good a job he did at putting this convention together this year. Okay, let's go; let's hear it for Ole Ron. [Thunderous applause by the audience of approximately one thousand persons] Who-e-e-e-e, come on, let's hear it again! [Continued heavy applause]"

Allgood began at that point to tell of the time that Williams, "a bear hunter from way back," went bear hunting:

Ole Ron got out one day in his pickup truck and he went to the woods. Going to hunt these bears. He got his shotgun and he got his shells.

Well, he looked for bears all day long. All morning and all afternoon, and it was coming night. He didn't find no bear. He got tired. Started gettin' dark; had to go back to the truck. So here he come on the way back. Said to himself, 'Well, I ain't going out for nothin.' So he started just shootin' them shells.

"Bam," "there's one."

"Bam," "there's one."

"Bam," "there's another'n."

Well, he shot up all his shells! So he's going back to the truck. Guess what? [Audience chuckles] You're right! You're ahead of me! Here comes the bear. That's right, a real bear! [Audience laughter]

So he takes off. He can't go to the truck. So he takes off runnin' hard and the bear right behind him. And he runs up to this place what looks like used to be a waterfall. And he can't go no further. The only thing he can think of is to pray. So Ron says, "Dear Lord, please let this be a Christian bear." [Audience continues to laugh]

And shore 'nuf he turned around and that bear was down on its knees, saying, "Dear Lord, thank you for this food I'm about to receive." [Thunderous applause and laughter by the audience]

Other types of singings that feature one or more quartets on program include regularly scheduled gospel music events in non-church settings such as those convened in Glasgow by Rex Agers at the Mitchell Clubhouse and in the parking lot at Louise's Bible Bookstore. Outdoor singings and benefit singings are likewise typically held in nonreligious settings, as in the cases of those infrequently convened in Metcalfe County at Branstetter Park and the Metcalfe Lake and Park, at Houchens Park near the Barren River Reservoir in Barren County, at the old Tabernacle in Scottsville, and in the Bertram Gospel Music Barn in Wayne County. Regardless of the settings, all of these singing events begin with prayer, and testimonials are occasionally given by singers who feel led to testify.

Benefit singings are conducted fairly frequently across the region as fund-raising enterprises designed to help a neighbor or fellow singer in need. The typical financial plight represented here is caused by loss due to fire, or prolonged sickness in the face of health insurance inadequate to cover physician, hospital, and medical costs. More often than not, the needy one has no health insurance at all. Typically, four to five visiting quartets sing at the benefit, perhaps joined by a singing group comprising family members of the person in need. Benefit singings are broken at midpoint to allow time for donated canned foods, clothing, and an assortment of household items to be auctioned off to the highest bidder. Proceeds from the auction, along with a love-offering taken in lieu of an admission charge, range anywhere between one thousand and six thousand dollars. No money is expected by the visiting groups; everything goes to the individual or family in need.

Outdoor singings may be held as integral parts of community events such as arts and crafts fairs or old-time days. Listeners are seldom seated at these events, distracting singers and other listeners alike. The attention factor is much better at outdoor sings held on school athletic fields, however, as persons in attendance are there to hear and see gospel music performed. Outdoor singing events held at night are sometimes referred to as "singing under the stars." It is not at all uncommon for a local amateur quartet to schedule a singing under the stars to commemorate its anniversary in gospel music. Four or five invited groups may be present, and all are expected to sing prior to the grand finale that features the host group.

Inherent in all these singing functions is the leadership role of the local arranger (my term), a person who acts on behalf of the host institution. A church example best illustrates the nature of the work involved in serving in this capacity. The church's arranger knows the emotional and spiritual temperament of the church's members and their expectations of a visiting groups' singing quality. The arranger is constantly on the lookout for gospel groups that fulfill congregational expectations, and sees and hears a gospel ensemble in actual performance before asking that group to fill a regular monthly singing slot on the church calendar. Outfits that do a lot of testifying and/or sermonizing, or perhaps use a full set of drums, need not seek an invitation into certain local churches—churches that expect the guest groups to primarily sing. On the other hand are those congrega-

The Madison Brothers Quartet surrounds a beneficiary family near Brownsville in 1989. *Photo by the author.*

Preparing for an outdoor singing at a residence near Edmonton in Metcalfe County in 1987. *Photo by the author.*

tions that look to the guest group to conduct an evangelistic song service and are disappointed with anything less.

Once a decision is made as to which singing group to invite, the arranger calls or writes the group's designated leader and asks them to sing. The leader has authority by virtue of group consent to book any and all weekend dates that are still open. Should the group have a previously booked engagement on the desired date, the arranger and leader look ahead to a date open for both parties and proceed to firm it up. That done, the arranger chooses another gospel group that fulfills congregational criteria, then picks up the telephone again. Eventually, all dates on the church's calendar set aside for singings are filled.

The local arranger is always on hand at church when the visiting quartet, complete with family members, arrives on the scene. Travel was once done primarily in cars, one of which had a trailer in tow. Now, however, quartets typically travel in shiny vans bearing the group's name painted prominently on the side of the vehicle. The vans are filled with singers, musicians and, space permitting, family members. It is not at all uncommon for the van to be escorted by two or three automobiles containing additional family members and fans. Fan following is commonplace. Hazel Bryson, then of the Southern Harmony Quartet, commented in 1986 that her group had three singings slated for the forthcoming weekend. She fully expected certain fans of the group to be present at all three events. And Debbie Reece commented in this connection, "I could almost tell you who was going to be there, depending on what group is singing."

Once greetings have been exchanged between the arranger and the visiting singers, the former takes the group leader inside to look over the physical layout of the church sanctuary. The other singers and musicians begin immediately the twofold task of unloading and setting up the PA equipment in the sanctuary in preparation for the evening's program, and mounting an exhibit of their tapes, albums, and other gospel music memorabilia in the church foyer. These jobs take upward of forty-five minutes, especially for the ones working with the sound system. Speakers and mikes have to be balanced with the accoustical character of the auditorium. Typically, the men set up the sound system, and the women prepare the sales table. These chores done, the singers wait for program time to arrive. Until then, they go outside to smoke a final cigarette, or mingle with arriving church members and still other fans who, as in past weeks, are on hand to witness their favorite gospel group in action once more.

When program time arrives, the arranger stands up to thank the home folk in the audience, along with the singers and visitors, for

Singers in the Crossroads Quartet of Columbia/Russell Springs have been together for twenty years without a change in personnel. *Photo courtesy of the Crossroads Quartet.*

being present at what promises to be a wonderful evening of worship in song. The arranger nods to the church song leader and pianist to lead the congregation in an opening number. A prayer follows, then another song by the entire congregation. Without further ado, the arranger briefly introduces the visiting quartet and turns the program over to the singers.

The opening format in more evangelical settings does not change all that much. The prayer may be more emotional, perhaps with several persons praying aloud in unison. And the congregational singing may cause someone to lift a hand upward in praise. Perhaps an occasional "Amen" is uttered during the introduction of the visiting singers. All in all, however, the structure of the opening portion of the program (generally referred to as a "service") is essentially the same in every church setting. All eyes and ears are now focused on the pulpit area where the singers are located, ready to begin.[4]

Most of these gospel music ensembles allow the words to the songs, along with the metaphors and vivid images contained in the verses, to act as the primary evangelizing agents during the song service. Although individual singers may provide occasional spoken testimonies, minisermons are rarely delivered by any of them. Spontaneity is extremely important, however, as singers and audience alike respect the informal atmosphere associated with the singing events. Thus it is that friendly humor is also accorded a place in these services.

"We're glad to be here tonight to witness to you through the power of song," the quartet leader says, looking out over the audience. "The altar is always open in the event you feel the power of the Spirit speaking to you here tonight," the leader continues. "For our first number, we've chosen 'Standing on the Solid Rock.'" The audience mildly applauds the ensemble at the conclusion of the song.

"Thank you for that good hand. My, my, it's good to be here with you," the group leader says, and then announces the next song. "We'll continue with another up-tempo number that features all members of the quartet, 'Give the World a Smile Each Day.'"

At the end of the second verse, someone in the congregation applauds the performance. Others may join in to demonstrate their appreciation of the singers. A hearty round of applause is given by all at the completion of the song.

"Thank you so much. Thank you. Thank you," the group emcee says with a real show of enthusiasm. "We'll slow things down a bit right now with a very beautiful song that we've been practicing on, 'Child, Child, O Why Do You Wander.'"

By the end of the third number, a discerning member of the quartet is able to analyze the audience's song preferences with rather amazing accuracy. In so doing, the group knows the types of songs to sing during the remainder of the service. Not all singing groups have such a person in their midst, however, thus forcing the ensemble to sing from a prepared list of songs. A highly successful group plans only three or four songs in advance, then improvises on the spot by calling upon a sizable performance-ready song repertoire. Garry Polston offers some interesting observations about reading audiences:

I'd plan the program after I'd dressed and set down to rest before singing. I made out two copies; one for myself and one for the group.

Once we began to sing, we'd sing three songs before I said a word. During these three songs, I would read the congregation. It might be that the program would change after those three songs. We always had more than 100 songs that we could sing at any time.

We'd always sing so many songs from our albums. Then, we'd do other types of songs. You can read a congregation. Some people want a slow, touching song. Others want to clap their hands and pat their feet. Some churches want to hear some of the old hymns. We might be in a large, stiff United Methodist Church that wasn't used to this kind of singing, and we'd walk in and do the old hymn, "Holy, Holy, Holy," and by the time we'd finished, we'd already sold ourselves to them. After you've done that, you can sing anything you want to.

I don't read a congregation by their applause. I can tell by their eyes if they're liking what they hear.

S.D. McGaha of the Crossroads Quartet also spoke of an intuitive ability to discern audience preferences. "Within five minutes, I can tell you what an audience wants to hear," he said.

"That's absolutely true," vouched McGaha's son Vernie. "I always look at him instead of the crowd as a means of knowing what they like."

The elder McGaha then made a revealing statement regarding the tactics of their highly successful, long-lived ensemble. "If we can't reach an audience after three to four songs, we start singing to each other and joking around much like we do in a practice session. Pretty soon, we have the crowd pulled in, too."

On occasion, an audience is receptive to slower songs that, say, compare the trials and temptations of living in the present with the peace and beauty that awaits the believer in heaven. The group spokesperson may implore persons in the audience, "Don't listen to the way we sing the next song; just listen to the words." Or, perhaps sensing someone's need for salvation, the emcee may comment, "It's not possible for us singers to save anybody, but God can. Just listen to the words of this beautiful song 'I Know a Man Who Can.'" The speaker is well aware that gospel music is unlike any other form of music; it is intended to convey a message that goes well beyond the actual performance of the song itself. In this context, words are powerful tools.

When the alto or baritone takes a solo lead at some point in the song, a fellow singer may encourage the vocalist with softly spoken, meaningful words such as, "Praise the Lord," "Yes, yes," or "Sing it for Jesus." The congregation remains silent with an air of expectancy. Light applause following the song signifies an attitude of reverence, not disapproval of the singing itself. If no one in the audience responds outwardly to the singers' invitation to seek God, an up-tempo song will likely follow.

When the song service is drawing close to the midpoint, or break, one of the singers may blurt out something in a humorous vein.

Bus ownership remains a hoped-for luxury for most area singing groups. Members of the Glasgow-based Gospel Crusaders proudly pose by their bus in 1986. *Photo by the author.*

George Abney of the Faith Singers jokingly confessed his group's ignorance of sight-reading music. "We don't know parts and we don't know notes," he commented in a very serious manner. "All we know is the 'open letter C.' We just *open* up, *let 'er* fly, and *see* what happens."

Clayton Lindsey of the Southern Harmony Quartet listened to the applause that Hazel Bryson received for one of her solo leads, then, with tongue in cheek, stopped the song at midpoint with the words "Hazel and Mae [pianist] get all the applause! Me and Mike and Frank here are studying to be astronauts. We're just taking up space."

One of the funniest routines in local gospel music circles is carried out by the Lyles. It features comedy interspersed with song during the entire course of the evening. The group's personnel include Genell Lyle, pianist and low alto; her husband, Bobby, on the lead; Carol Thomas, alto; and W.D. Martin, bass. Odie Ray McReynolds plays bass guitar. All of them bear the brunt of the humor dished out by Genell, Bobby, and Carol at various points during the service. On one occasion, Bobby interrupted Carol right in the middle of a solo performance in a humorous attempt to confuse her. "Do that verse again Carol; I sure do like it!" he teased.

When she was finished, Carol threatened to tell everyone about the "fool blunder" he made while driving to a singing the other night. Without breaking stride, Bobby turned to the audience to introduce their next song. "When we first started practicing on 'Can He, Could He, Would He,' Carol said that we'd never learn it," he said. "She was right! But we're going to sing it anyway."

Following completion of the song and heavy applause by the audience, Genell pretended to squint frantically into the sheaf of songs on the piano stand in front of her. Jokingly she remarked about her poor eyesight, "I can't see a single one of these songs," she chuckled, "but you can't imagine how good it makes me feel just to know that they are there!" Without the slightest pause, she began playing the introductory chords to "I Think I'll Read It Again and Let It Bless My Soul." The message of the song had no relationship to the joking. A polished interpretation of the song was provided by the Lyles, followed immediately by "I Want to Be Just Like My Lord," a song that describes a dedicated Christian's desire to achieve a higher earthly plane.

Genell continued the banter at the end of the song, this time by singling out the bass player, Ray. "A year or so ago we were singing in Glasgow, and this little old lady walked up to me. Said, 'Honey, is that your son that's playing the guitar?' And Ray's just three years younger than me!"

Bobby interrupted her and took over the narration at that point. "And when the lady was leaving the church that night," he said, laughingly, "Genell kicked her on the shin! [The crowd erupts with laughter]"

"Every since then," Genell told the still-laughing audience, "Ray makes it a point to call me 'Mom' in public. And me just three years older than him!"

She had continued to play the piano while telling the story. Both Genell and Bobby, and Carol to some extent, have the ability to take events from everyday life—things that happened last week or this morning—and translate them into humorous narratives suitable for retelling at singing events. Some of their stories serve nicely as appropriate introductions to songs in their repertoire. Their comic antics in no way represent fake showmanship. This is honest-to-goodness humor designed and used to poke fun at each other. And the audience loves every minute of it.

Toward the end of the service, Genell employed a stock joke heard at other singing events. She leafed through a stack of notes presumably submitted by persons in the audience. "We've had an unusual

The Lyles in concert at Pleasant Grove in Warren County in 1987.
Genell Lyles is seated at the piano on the far right.

number of requests tonight," she observed, "but we're gonna go
ahead and sing awhile longer anyway."

After the featured group has sung eight to ten songs, the group
emcee follows customary protocol by announcing, "We'll sing one
more song, and then let someone else get up here while we catch our
breath." At that time also, an announcement is usually made regarding the availability of tapes and albums for sale in the foyer.

During the break, the program arranger calls on the home quartet, if there is one, to sing three or four songs. Next, the arranger asks
if other individuals came prepared to sing or play a piano solo.
Following these performances, a love offering is taken for the visiting
singers. In rare instances, the home church has made budgetary
provisions to pay the visitors a set amount, thus negating the need for
an offering.

Upon completion of these interim activities, the featured group
resumes the spotlight to sing four or five additional songs. For these
concluding moments, some quartets intentionally choose slower
songs that deal with salvation and Christian living, facing the reality
of death, and/or going to heaven. They strive for an attitude of prayer
and rededication among listeners in the audience.

While most gospel groups witness primarily through song, a few
ensembles are made up of individuals who both sing and sermonize
during the service. To them, "singings" should be revivalistic in tone.

Also, the churches that invite these groups typically expect an emotion-charged service, in both testimony and in song. Members of such congregations are often prone to emotional religious experiences. They are ripe for triggered releases that are manifested through shouting and arm waving on the one hand and by closed eyes and gentle swaying from side to side on the other. At this type of singing event, it is difficult to know who it is—the congregation or the singers—that dictates the emotional level of the service. One gospel singer who frowns on the emotional school feels that the visiting singers trigger people's emotions. He commented that such singing groups "don't read people as to song preferences, they orchestrate them."

Wanting to check this out for myself, I went to a small church in a nearby county seat town to witness a singing of this variety. It was Saturday night. Sixteen persons had attended Sunday School the previous week; only ten the Sunday before that. But by the time the singing began that evening, the sanctuary was filled to capacity (approximately one hundred people) and some people stood along the walls.

I had gone early in order to set up my recording equipment. As I opened the door to the church, I was greeted by the sounds of the visiting singers warming up for the evening's service. A rather big fellow in his mid-fifties extended his hand to me and introduced himself as the pastor of the church in a genuinely warm manner. We chatted for a moment and were then joined by three other men who came over to welcome me. The pastor's wife also dropped by to say hello.

Soon, one of the singers was helping me set up my recording equipment. I had never been treated more royally and felt totally at ease mixing with the crowd and talking at greater length with the pastor and the singers. No one present seemed to mind the extremely hot sanctuary, overheated by both a woodburning stove and a gas heater.

The service began with the pastor asking three women, perhaps in their late sixties, to come to the front and lead the congregation in singing a song or two. They obliged by choosing two selections from a Stamps-Baxter songbook. The pastor again took to the podium and made a rather lengthy introduction to the evening's program before calling on the congregation to have "a season of prayer." Numerous persons went forward to the altar area to pray aloud simultaneously. Two solo song performances followed the prayer. After about thirty minutes of preliminaries, the visiting singers were invited to "take over the services." And take over they did!

Their very first song was "Just Any Day Now," a powerful song that warns of Christ's Second Coming. Before their heavily amplified voices had completed the first verse of the song, an elderly woman, filled with emotion, lifted her hands and arms heavenward and began to shout praises to God. A second woman in the congregation left one of the pews and moved hurriedly toward the singers, tears of joy streaming down her face. She embraced all of the singers who, by then, were also weeping openly.

The group spokesman preached for a few minutes on the immediacy of the rapture of the saints. An adult male shouted praises from the rear of the church; several "amens" were sounded across the small auditorium, and a six-year-old girl with tear-filled eyes and quivering lips ran forward to embrace one of the male singers. The pew on which I sat began to shake because of the movements of a woman worshipper who had apparently achieved a trance-state.

People continued throughout the emotional song service to manifest ecstatic feelings, and the singers employed vivid imagery in their trembling-voice testimonials. As the evening progressed, emotions subsided, and both the singers and the audience seemed to relax a bit more. By the end of the longer-than-usual service, the singing was just that—a singing.[5]

It is not uncommon for singers at any singing event to give an emotionally charged personal testimony. This is especially true if they link a personal experience with the lyrics, such as sickness or death of a loved one. By way of illustration, a Mr. Barnes of the Faubush community in Russell County was present at an old-time congregational singing at Coffey's Chapel Methodist Church in June 1987. Mr. Barnes entered the church that day with his retarded son in his mid-twenties holding onto his arm. The two lived together, alone.

Mr. Barnes, a farmer all his life, stood up to take his turn leading the congregation in one or two songs. He commented to the audience that he had lost his wife twenty-six months ago "and I still miss her so very much. I miss her voice." Then, with tears in evidence for all to see, he asked the singers in the congregation to join him in singing "No Tears in Heaven Will Be Known." His was a beautiful example of authentic, nonorchestrated emotion. And so it is with all these singers who personally depend on and believe in the messages contained in the songs they love most.

Folklorist Ray Allen writes that gospel songs "carry messages of Christian love, salvation and the possibilities of liberation from the burdens of an often hostile world."[6] Folklorist Bill Malone, writing about the ever-popular repertoire of the Chuck Wagon Gang, de-

scribes their songs as "comforting, . . . with visions of a caring Sav-
iour and a Heavenly reward."[7] Former music teacher C.E. Deweese
commented that "most of our songs point toward heaven. They may
start out on earth telling of our conversion, but we wind up looking
forward to that heavenly home." And church music historian Stanley
Brobston notes that the bulk of the gospel songs sung by the Georgia
groups he studied were written in the first person. The most frequently recurring theme there is the anticipation of heaven, with the
joys and rewards of conversion running a distant second.[8] Themes
contained in the songs found in the repertoires of singing groups in
south central Kentucky are certainly no different from the themes
already enumerated. Singers here use the same songs as their amateur
singing counterparts elsewhere. All of them, in turn, borrow from the
professionals. Themes not mentioned thus far but which belong in
the list include the family circle, efforts to live a Christian life, death,
and the believer's victory over death.

These observers all agree that gospel songs are future oriented.
Collectively, the song lyrics comment that Christian people are moving forward and ever upward to heaven during their earthbound
journey—a journey that is often filled with trials, tribulations, and
sorrows. The Christian life is thus never static. There are things to be
done along the way, including helping others materially and witness-
ing to those who need the Lord. Since so many of these songs focus on
the question of "when," not "where," the indication is that singers
are concerned with future time, not future place. They know and sing
about where they will spend eternity, but do not know when it will
begin.

Gospel songs not only anticipate heaven and the hereafter, they
often talk about what the believer is leaving behind. There will be no
more sickness, blindness, burdens, partings, or deaths there on that
Bright Shore. Nor will there be a need for wealth and the worldly
amenities that money can buy.

No more than a half-dozen recent songs address the themes of
judgment, hell-fire, and eternal damnation. Instead, gospel songs
address such themes as "the Cross, Calvary, Christ's suffering, His
dying, the blood, cleansing, etc."[9] "Basically, these songs offer hope,"
Vernie McGaha commented. "Whether intentional or not," he went
on, "we dwell on the positive aspects in our singing. How many
people are going to enjoy our singing if we stand up and sing, and
when we get done we have sung them into hell?"

Although songs with sentimental themes had been present in the
gospel repertoire from the 1930s, they became more common about

1970. Prevalent indeed were songs about praying mamas, family Bibles, Mama's Bible, the death of parents, family reunion in heaven, and other emotional themes. Connor B. Hall, editor of *Vaughan's Family Visitor*, bemoaned the tendency to publish and sing "more and more songs that are no more than folk themes about home, hills, cabins, mother, father, seasons, and flowers." [10] Perhaps the accelerated interest in sentimental themes is indicative of the loss of the kind of life-style represented in the songs. Such songs perhaps afford the composer, singer, and listener a vicarious means of returning to a more carefree past, perhaps even a past that never was.

Gospel music's popularity may be attributed to its familiarity to singers and listeners alike. These days, some people argue, it is possible to go to a large city church and not enjoy the singing heard there. The emphasis is on the new, the modern, in both lyrics and sound. People who feel this way about contemporary music are typically receptive only to the sound of old-time southern harmony, perhaps because of lifelong familarity. They are moved by the images and metaphors used in the songs that are biblically based or that derive from more than two centuries of rural southern life and thought.[11] Folklorist Charles Wolfe illustrates this point in describing Dottie Rambo's very popular song "I've Never Been This Homesick Before." He comments that she borrowed the imagery of the rural homecoming while managing to suggest that it is only a metaphor for a more profound religious experience.[12]

Life on earth is often described in gospel songs in terms of natural landscapes—roads, hills, mountains, rivers, weather conditions, and other familiar features seen on an everyday basis. The afterlife in heaven is often portrayed as a kingdom or a city with golden streets, palatial mansions, walls of jasper, pearly gates, and other wonderful, unfamiliar attributes. Since southern gospel lyrics spring from a rural culture, it is quite natural for the descriptions of heaven, which is the future "home" for all believers, to focus on imagery that is totally different from what people have known in this life. In more recent times, however, song lyrics have described heaven as a place of green pastures, green fields of clover, gentle breezes, and beautiful flowers. Perhaps these lyrics, like those with the sentimental themes of hearth and home, reflect a shift in southern population from farm to city, and the attendant feelings that the good things of life were left behind. Such things will be awaiting the pilgrim's arrival in heaven.

All imagery about God the Father is biblically based. Jesus on the other hand, is portrayed as a friend, a light, treasure, a bridge over troubled waters, shelter from a storm, a ship's captain or pilot, and a lifeboat at the believer's death. Numerous physical interactions take place between Jesus and those who have been redeemed. They may lean on Him, shake hands with Him, feel His hands touching them, hear Him speak audibly to them, be healed by the touch of His hand, feel His arms around them, walk through life holding His hand, and feel Him holding their hands at death. Jesus' love is like pure gold, a light, a fountain, a rainbow, and water.

In these songs, the Holy Spirit is symbolized in the Christian's life both as a wind and as a tug ("I know He lives within my heart, for I can feel the tug"). The Bible is a great speckled bird, a road map, and a compass. Life is portrayed as a river to be crossed, a raging sea or storm, travel on a wearying road, a battle, a fight against Satan, a fight against the forces of sin, a narrow path to heaven, an unbroken chain, a trouble-filled journey, a journey filled with physical obstacles— rivers, valleys, mountains, desert sand—a pasture, a vapor, a flower that will fade, a ship drifting away from the shore, a wrecked ship in need of rescue, a ladder to be climbed, sinking land, a flight to heaven, a railroad, a rocky road, a bridge-building process, a race to be run, a stairway to be climbed, and a lot of broken pieces.

Christians are children of light, children of the King, little servants, kings, soldiers in the Lord's army, faithful sheep, range riders for Jesus, people in love with Jesus, empty vessels in need of being filled, flowers to be gathered by God, business people, and future millionaires. The human body is a prison, a house of flesh, a house of clay, and a temple of the Lord. Sin is portrayed as darkness and as shackles. Trouble is bad weather, a storm, raging water, and a nightmare. The Christian's salvation is seen as a fountain, a river that never runs dry, a crossing over River Jordan to get out of the wilderness of sin, a lifeboat, a bridge over a river, the Ship of Zion, a door to heaven, a light, a pardon from sinful living, a treasure, new construction on a mansion in heaven, a title to a place in heaven, a deliquent account paid in full, a ticket to heaven that was purchased at the altar, and a reservation for a one-way flight to heaven. While a host of songs deal with the theme of salvation, very few of them describe the actual details of the conversion experience. A notable, emotion-filled example is the song "A Child's Request," made famous a few years back by the Sego Brothers and Naomi.

A rock, a ship, and a flame are metaphors for the Christian faith, a bridge signifies the church, and a ship is employed to represent a body of believers. Numerous songs, such as "Gone," deal with the triumph of Christ over death and the assurance of a future life for believers.

Christ's Second Coming to establish His earthly reign is frequently addressed in gospel lyrics. This event is represented as a thief in the night, a meeting in the air, and Christ's wedding day. His return will be signaled by audible footsteps. The final resurrection will be a morning, a roundup, a wedding, and a meeting in the air.

The end of time and the final judgment are rarely dealt with in this body of religious song. There are notable exceptions, however, such as "Payday, Someday," and "Oh, Sinner, What Will You Do When the Stars Begin to Fall?"

As previously indicated, most gospel songs lead to heaven—a place where all the imperfections of this present world are made perfect, where human sorrow is unknown, where Christians live the full life not possible in the present world. "I want to stroll over heaven with you," run the words to a currently popular song. Heaven is vividly portrayed in wonderful images and metaphors. At death, travel to this celestial home is accomplished by means of a flight through outer space, by riding on a ship or chariot, by stepping on the clouds or from star to star, and by walking on the milky white way. Heaven is a place of family reunions, a meeting place for the redeemed, where Christians shall reign forevermore; it is a treasure-filled place, a kingdom, a place where no cabins fall, where only mansions are found ("Just wait 'til you see my brand new home"), where regal clothing will be worn. Heaven is home, a place of unending day, and a land of uncloudy skies. These "heaven songs" are the salve that heals the hurts of Christians who are living in what they believe to be the last days. And when they finally get to heaven, according to the songs, believers will worship, eat at the Lord's table, rest beneath the evergreen tree, stroll over heaven, run through the green fields of clover, feel the gentle breezes, and look at the gently flowing river.[13] Heaven will be a place for God's chosen people to do these simple things that a life of hard work and responsibility denied them on earth.

That these song lyrics appeal to local singers and audiences alike can be attributed to the fact that, while most of the songs were composed by individuals, elsewhere, such composers' lives resemble those of the people who sing and listen to the songs. The hillcountry of south central Kentucky has also produced countless song composers, past and present, some of whom achieved measurable success in having their creations published in convention songbooks,[14] distributed as sheet music, or recorded and issued on the tapes and albums of local singing ensembles. Most of their compositions nurture a deep respect and reverence for biblical themes. Yet, like gospel song composers elsewhere, local composers exhibit a tendency to employ vivid images and familiar metaphors.

Arlis O. Harmon is one of the most prolific gospel song composers in the Upper South in recent times. Harmon has seen forty-two of his compositions published since 1961, and in 1990, had three others in the hands of publishers. He has in manuscript form another two hundred songs and approximately one thousand poems. While Harmon's early compositions appeared in songbooks bearing the imprints of Stamps Quartet Music Company, James D. Vaughan, Tennessee Music Company, Convention Music Company, and Hartford Music Company, most of his more recent songs were published by Leoma Music Company, Leoma, Tennessee.

Born April 1, 1905, in Allen County, Harmon worked as a private investigator for thirty-one years, traveling in twenty-four states, the District of Columbia, and Canada. All the while he contributed a regular column to his hometown newspaper, the Scottsville *Citizen-Times*, writing under the pen name of the Lone Traveler. In June 1959, Harmon retired to his native Allen County to pursue his love for gospel music that began as a six-year-old boy when he studied under shape-note teacher Fletcher Wolfe.

Harmon's first song to be published was "Coming Home on a Promise and a Prayer." Also in 1961, he co-authored "They Have Gone to Glory," which was published by James D. Vaughan Music Publisher. It was not until eight years later, in 1969, that two more of his songs appeared in print. "Those Sacred Hands" bore the imprint of the Tennessee Music and Printing Company, and "Angels Will Fly My Soul" was issued by the Convention Music Company, Montgomery, Alabama.

Two more of Harmon's songs were published in 1970. These were "On the Streets of Gold" (Convention Music) and "I Live in Faith" (co-authored), recorded by the Spicer Family of Hamilton, Ohio, as the first song on side A of their album. His next six songs were published by Albert E. Brumley's Hartford Publishing Company of Powell, Missouri. These were "Precious Lord, I'll Meet You" (1971; co-authored), "I'm Gonna Ring Those Golden Bells" (1971; co-authored), "I See Beyond the Shadows" (1972), "As I Walk Through the Valley" (1973; co-authored), "It's A Wonderful Day" (1974), and "Jesus Changed The Melody in My Heart" (1975). About two dozen of Harmon's songs have been published since 1979. Two of these were issued by Vaughan in 1979 and 1980; the Cumberland Valley Music Company of Maryville, Tennessee, published one of his songs in 1988 and two others in 1990; two were included in the National Music

Company's 1989 songbook and one in its 1990 book, *Beautiful Songs,* and a whopping nineteen of Harmon's creations were published by the Leoma Music Company between 1979 and 1990.

I wrote Harmon in early 1989, asking him to explain his prolonged affiliation with Leoma. His response reads as follows:

The reason Leoma has used more of my songs is they are still in business. The Hartford Music Co. used six of my songs and quit publishing convention type song books. The Convention Music Co. and The Gospel Song Publishers Association went out of business and Vaughan cut down to one book a year. The Stamps Quartet Music Co. also went out of business. Only Hartford and Tennessee gave royalty contracts. All others were on cash terms which was very low. The main thing I was interested in was to get my name established as a song writer and to get some of my songs published. My dealing with all the different publishers was friendly and all treated me nice.

Harmon acknowledges the role played by inspiration in helping him with the words and music to his compositions. He feels the Lord guiding him when he "gets a tune" in his head. Once this happens, Harmon thinks about the tune for awhile, then plays it on the piano. "I get one score and then I'll add another," he stated. "Then, when I get that piece of music to sound like I want it to, I put it on paper and begin to hunt up some words to go with the music." Arlis O. Harmon is known across the South for his ability to set music to words, thus explaining why numerous southern lyricists have come to him for help with their creations.

Many individuals associated with singing ensembles around the region have written religious poems in recent years, some of which have been set to music and sung during public performances by one or more area groups. Most of these creations have never been published as sheet music, however, or recorded on albums or cassettes. Such is the case with Toby White Cockriel of Bowling Green, who has written numerous songs, three of which have been copyrighted; however, "Most of her compositions are still confined to her notebook," observed her husband, Lonnie. "She has to be in a sad frame of mind before she can write. She has to be down and out and needing the help of the Lord more than anything in the world. She couldn't ever write a song if she was happy."

Toby broke in, "They usually have to come from the heart; reflect how I feel," and then added, "I've got to be really depressed."

Lonnie added, laughingly, "She's already told me that if she dies before I do, and if somebody comes around and don't cry, hand them an onion to make them cry." Lonnie began to sing one of Toby's compositions: "Walk with me Lord, all the way, / Til I reach the land of unending day."

"She's low, see. So she starts to thinking about a better time that surely is coming," Lonnie observed.

"I get to thinking 'So what?'" Toby broke in. "'So you got a little problem. Well, the Lord *died* on the cross. I don't have any problems like the Lord went through.' After I express it all, get it off my chest how bad I feel, then I feel pretty good. I compose a song right then. If I can't write it and finish it right then, then I can't finish it at all." Three of her songs were recorded by the Cockriel Family on their 1967 LP album "Singin' and Shoutin'."

Charles Witty of Glasgow, formerly of the Servants Quartet from Campbellsville, is known among area singers for his song compositions which, in the words of one-time colleague Donnie Parker, "are great for our kind of music. They're doing good; will probably make some big bucks." And Gary Martin of the Singing Martins of Scottsville has written numerous songs, including four that appeared on their 1988 album. His well-received "No One Can Wear My Robe But Me" has commanded a lot of air time on area radio stations, and is currently being sung by several groups in the Nashville area.

Most of Garry Polston's compositions deal with the issues of being a Christian in the contemporary world, rather than focusing on "the themes that people like to hear about, such as the resurrection and heaven." Polston came under some criticism for a song he wrote in the late 1970s, called "It's More Important that He Tarry than He Come." "Getting ready to live in the world," he said, "is more crucial than sitting around longing for the next life on the other side of death."

Christell Wells Bennett of the Wells Family Quartet in Horse Cave is another of the present-day composers who, like her mother, Lucille London Wells, and countless other area singer-composers, has not pursued publication possibilities for her compositions. Bennett, who is a granddaughter of early shape-note teacher J.W. London of Metcalfe and Hart counties, works on her creations only through inspiration, pondering themes and words for several days before actually attempting to commit her thoughts to paper. Because of society's fascination for space ships and flights in the early 1970s, Christell's pastor delivered a sermon in 1972 on this subject to make the point that God's plan of redemption would carry His believers on a safe flight through space. His message inspired her to pen the words and music to "A Flight Through Outer Space," a verse and chorus of which are as follows:

> We've heard so much about the flights in space
> and trips up to the moon,
> One of these days I'll make a flight in space.
> It could be very soon;
> I'm just waiting for the count-down,
> when the Master calls his own,
> Then I'll get aboard a space ship,
> fly away to worlds unknown.
>
> Chorus:
> There's no danger in this space ship,
> for its, oh, so well equipped,
> Everything is now in order
> for that long awaited trip;
> Yes, my trust is in the pilot
> for I met Him face to face;
> At the altar I got ready for
> my flight thru outer space.

Some members of the Lowell Davis clan of Lindseyville are gifted song writers and have numerous recent compositions to their credit. The Masseys of Glasgow-Madisonville have written and recorded some very fine gospel songs, including "That Same Spirit." So it is, too, with Johnny Johnson of Jamestown, the James Turner Family of Bowling Green, Vernie McGaha of Russell Springs, and Lottie Marr of Greensburg, among other unheralded composers of south central Kentucky. Many of their songs, which nicely illustrate mastery of biblical themes and time-tested metaphors, have been published and sold in sheet music format in regional bookstores, music shops, and at singing events.

Most gospel music groups today are aware that if they aspire to recognition on the semi-professional circuit, they must issue professionally recorded cassette tapes and albums that contain songs of their own creation or that are at least new. It is these recordings that demonstrate the group's distinctive sounds and to a listening audience beyond the parameters of home base.

9

SINGING FAMILIES

"We were just a family that went around singing." Those words uttered by Junior Selvidge of Wayne County are filled with meaning for numerous persons in south central Kentucky who now are or once were part of family singing ensembles. Like Selvidge, these people know how important family groups are to gospel music and, conversely, how meaningful gospel music is to family singing units. By family group, I refer here to any singing ensemble that utilizes the services of at least three vocalists (two in the cases of trios) from the same family. Although many gospel music performers work outside their own family groups, the family was and still is the backbone of four-part southern gospel music.

Of the 825 known groups in south central Kentucky at various times between 1900 and 1990, 146 (35 percent) of them had at least three singers and/or musicians (two in the instances of trios) from the same immediate family. There were forty-eight such groups active in 1990. Other kinship groupings not counted in the above statistics include those that comprised, for example, two sisters and their husbands; three brothers and a child of one of them; or two sisters and the children of a nonsinging sister. If all kinship ensembles such as these were to be included in the family statistics, more than 40 percent of all singing groups, past and present, were familial in their basic composition. Family-based groups account for 52 percent of those that are currently active.

Family-based ensembles are typically of two different generational varieties. First are those groups made up entirely of siblings. These include(d), among others, the Wooten Four and Keith Sisters of

Casual attire is quite acceptable at outdoor singing events, as demonstrated by members of The Guiding Light from Columbia. *Photo by the author.*

Eubank, Stuart Sisters Trio of Bowling Green, Guffey Sisters and Bertram Sisters of Wayne County, Templeman Sisters of Munfordville, Harmoneers of Lewisburg, King's Daughters of Columbia, Eaton Trio of Salmon, Madison Brothers Quartet of Brownsville, McCubbins Brothers of Munfordville, Haste Brothers of Bethelridge, and the Madison Family of Smiths Grove. There are forty-one such groups, past and present, fourteen of which were still singing actively in 1990.

The second type of generational grouping comprises parent-

The Braswell Family, pictured here in 1972, is still actively singing in the Dale Hollow Lake area of southern Clinton County. *Photo by the author.*

children ensembles. Eighty-five known singing families fell in this category across the years; a rather surprising forty-three of them are still active. Included here are such current kinship groups as the Hanners, the Holders, and the Wolfes of Scottsville; the Crisp and Pierce families of Glasgow; the Braswells and the Smiths of Albany; the Minyards and Skaggses of Edmonson County; the Marrses of Greensburg; the Dorseys of Munfordville; the Bowleses, the Dicksons, and the Thrashers of Metcalfe County; the Clarence Bertram family of Campbellsville; the Burches, the Howards, and the Turners from Bowling Green; and the Anderson, Bradshaw, Corder, and Davis families from Wayne County.

I know of only two instances—current ones, at that—of singing groups in which three generations of performers from the same family are teamed up. Lela Pond, her daughter Jennifer Godby, and Jennifer's daughter Tammy all participate in the Builders for Jesus (1988–), along with Jennifer's husband, Lewis Godby, and Opal Haste Roy. All of them are members of the Kingbee Baptist Church near West Science Hill in Pulaski County. The House of Prayer Singers from Calvary Ridge in Casey County are also a mother-daughter-granddaughter combination.

Family singing units have long been a part of the gospel music scene, attested to by such stalwarts as the Chuck Wagon Gang, the Blackwood Brothers, the Speer Family, and the Happy Goodmans. Gospel musicians often learn to read music, sing, and play musical instruments from others in their family. Cora Davis Meredith, who grew up in a singing family in Lindseyville and who currently sings in the Davis Family ensemble, mused, "I guess when I was a child, it was odd to me when other families couldn't sing. It just seemed to me like everybody could sing. It was such a big part of my life growing up."

Cora's son, David, singing pianist for the Davis Family, commented on the value of growing up in a gospel music family:

It's almost like something that we've taken for granted. I never really thought about it until I started singing with some other people who had trouble picking out the harmony parts or whatever. I think it definitely has something to do with Grandpa Davis [also a singer].

As kids, we used to sing harmony parts to TV commercials. We can whistle all the harmony parts to Andy Griffith and stuff like that. Harmony is just something that happens in the family. It's just something that I was brought up with; almost natural, I guess. It's not anything I was trying to learn or anything like that. It just happens.

As articulated by David Meredith, and commented on by a host of other singers as well, the striking harmonic quality of family voices, especially those of siblings, is rather easy to spot. Such genetically related voices, properly assigned to the right vocal parts in a family ensemble, produce a balanced sound that stands largely unchallenged by nonkinship groups. Ivis Roy, of the Roy Family Singers, was rather emphatic about the advantages. "Whenever you have a family group, you have better harmony," he said. "In some way or another, that blood tie causes you to harmonize better."

Family singing groups are drawn together by kinship ties and their common love for gospel music. For them, this music helps to create and maintain generational continuity. Singing provides young family members with an added emotional identification with older singing members of the family. And because family ties are so very important in this geographical area, singing is a means of perpetuating the family's association and identification with the gospel music tradition.

Young people who are actively continuing the family tradition, even those just beginning to work within this framework, are made to feel important and needed. Being part of a singing family and having a vocal part that is theirs, and theirs alone, makes youngsters feel just as important as the adult performers in the family ensemble. Margaret Martin of the Singing Martins commented on this positive attribute of family-based gospel music. "When the kids are standing up there with Mom and Dad," she said, "they are on an equal footing with the parents."

"When a group is made up of all family members," Martin continued, "each person feels free to disagree with the others about certain facets of the music." She pointed out that younger children do not always voice their feelings openly, however, as such utterances might be construed as disrespect. Other than this one potentially negative facet, Martin felt that family singing groups had the best of all possible working conditions for gospel ensembles. She commented on the fact that working in a nonkinship gospel group is extremely disruptive to the families of those persons involved. An inordinate amount of time spent away from home and family members is normal for the singers and musicians who perform with a popular gospel group. While nonsinging families are free to use their weekends for family-based activities, gospel music participants are almost always gone from home on Saturday and Sunday nights, and often Friday evenings as well. On the other hand, when the entire family is involved in gospel music, the family is not torn apart; rather, the family unit is on the road together. By providing all the singers and musicians necessary for their group's performance needs, a family-based outfit does not disrupt the weekend activities of several other families.

Ivis Roy talked about the convenience of family groups. "I liked our family group because it was handy," he said. "We didn't have to wait on other singers, or have to go to get them. When we got ready to go, we just milked the old cow and took off and went to where we were going."

Some of the families trace their gospel music roots back to the days when singing was learned at shape-note schools and practiced at home by siblings, parents and children, grandparents and grandchildren. Numerous persons told of singing with other members of the family while at work in the fields or while riding down the road in a horse-drawn conveyance. These informal song sessions also took place in the home at night with family members sitting around the fireplace during winter months or on the front porch in the summertime. Such singing involvement provided a welcome relief from the routine of daily life for many area families, and did so until the introduction of the automobile, radio, and television changed their

The Ransom by The Bertram Sisters

The Bertram Sisters of southern Wayne County are one of the few all-sisters groups produced in the Lake Cumberland area. *Photo from the jacket of their album.*

way of life and, to a large extent, took away their reliance on this music genre as a sustaining force. Many oral accounts provide insight into the importance of shape-note gospel music before technology so radically changed the character of local life and thought.

For example, Noble Stuart, a product of the Stuart's Chapel area of north Logan, recalled that his father purchased the first battery-powered radio set in the community about 1927 or 1928:

Until then, we had to create our own entertainment. After supper, especially in wintertime, there was nothing to do but stare into the fireplace or read a book. There was no use talking, because you'd already talked about everything during the day.

So when I was six years old, my Dad taught me the shape-notes of singing. Then he and I would sing. By the time I was eight, I could sing the alto part to a new song. So after supper back then, it was either read or sing—until the radio come in.

Maude Bowles of the Summer Shade community in Metcalfe County described how teaching the shape-notes at home eventually led to the origin of the Bowles Family singing ensemble:

Singing schools were one of the things that got quartets started. When Troy and I were married, he didn't know a note of music. He couldn't sing at all. I learned him the notes.

In the wintertime when our children were small—before they were big enough to get out and sing—we'd put up a big board on the wall with the notes on it. And when it was bad at night, the kids had to sing them notes; learn them notes. And they learned the notes that way. We got to practicing and singing. Did that for a long time, then we just decided we'd start out singing [in churches].

Mary Hurt, also a Metcalfe native and co-founder of the Grace Union Quartet, recalled how she was introduced to gospel singing. "My mother was a great singer and we sung every night," she stated. "There were eleven of us children, so you can just imagine how we'd raise the rooftop. We sung every night!"

John W. Norris, of the Bow community in Cumberland County, taught his three sons, Albert, Leonard, and Dade, to read music notes by taking charcoals from the fireplace and using them to sketch the shapes of the notes on the hearthstone. Influenced by their mother as well, who was a part of the singing Wray family of local fame, the Norris brothers would later be numbered among the most prominent singers ever identified with the Dale Hollow portion of the region.

Singing at home during his childhood in the Jabez community of Russell County also explains how Garry Polston, founder of the Brotherhood Quartet, was first introduced to the shape-notes:

I grew up in a family of seven kids—kids who sang along with our parents. They taught us to read music and to sing any part. We sang at home; we sang in the field; we sang in the barn; and we sang while we milked the cows.

I had a twin brother, Larry. When we were eight years old, Dad decided it was time for us to sing in public. So we worked for two to three weeks on a particular song in a Stamps-Baxter songbook. First, we learned to sing the music to it, then we learned the words.

I sang the baritone, Larry sang the bass, Mom sang the alto, and Dad sang the lead. The reason Dad wanted us to sing that song, it featured every part. One Wednesday night, we sang it at church. It was exciting to me, especially the part when the people applauded. I loved it!

Above: The Bowles Family Singers of Summer Shade are accompanied by their mother while performing in their home church in 1986. *Photo by the author.* Below: The Polston Family of Jabez sings the music exactly as it appears in the songbook. *Photo courtesy of Garry Polston.*

Sunday afternoons during summer months often found the Savage family of north Logan out in the yard under the big shade trees. Some member of the family would invariably say, "Well, let's sing," according to Curtis Savage, who later taught shape-note schools in the Logan-Todd area. "We'd all sing together; me and my brother and sister and our father. We'd sing as a quartet out of the old songbooks." Parent-children ensembles were, as indicated, fairly numerous across the region. However, three continuous generations of involvement in gospel music was and still is uncommon. Even more rare are families that boast of four continuous generations of gospel music practitioners. Those who lay claim to this rare distinction include the Davises of Edmonson; the Londons of Metcalfe-Hart counties; the Pattersons of Simpson; the Reeder family of Allen County; the Stuarts of Logan; the Templemans of Hart; the Godbys of Pulaski; and the Hume family of Monroe County. If so few known families produced singing groups spanning four generations in the ninety-year history covered by this study, that makes the Haste family, with its five continuous generations of singers something to be prized and treasured.

The Haste family name and gospel music are synonymous in the wooded hillcountry along the Casey-Pulaski line. Although the Haste family singers originated in the Sardis Christian Church of western Pulaski County, churches of all denominations in the local vicinity have been home to one or more of the Haste ensembles across the years.

The Hastes featured in this account began with the marriage of George Haste, native of North Carolina, to Jane Wesley of Bethelridge, Casey County. The newlyweds set up housekeeping on the banks of Fishing Creek, a stream made famous during the Civil War for its association with the nearby Battle of Mill Springs. James Frank, their oldest son, was born in 1864 while the War was still being waged. Four additional boys were born to them—Huston, John, Andrew, and Robin. All but the last were gospel singers and became legendary at home and in adjacent communities at a time when they either walked or rode horseback to keep singing engagements.

The four singing Hastes learned both round and shape-notes from Mark DeBord, a neighbor from nearby Bethelridge in Casey County. All of them preferred the shape-notes, however. Jim Frank and Andrew became music teachers themselves and taught singing schools until the 1930s. Their enthusiasm for gospel music was passed along to their children and their children's children. Jason, one of Jim Frank's sons, mused, "I grew up with a songbook in my hand and became a lover of southern gospel singing. There was just nothing like it."

The four Haste brothers began singing as the Haste Quartet "by 1900, maybe earlier," claimed Jason, who was born in 1905 and recalled hearing them sing and talk about their early years in music before he was around. He recalled that the original Haste Quartet (Jim Frank, lead; Huston, bass; John, baritone; Andrew, tenor) keyed their songs with a tuning fork. Theirs was the only known group in the eastern portion of the region until the early 1920s, when Andrew, by then a Church of God minister, moved to Bedford, Indiana, where he sang, taught, and composed songs, in addition to his pastoral duties. The three remaining brothers continued to sing on occasion as a trio through the late 1920s, and all of them regularly sang in church choirs for the rest of their lives.

The last time the four brothers performed as a quartet was in 1924. The emotional occasion was a homecoming at Sardis Christian Church, the church of their childhood. Lewis Adams, an old-time music teacher and lifelong friend of the family, recalled, "The brothers were getting older at the time of the homecoming, and they were at home again. When they sang 'Look How This World Has Made a Change,' everybody's eyes were wet." Adams began immediately to sing for me the words to their song that had first appeared in Vaughan's *Praise Divine* (1917):

> Look how this world has made a change,
> Look how this world has made a change;
> You can see every day
> How the people pass away;
> Look how this world has made a change.

"They couldn't hardly sing that song," Adams said, "it was so hard on them."

Later in the 1920s, the Sardis church had a quartet that sang on an irregular basis. Jim Frank was a part of this unnamed group, along with Richard Adams, Isaiah Godbey, and Jack Godbey.

Jim Frank was married twice. George Willie Haste was the only child born to the first union. Willie taught some singing schools and frequently led singing in area churches. He was known far and near as "the left-handed song leader from Poodle Doo Ridge [located in eastern Casey County]." Willie, now deceased, was one of the founders of the Jacksonville Baptist Church there.

With the death of his first wife not long after Willie was born, Jim

Frank next married Sarah Wesley, whom he had known since child-hood. Their children were Jason, Vernice, Arnold, Andrew, Ransom, and Herman. All became singers except Herman. Jim Frank, who died in 1932, was remembered by Lewis Adams as a man who "never went anywhere but what he had a songbook in his pocket. You could meet him on the road anyplace and he'd have a songbook with him," Adams went on. "Why, back in the days when they cleared a lot of new grounds, Jim Frank and his sons would take their songbooks to the new ground where they was clearing, and set down to rest on them old stumps and have a singing. Every day! Just their family."

Jim Frank, Sarah, and their children were all active members of the Bethelridge Methodist Church, a handsome rural Gothic edifice that stands atop a high knoll overlooking the countryside in all directions. The history of this church and of many of the Hastes is inseparable. Haste singing ensembles were spawned in this building, and two present-day Haste groups still call it home. Additionally, Roger Haste of the Happy Travelers leads congregational singing there, and his niece, Helen, plays the piano.

Some of the second-generation Hastes formed the Bethelridge Quartet in 1930, named after their home church. That ensemble consisted of two of Jim Frank's sons, Andrew and Jason (who were both music teachers by then); Jason's wife, Abbie Warren Haste, whose brother, Rev. Lloyd Warren, still heads up a group in Indiana called the Faith Builders; and Tom Phelps, also a member of the Bethelridge Methodist Church. They sang together until 1936, at which time Phelps left the quartet to join another group. For the next few years, all slots on the Bethelridge Quartet were filled by four of Jim Frank's sons. Andrew "Drude" sang tenor; Jason "Jake" sang lead; Vernice "Vern" sang the baritone; while Arnold "Monge" and Ransom shared the bass part. Monge is remembered locally as one of the area's very finest deep bass singers. Like their father and uncles before them, members of the Bethelridge Quartet used only a tuning fork to key their tunes. A guitar played by Drude was introduced in the late 1930s, however.

Monge and Ransom left the group about 1942 and were replaced by Arvil Dick and Anthony Ashley, also of the Bethelridge congregation. These two subsequently departed the group in 1946 because of demands made on their personal time. The vacancies created by their departures were filled by Hobart "Red" Haste, son of Jason, and Delbert Spears, who was married to Martha Warren, Abbie Haste's sister. (Today, Delbert and Martha's son, Gerald, heads up the Firm Believers of nearby Science Hill. Another son, Lonnie, played bass guitar for area groups for many years.) The 1946 Bethelridge ensemble comprised Drude Haste, baritone and guitarist; Jake Haste, lead; Delbert Spears, tenor; and Red Haste, bass. Their guitarist was Bass Hodges, who was later replaced by Reid Haggard of nearby Lizard Lope Ridge. Rev. Hollis Wilson of West Science Hill occasionally substituted as vocalist for ill group members. The others like to tell of the time when Wilson was with them at a church homecoming in neighboring Wayne County. When the group was introduced, Wilson assumed the role as spokesman, Reid Haggard explained. "Now ladies and gentlemen," Wilson began, "We're awful busy. So we'll just render you a song or two and then pass out quietly."

Jason Haste added more to the details of that embarrassing episode. "And there we were without a thing to do!" he said. "Wudn't busy a-tall. I don't know why he said that. And then Hollis got to feeling so bad over all our teasing that he wanted to go back in and sing some more!"

The superior reputation of the Bethelridge Quartet kept the group in heavy demand in Casey, Lincoln, Pulaski, Russell, and Wayne counties. Additionally, the quartet made frequent visits into Indiana and Ohio to sing in churches where former friends and neighbors were members at the time. Back in the 1940s, their reputation for excellent shape-note singing won for the Bethelridge group an invitation to sing as part of a radio ministry over WNOX in Knoxville, by the Rev. Randall of Science Hill. In 1947, they became the first regular gospel group to do a live weekly broadcast over WSFC in Somerset. This latter affiliation lasted for seven years, during which time the Bethelridge Quartet also made numerous appearances on a Lexington radio station.

In the mid-1950s, the Bethelridge group appeared on a publicity film entitled "Somerset," produced by the city for business and commercial reasons. With one plaudit after another heaped upon the group, and because of continued fan pressure for an LP album, they issued "He'll Hold to My Hand" through Rose Records of Cincinnati in 1975. Jason turned over the vocal lead to his son, Virgil, in 1965. Darrell Smith was added as the group's first pianist about that same time. The Bethelridge Quartet disbanded in 1985, ending fifty-five years of active service. When this historic group finally called it quits, it was composed of Virgil, Hobart, and Andrew Haste, along with Delbert Spears. Darrel Smith was the group's pianist.

This quartet sang at more funerals than any other local group after 1950, according to both Jason and Hobart. Once, they sang at three funerals the same day. Another time they sang at seven such bereavement services in eight days. The demands on their time for this purpose were so heavy that funeral home directors in the surrounding towns worked around the quartet's schedule. Often, the group sang at one o'clock in the afternoon for one funeral and at another an hour later. When asked about their fees for such occasions, Hobart responded, "We didn't charge, but we generally took what they offered. Some of them would just put the money in our pockets. But when we knew that they couldn't afford it, we'd make them take the money back."

The Bethelridge Quartet no longer books regular singings, but it still functions as a funeral group comprising Hobart Haste and his three children. He sings the bass, Darlene Haste Godbey sings alto, Roger sings lead, and Lewis Randolph sings high tenor and plays guitar.

Another Haste ensemble now sings under the name of the Happy Travelers. This group is known for some of the finest four-part harmony ever produced in the Lake Cumberland region. Lewis Adams said of the Happy Travelers, "I'd rather listen to them than anyone I know of. And they're the best Haste singing group of all time. Lewis Randolph, their tenor, is the best tenor singer I know of anywhere." Made up of third- and fourth-generation Hastes, the Happy Travelers began so early in life that they personally find it hard to identify their actual year of origin.

Their story seemingly began in 1948 when two of Jim Frank's grandsons and two of his great grandsons were overheard singing four-part harmony in one room while the Bethelridge Quartet practiced in another. They came together at the urging of other family members to form the Bethelridge Junior Quartet. The group comprised Jason's two sons, Virgil, ten, as the lead singer, and Harold, six, doing the baritone. Hobart's two sons, Lewis Randolph, eight, and Ronald, six, sang high tenor and bass. Drude played guitar for these highly acclaimed youngsters. Their fame soon spread to the extent that John Lair invited them to appear on his All-Night Singing and Sunday Morning Gathering at Renfro Valley. Their reputation grew quickly when they were heard over WHAS in Louisville, the station that carried the Renfro Valley shows at that time.

"When the boys would sing 'Way Down Deep in My Soul,' Hobart recalled, "Ronald would sink toward the floor when he sang the words 'way down,' and the crowds would go wild. And there were about fifteen thousand people there at one of the shows." Lair extended the Bethelridge Junior Quartet a standing invitation to appear on his program at their convenience. They continued to make occa-

The Bethelridge Junior Quartet, now called the Happy Travelers, with John Lair at Renfro Valley, c. 1950. *Photo courtesy of Ronald Haste.*

sional return trips until 1953, at which time they temporarily called it quits. Some of their voices had begun to change and played embarrassing tricks on them!

Ronald and Lewis moved with their parents to Cincinnati, where they lived until 1967 and 1970, respectively. The boys were involved in gospel singing in the Queen City during their years there, mainly at gatherings of family and friends from back home.

In 1971, three of the former Junior Quartet members—Lewis (high tenor and guitar), Ronald (bass), and Harold (baritone)—united with their great-uncle Drude (lead and guitar) to form a gospel ensemble that was also known, to everyone's confusion, as the Bethelridge Quartet. Two quartets from the same church bearing the same name and both groups made up of Hastes! People in area churches referred to them as the Haste Boys and the Older Bunch of Hastes, or the Younger Bethelridge Quartet and the Older Bethelridge Quartet. Drude also played guitar for the older set. To simplify his own life, Drude told the young group that he would sing for them only until they could find a new lead vocalist. Thus it was that Roger Haste, another of Hobart's talented sons, assumed the vocal lead. Drude continued to play guitar for them until 1975, when he was replaced by Bobby Moore, a distant cousin.

In late 1975 or 1976, the Haste Boys decided it was time to choose another name, one that would distinguish them from their elders and, at the same time, make a statement about their Christianity. The name Happy Travelers was suggested within the group and agreed upon by all of them, including James Clark, another cousin who joined them in 1976 as the group's first pianist. From 1974 to 1977 Lonnie Spears played bass guitar for the group.

The renaming of the group as the Happy Travelers coincided with the release of their first album in early 1977, "Leaning On the Everlasting Arms," bearing the Cincinnati-based Jewel Records imprint. Their second album, "He Did It All for Me," also pressed by Jewel, was issued in 1979.

The Happy Travelers disbanded on New Year's Eve, 1979, due both to Harold's sickness and the fact that the others in the group were dairy farmers hard pressed for spare time. Unable to lay gospel music aside for long, however, Lewis, Ronald, and Roger, along with their uncle, Virgil, resumed singing later in 1980 under the same name. Clark remained on as pianist. Charles "Mutt" Godbey, descended from the singing Godbey family of West Science Hill, joined the group as bass guitarist in 1985. The Happy Travelers again called it quits in early 1987 because of sickness and personal problems.

The group experienced a rebirth on January 17, 1988. On that date, Lewis, Ronald, and Roger were joined by Harold, now healed and an active member of the Christian Messengers, a Casey County bluegrass outfit from King's Mountain. Together, they staged a special singing for me at the Bethelridge Methodist Church. Still intact, the same personnel performed at the Haste family reunion in June 1988, and again at the church's annual outdoor singing in July 1988. A half dozen other singing ensembles were present at the latter event, including the Lloyd Warren family from Indiana. In October 1989, with Charles E. Godbey as lead guitarist, the Happy Travelers issued a cassette tape, "Ring the Bells of Heaven," under the RS Recording Service label (formerly Atwell Records) of Lafayette, Tennessee. The tapes in that first issue sold out in less than a month.

Arnold, another of Jim Frank's sons, spawned an equally rich legacy of Haste family singers in the Mt. Zion community just west of Science Hill. When Arnold "Monge" left the old Bethelridge Quartet back in the 1940s, he helped to form and sang bass for the Ansel Quartet of West Science Hill. Other members of that quality quartet

The Happy Travelers on stage in Glasgow, with Jason Haste (center) and Hobart Haste (right) in 1988. *Photo by the author.*

included Eloise Wiles Godbey, soprano; Ella Vaught, alto; and Jerry Warren, tenor. The group remained intact with the same personnel from 1948 until 1964, the year the group disbanded. They sang a cappella the entire time, with Monge vocally pitching the tunes.

Immediately after the Ansel Quartet disbanded, Monge began singing with his three sons, Junior, Glen, and Carroll, in a new group called the Haste Family Quartet. They sang together from 1964 to 1967, when failing health sidelined Monge, who died in 1976. In 1968, however, his three sons, along with their first cousin, Virgil (son of Jim Frank), reactivated the Haste Family Quartet. Virgil's brother Harold sang with them as a fill-in when his services were needed. Virge and Junior dropped out of the group in 1972 and were replaced by Glen's daughter, Joyce Ann, and her singing husband, Barty Bullock, whose parents still sing in the Jacksonville Quartet. When the Haste Family Quartet issued its LP album "I've Never Been Sorry" in 1978, personnel included Carroll Haste (lead), Joyce Ann Haste Bullock (alto), Barty Bullock (tenor), and Glen Haste (bass). Ray Lee Haste, son of Monge, was guitarist. They sang together as a formal ensemble for the last time in 1984. At that time, Barty left them to join the fast-rising, widely booked New Covenant Quartet of Somerset. In this affiliation, he sings baritone; Richard Edwards sings tenor; Lisha Martin is group alto; and Mitchell Wesley does the bass vocals.

Andrew Haste, still another of Jim Frank's sons, produced the greatest number of singers in the extended Haste clan. Drude, as he was known far and near, had an even dozen children—nine girls and three boys. They were Margaret (Dick), Mildred, Opal (Roy), Ila (Godbey), Alta (Phelps), Agnes (Jasper), Sandy (Hatter), Patricia (Elliott), Christine (Haste), Andrew Glen, Lester, and Victor. The last is the only one not involved in gospel music. Margaret, Mildred, Ila, and Opal made their singing debut as the Haste Girls Quartet in the late 1940s. Drude doubled as guitarist for his daughters and the Bethelridge Junior Quartet. On later singing occasions, often on the spur of the moment, Drude would call his daughters to the front of the church by motioning to them in the audience and saying for all to hear, "Come on, little children, let's sing." One of his daughters recalled those instances with both fond remembrance and humiliation. "He would embarrass me to death by calling us little girls," she told me. "There I was, a teenage girl trying to court the fellows," she laughed, "and Pop calling me a little girl."

The Haste Girls Quartet increased in number by the late 1950s until six of the sisters rotated the singing. By then, they called themselves the Haste Family Singers. When Drude died in 1985, his daughters took the name Haste Sisters. Eight of them began rotating the singing assignments at that point. One of their cousins commented to me, "When Drude died, seems like they all wanted to sing." They are still active, but most of their singing these days is done at revivals in area churches. Five of the girls were present at the Bethelridge Methodist Church for the Haste reunion in June 1988. At the request of some of the other Hastes present, they sang four of their father's own compositions: "That's the City That I'm Looking For," "One Day He's Coming Again," "I Left It All in the Master's Hands," and "Reach Out." The atmosphere was emotionally charged as Drude's "little children" rendered their father's songs in beautiful, poignant tones.

Two of the sisters, Opal Roy and Sandy Hatter, were then and still are involved with other singing ensembles in the area. From 1984 until 1987, Opal sang with the Trinity Quartet of West Science Hill, along with her cousin Margie Haste Tilley, Margie's husband, Steve, and Jimmy Godby. Opal was forced by illness to leave the group, but she is now singing with the Builders for Jesus, a group formed in early 1988 by members of the Kingbee Baptist Church.

Sandy Haste Hatter sang alto from 1976 to 1979 for the Gospel

Six, a Casey County group led by Robert Durham of Walltown, who sang the tenor. Other members included Bobby Clarkson (lead), James Arnold Hatter (bass), Sheila Dunham (soprano), and Gary Hatter (baritone). The Gospel Six's LP album "Just Any Day Now" was issued in 1977 on the Gloryland Records label. Sandy was affiliated with another area group for some years in the early 1980s and then joined the Trinity Quartet in 1987 as Opal's replacement.

John Thomas Haste, one of the original Haste Quartet members, was remembered by Lewis Adams as "a good-turned fellow who never got in a hurry. When he went to a singing, it would be partly over by the time he got there. But when he began to sing in that high tenor voice, you could tell a difference in the singing class. I never could place his voice; didn't know where to put it on the staff. It was higher than any tenor voice I ever heard."

John Haste married Margaret Wesley. They raised a family of seven children on Lizard Lope Ridge. While none of their children ever sang in an organized group, six grandchildren, all born to their son Oscar, made an important contribution to the local gospel music scene. Oscar's daughter Mary Haste Mofield is a member of the Jacksonville Baptist Church and sang with the Jacksonville Quartet from 1972 to 1982, along with her husband, Ralph Mofield, and Barty Bullock's parents, Denton and Katherine Bullock.

Three of Oscar's other children, Jim (bass), Doug (tenor), and Matra (alto), along with Barty Bullock (lead), and Wayne Mofield, Mary's son (baritone), formed another ensemble also known as the Haste Family Quartet. This outfit, composed of members of the Jacksonville Baptist Church, began singing together in 1980. They still take bookings when Barty is available to sing with them.

Matra Haste Dunham was a member of the Calvary Ridge Singers of Casey County from 1974 until 1978. Matra's daughter, Marsha Brown, and Marsha's daughter, Jessica, along with Oak Douglas, organized the House of Prayer Singers, also of Calvary Ridge, in 1983. Prior to this affiliation, Marsha, Oak, Oak's wife, and an unidentified fourth member, sang together in an unnamed gospel singing group that was formed in 1965.

Shirley, Oscar Haste's daughter, married the brother of Delbert Spears and moved to Mt. Vernon, Indiana, where she now heads up a gospel singing group. Marjorie, the youngest of Oscar's daughters, sings with the Trinity Quartet, previously identified.

The last member of the original Haste Quartet that began about 1900 was Huston Haste, a fellow who, according to Lewis Adams, "was an awfully religious man, him and his whole family. They were great Nazarenes. Revivals didn't get too far away for them to hitch the mules to the wagon and go—as far as twenty miles there and back. And maybe the next night, they'd go again."

Huston began singing with his three daughters, Ebbie, Anna, and Samantha, in the 1920s, perhaps about the same time that Andrew moved to Indiana. Huston and his girls, billed as the Huston Haste Trio, sang together until both Samantha and Ebbie married and left home in the late 1930s.

Almost all of the Hastes have been described as fine singers: John with the highest-pitched voice of any male singer in the region; Lewis Randolph as the finest tenor voice anywhere; Arnold as a superior bass singer; Jason as "the best lead voice around;" and Mary Mofield with a voice so high that it "goes to the moon." Certainly, these are prejudiced opinions in some instances, but these accolades all point to one conclusion—"any of the Hastes can sing if they want to, and most of them do." One person observed, "All of the Hastes were singers. Show me a Haste and I'll show you a singer."

The original Haste brothers' offspring have founded approximately two dozen quartets, trios, and other organized singing ensembles since 1900. Their singing tradition extends to the fifth generation in both Jim Frank's and John Thomas's offspring. Moreover, the sixth generation is already visible in the Haste singing picture, as some of the smaller children are now singing specials at church.

The Haste singers originated as a product of singing schools and, subsequently, provided that revered socioreligious movement with several shape-note teachers who taught others in their part of the region. They gave the entire region its first quartet, promoted congregational singing from the earliest days of the century to the present time, supported the singing convention movement throughout its days of glory from the 1920s to the 1940s, and contributed more small gospel ensembles by far than any other family in the region.

Whatever the fate of gospel music in the future, history will always provide a place for the important contribution the singing Haste family made to its performance for almost a century. The Hastes' success can be attributed to their unabashed love for the music and for their Lord. When I asked Jason Haste in 1986 what he liked best about gospel music, he responded, "All of it," and then, filled with fond memories of the years that he and numerous family members had devoted to southern gospel music, he broke down and wept.

CONCLUSION

Gospel music developed in south central Kentucky at the beginning of the twentieth century within the framework of the seven-note musical system established primarily by and for singers in rural and small town settings. Teachers taught this much-needed, much-loved music in shape-note music schools whose fundamental goal was to stimulate and promote four-part harmony congregational singing. Local singing conventions originated beginning around 1915 in response to quality congregational singing and heightened public interest in shape-note music.

Both the schools and conventions were venerated institutions that flourished until the 1940s only to decline rapidly following World War II. Their demise can be attributed largely to the growing importance of local amateur quartets and the presence of touring professional groups, to the loss of one-room schools in the rural communities brought about by the forces of consolidation, and to the declining vitality of many small churches caused by the prevalence of automobiles and radios. Community schools and churches had been the two places that nurtured religious music events. Shape-note schools and singing conventions died almost overnight when confronted by the forces of a new social order that caused local residents, especially young people, to look elsewhere for entertainment and socializing. But the amateur gospel quartets remained.

These small singing ensembles developed concurrently with the music schools and singing conventions during the first half of the present century. They originated as a means of showcasing the singing talents of four individuals within a singing school class who had mastered their particular vocal parts. Quartet music grew rapidly, both as a form of entertainment and as a channel of worship for singers and listeners alike. This happened because of changing attitudes toward God, religion, and the social order in general. Post-1950 church services were attended by passive observers and listeners who often chose to forgo personal involvement in matters of the church. This same pattern extended into the singing realm as well. The same church members who once sang in choirs and participated in singing conventions now depended on visiting quartets to provide them with entertainment.

With their supremacy unchallenged in the realm of gospel music, certain community quartets, led by their professional counterparts, slowly began to pursue certain fundamental changes in sound and performance that would take gospel music far from its singing school roots. By the late 1960s, many quartets had moved away from four-part harmony to an emphasis on solo performances by one or more of the members. Individuals sang while their colleagues stood there with arms folded, or perhaps clapping their hands in time with the music. Also, these small ensembles chose to add amplified instruments, even full drums in some instances, to the traditional lone piano or guitar. By the early 1970s, many local gospel music groups had a sound unlike anything heard during the formative and middle years of this music genre. New sounds continued to develop into the 1980s, as an upbeat, rocklike tempo was employed by two dozen or so groups in hopes of producing a modern sound that would appeal to contemporary musical tastes.

Regional radio stations have also been instrumental in producing the changing sounds in gospel music. As I write this, there is a disappointing absence of locally based gospel groups featured on area broadcasts. Although a half dozen stations devote regularly scheduled time slots to the music of community groups and announcements of their singing engagements, the unstated philosophy of most station managers is that local gospel groups should step aside in favor of professional quartets and soloists performing in a more universal, southern—even national—style of gospel music. Subregional vocal and instrumental performance styles are sub-standard, they feel, and thus are to be scorned.

In my capacity as president-elect of the Kentucky State Singing Convention in 1988, I approached station personnel associated with an all-gospel radio station in Bowling Green about the possibility of broadcasting a live segment of that year's convention. "Oh, no," the response came back. "We don't play *that kind* of music on this station. We're the only contemporary gospel station between Louisville and Nashville." Ironically, a year later, this same station began featuring tapes and albums by local singing groups on Saturday morning broadcasts.

In contrast to other area television stations, WGRB-TV (Channel 34), the voice of the Green River Broadcasting Company in Campbellsville, began broadcasting a daily thirty-minute gospel music program in January 1990. It features only community-based groups, mainly from south central Kentucky. The station's film crew is a familiar fixture at many local singing events, especially when two or more groups are involved.

The rich tradition of shape-note schools and singing conventions still influences gospel music as it enters the final decade of the twentieth century. A few singing schools are still conducted each year by surviving old-time music teachers; songs from the 1930s to the 1960s are still sung by quite a few quartets that stress early, convention-style, four-part harmony; and gospel music remains essentially a rural phenomenon. Close to one-half of today's singers and musicians still live in rural settings, and the Protestant churches that host singings on a regular basis are primarily rural. Certain evangelical churches in county seat towns and small cities in the region that have not succumbed to criticism by denominational and other Christian publications of this brand of religious music run a respectable second.[1]

Some of the rural and small-town churches that host regularly scheduled gospel singings have managed to maintain strong memberships and are financially stable. Such institutions—and there are many of them scattered across the region—have programs that still attract and appeal to people. They continue to proclaim an old-fashioned gospel of salvation through belief; they emphasize revivalism as a necessary component of Christian living; they place a low emphasis on money; they demonstrate genuine friendliness; and, to reiterate, they stress and support old-time singing.

This book is thus a paradox. It is a study of a music that ebbed and flowed with, and sometimes borrowed from, the main currents in American popular culture—automobiles, radio, school consolidation, television, rock and roll, contemporary music. Yet it is also a study in the continuity of tradition. In spite of seemingly insurmountable odds at times, traditional gospel music sung in southern harmony style continues in the present and shows no real evidence of succumbing to contemporary pressures for conformity. This is a music that, in performance, is unlike any other kind of music. Simply stated, old-time gospel music has a function that reaches far beyond

its performance. While it may be a form of entertainment, it speaks
to deeper emotional, temporal, and spiritual needs. Gospel music
provides the singer and the listener with a sense of well-being and
with a strong feeling of spiritual and cultural continuity.

Some of the singers are concerned that attendance at gospel
music events is declining. They attribute the decrease to several
factors, including over-saturation because of the constant airing of
contemporary gospel music by radio stations, the availability of
tapes, albums and videos issued by professional ensembles, and the
presence of an excessive number of local groups in need of bookings.
Excessive exposure to gospel music, the argument runs, "tends to
wear people out and they stop attending any and all singings." Those
people who claimed that gospel music was at a low ebb during the
1980s were quick to admit, however, that attendance at singing
events is somewhat cyclical in nature. It tends to go up for a few years,
plateau, then go into decline; up again, followed by a down period.

I have attended singing events since mid-1985 in all sorts of
locations—churches, school auditoriums, gymnasiums, recreation
parks, private homes—and in all kinds of weather. I have heard
inferior singing and I have listened to the best this region (or any other
for that matter) has to offer. Crowds have been small on occasion,
while in other instances people sat in the aisles and stood along the
walls in order to hear and see the groups. Audience sizes have not
diminished during the five years I have been attending these gospel
music events.

People attend these events because they love gospel music and
find comfort and satisfaction in the messages contained in the song
lyrics. These faithful attenders are there as well, however, because
they love, respect, and appreciate the singers who unselfishly give of
themselves to proclaim the message of love, redemption, sanctifica-
tion, and eternity in song. While there are exceptions here as in every
walk of life, these gospel singers and musicians by and large conduct
themselves in a manner befiting the ministry. They aspire to live the
life they sing about.[2]

Sincere dedication to the God they serve, devotion to the cause of
gospel music, and a love for people in general will enable these singers
to nurture and perpetuate this historic music genre. The sounds and
performance styles will undergo certain changes in the years ahead,
but the children of these singers and their children's children will be
around in the twenty-first century still telling the "old, old story" in
gospel song.

APPENDIX A

The active years indicated for each group are listed in accordance with information provided by one or more members of the group. When closing years are not listed after the dash (-), the ensemble was still singing in early 1990 at least four times a year by invitation. An asterisk (*) preceding a group's name indicates one or more known commercial recordings.

ADAIR COUNTY

* Bailey Family	Columbia	1968-
Bennett Family	Fairplay	c. 1950-
* Brotherhood Quarter	Milltown	1979-86
Chestnut Grove Quartet	Breeding	1938-51
* Commonwealth Singers	Columbia	1971-78
* Crossroads Quartet	Columbia	1960-
Cumberland River Boys	Columbia	1944-52
* Dixie Aires Quartet	Sparksville	1976-77
* Egypt Quartet	Columbia	1960-
* Feese Quartet	Columbia	1964-66
Feese Trio	Columbia	1940s only
God's Children	Columbia	1983-
God's Humble Servants	Knifley	1976-
Gospel Travelers	Columbia	1950-59
Gospelettes	Columbia	1961-68
* Green River boys	Knifley	1972-80

*Guiding Light	Columbia	1986-
Hadleys	Fairplay	1989-
Happy Four	Breeding	1954-63
Harmony Makers	Columbia	1961-69
Heaven Bound	Harvey's Ridge	1989-
Jubilee Five	Sparksville	1966-70
*King's Daughters	Columbia	1979-
*Lake City Quartet	Columbia	1983-88
*Melodyaires	Columbia	1960-
Mission Aires	Knifley	1985-
Rich Family	Barnett's Creek	1936-42
Singing Lights	Harrod's Fork	1983-85
Southernaires	Columbia	1956-65
Sparksville Quartet	Sparksville	1927-39
Sparksville Trio	Sparksville	
*Sunshine Quartet	Columbia	1963-74
*Tone Masters	Columbia	1956-69
*Tri-County Gospelaires	Columbia	1980-86
Trinity Trio	Columbia	1968-
Zion Singers	Fairplay	1989-

ALLEN COUNTY

*Allen County Gospel Singers	Scottsville	1978-84
Allen County Quartet	Scottsville	1934-38
Beech Grove Ladies Quartet		1912-?
*Bethelaires	Scottsville	1958-63
*Beulahland Singers	Scottsville	1980-82
Born Again	Scottsville	1981-82
*Christianaires	Scottsville	1969-77
Clifton Trio	Clifton	1960-83
[Conner-Cassaday] Trio	Settle	1918-20
*Conquerors	Scottsville	1985-89
Corder Quartet	Halifax	1922-37
*Counselors	Scottsville	1984-
Crusaders Quartet	Scottsville/	
	Bowling Green	1946-58
Deacons Quartet	Scottsville	1976-82
*Faithful Aires	Adolphus/Scottsville	1972-76
Followers of the Son	Adolphus/	
	Westmoreland	1986-
*Free Spirits	Scottsville	1976-82

* Friendly Five	Scottsville	1968-72
Friendship Five		1965-69
Friendship Quartet	Settle	1928-30
* Gloryland Five	Scottsville	1970-76
* Gloryland Singers	Scottsville	1982-
* Gospelaires	Adolphus	1970-77
Gospel Crossroads	Adolphus/	
	Westmoreland	1986-
* Gospel Crusaders	Scottsville	1960-77
* Gospel Sounds	Scottsville	1970-76
* Gospel Sounds	Scottsville	1984-
* Gospel Tones	Scottsville	1962-79
Hanner Family	Scottsville	1983-
Heavenly Echoes	Scottsville	1980-82
Heavenly Tones	Scottsville/Akersville	1988-
* Holder Quartet	Scottsville	1964-
* Holder Trio	Scottsville	1958-64
Holland All-Stars	Holland	1945-48
Holmes (Tommy) Quartet		1958-61
* Kentuckians	Holland	1980-
Kentucky Crusaders	Scottsville	1948-59
King's Trio	Scottsville	1984-
Liberty Quartet	Halifax	1916-20;
		1944-47
* Lyles	Scottsville	1969-
Melody Masters	Scottsville	1972-78
Memory Echoes	Adolphus	1984-86
* Messengers	Scottsville	1973-74
Midget Quartet	Holland	1931-38
Pardue Family	Maynard	1974-74
Peacemakers	Scottsville	1984-
Pioneer Gospel Singers	Scottsville	1975-75
Reeder Family	Midway	1941-
Reeder Junior Quartet	Midway	1946-49
* Reederettes	Midway	1955-70
Reeder Trio	Midway	1945-56
* Regals	Holland	1975-80
Scottsvilleaires	Scottsville	1953-
Scottsville Echoes	Scottsville	1956-
Settle Quartet	Settle	1938-40
Singing Echoes		1965-67
* Singing Martins	Scottsville	1984-
Smiling Girls Quartet	Scottsville	1939-47
Spiritual Five	Scottsville	1973-82

* Spiritual Four	Scottsville	1982-84
Sunshine Girls	Scottsville	1966-67
Sunshine Quartet	Scottsville	1938-46
* Sword and Shield	Scottsville	1970-74
* Thomas Quartet	Scottsville	1968-75
* Thomas Trio	Scottsville	1956-68
Travelers Quartet	Scottsville	1972-75
Wade Family	Adolphus	1970s
Walker's Chapel Quartet	Walker's Chapel	1943-44
West Allen Quartet	Halifax	1912-41
* Wolfe Family	Scottsville	1977-
Young Seekers	Adolphus	1986-

BARREN COUNTY

Attendants of Christ	Cave City	1983-
* Austin Aires	Austin	1966-72
* Barren County Harmoneers	Glasgow	1975-78
Barren River Boys	Glasgow	1976-78
Barren River Quartet	Glasgow	1978-80
Barrick Singers	Glasgow	1987-88
Believers Four	Glasgow	1980-82
Beulahland Travelers	Glasgow	1985-87
Bilbrey Family (Full Gospel)	Glasgow	1986-
Brotherhood Gospelaires	Glasgow	1982-83
* Canaanland Quartet	Glasgow	1980-
Carver Family and Nelda	Tracy	1979-80
Celeste Praise	Glasgow	1985-86
Chosen Generation	Glasgow	1981-82
Cornerstone	Glasgow	1980-81
* Crisp Family	Glasgow	1965-
Directors	Glasgow	1987-88
Eaton Quartet	Tracy	1947-51
Elmore Quartet	Glasgow	1947-49
Evans Family	Glasgow	1990-
Faith Travelers	Cave City	1986-87
Fellowship Quartet	Eighty Eight	1967-
* Freedomland Singers	Glasgow/Louisville	1984-
Friendship Quartet	Glasgow	1982-
Glasgow Four	Glasgow	1954-72
Glasgow Quartet	Glasgow	1941-49
* Glory Bound Quartet	Glasgow	1983-

Gloryettes	Glasgow	1968-71
* Good News Singers	Glasgow	1971-74
* Gospel Aires Quartet	Glasgow	1971-
* Gospel Crusaders	Glasgow	1984-
* Gospel Echoes	Tracy	1968-70
Gospelettes	Glasgow	1983-87
* Gospel Jordanaires	Glasgow	1984-
* Gospel Lights	Glasgow	1979-83
Gospel Revelations	Glasgow	1985-
* Gospel Travelers	Glasgow	1978-82
* Gospel Troubadors	Glasgow	1960-
* Happyaires	Glasgow	1963-85
Happy Five	Railton/Hydro	1948-56
Happy Five	Dover	1960-62
Happy Harmonizers	Glasgow	1954-57
Happy Rhythm Boys	Glasgow	1956-63
Happy Valley Quartet	Glasgow	1946-75
Harbor Lights	Glasgow	1981-
Harmony Echoes		1969-72
Harper (Buddy) Singers	Glasgow	1982-
Heavenly Echoes	Cave City	1985-86
* Homeward Bound	Glasgow	1986-
Jesus Mission Singers	Eighty Eight	1987-87
* Jubilaires	Glasgow	1960-63;
		1967-74
Keith Family	Glasgow	1981-85
* Kentucky Aires	Austin	
Kentucky Harmonizers	Glasgow	19?-54
Kingrey (Stanley) Family	Glasgow	1980-
Lamp Lighters	Glasgow	1973-75
* Liberty Quartet	Glasgow	1989-
* Massey Family	Glasgow/Madisonville	
		1985-
* Melody Singers	Glasgow	
Missionaries	Glasgow	1985-87
New Harvest	Glasgow	1990-
New Hope Quartet	Cave City	1962-65
Norris (Lee) & Bilbrey Family	Eighty Eight/	
	Smiths Grove	1977-86
Old Timers	Cave City	1945-48
Old Zion Quartet	Park City	1983-
Overlanders	Glasgow	1980-81
* Pierce Family	Glasgow	1969-
Pilgrims	Glasgow	1982-87

Redeemed	Glasgow	1981-84
Redeemers	Glasgow	1981-82
Sacred Five	Bon Ayr	1958-68
Sacred Four	Glasgow	1938-46
Sacred Harmony	Tracy	1962-65
Salmon (John G.) Family	Glasgow	1947-54
Salmon Tabernacle Singers	Glasgow	1955-
* Sons of Faith and Orena	Glasgow	1969-74
Sounds of Praise	Glasgow/Smiths	
	Grove	1988-
Southern Cross Quartet	Glasgow	1983-84
* Temple Trio	Glasgow	1959-89
Tonettes	Glasgow	1955-61
[Tracy Quartet]	Tracy/Glasgow	1970-71
Tracy Singers	Tracy	1989-
Union Aires	Tracy	1958-60
Voices of Faith	Glasgow	1972-75
Young Voices of Praise	Mt. Hermon	1984-87

BUTLER COUNTY

Barnett's Lick Quartet	Brooklyn	1938-43
* Beginnings	Welch's Creek	1974-83
Brooklyn Quartet	Brooklyn	1968-72
Brooks Brothers Quartet	Casey	1960-65
Brooks Family Trio	Casey	1964-73
Butler County News Quartet	Morgantown	1943-50
Butler County Quartet	Morgantown	1970-71
Byers Quartet	Welch's Creek	1940-41
Chapel Union Quartet	Welch's Creek	1942-50
Clark Family	Monfort	1974-79
Cool Springs Quartet	Cool Springs	1986-
Embry Quartet	Brooklyn	1946-59
Flener Boys	Aberdeen	1968-70
* Free Spirits		1987-
Friendly Four	Morgantown	1961-68
Happy Four	Casey	1950-51
Heaven Seekers	Morgantown	1972-82
Johnson Family	Morgantown	1956-64
Joyful Five	Brooklyn	1965-68
* Joyful Four	Brooklyn	1968-80
Kessinger Trio		1955-73

Melody Echoes	Morgantown/	
	Caneyville	1977-81
Messengers Quartet	Casey	1960-65
Pathfinders	Casey	1956-70
Pisgah Quartet	Pisgah	1927-32
Reid Quartet	Casey	c.1935-69
Renfro Family Quartet	Brooklyn	1957-
* Rhythmaires Quartet	Morgantown	1980-83
Royal Aires	Morgantown	
Smith Brothers Quartet	Quality	1946-72
* Travelers	Aberdeen/	
	Morgantown	1970-80;
		1988-
Trebleaires		1968-69
True Believers	Morgantown	1986-
Ward Quartet	Morgantown	1929-44

Casey County

* Believers	Liberty	1976-
* Bethelridge Quartet	Bethelridge	1930-
Bethelridge Jr. Quartet	Bethelridge	1948-53
Brackett Family Trio	Liberty	1963-72
Brown Brothers Quartet	Liberty	1952-85
Brush Creek Church Quartet		1970-80
[Calvary Ridge Quartet]	Calvary Ridge	1965-82
Calvary Ridge Singers	Calvary Ridge	1974-78
Casey County Quartet	Yosemite	1950-59
* Christian Messengers	Mount Olive	1982-
Community Quartet	Middleburg	1966-71
Coppage Family	Liberty	19?-85
* Country Church Singers	Middleburg	1976-
* Crestonaires	Liberty	1980-
* Cumberland Mountain Boys	Mintonville	1976-
First Baptist Church Quartet	Liberty	1955-62
Gospel Connection	Liberty	1982-83
Gospel Seven	Walltown	1979-81
Gospel Six	Walltown	1976-79
Gospel Time Singers	Liberty	1980-
* Happy Travelers	Bethelridge	1971-
Harvest Time Gospel Singers	Liberty	1981-
Haste Boys [Quartet]	Bethelridge	1971-76

Haste Family Quartet	Bethelridge	1900-84
Haste Family (Andrew)	Bethelridge	1948-
Haste Sisters	Bethelridge	1948-
House of Prayer Singers	Calvary Ridge	1983-
Liberty Trio	Liberty	
Melody Trio	Windsor	1974-78
Melody Trio/Quartet	Liberty	1950-60
Price Quartet	Walnut Hill	c. 1932-34
Rogers Family	Clementsville	1980-83
Scott Family Singers	Liberty	1965-78
* Southern Gospel Quartet	Yosemite	1957-64
* Spirits	Liberty/	
	Russell Springs	1975-85
* Tributes	Liberty	1974-78
* Walltown Quartet	Walltown	1978-81
Williams Family	Liberty	1961-
Young Believers	Dunnville	1980-88

CLINTON COUNTY

Born Again Singers	Shipley/Albany	1980-
* Braswell Family	Caney Branch	1970-
Central Grove Singers	Albany	1985-
Clear Chapel Trio	Albany	1966-68
Clear Fork Trio	Albany	1962-66
Clintonaires	Albany	1952-57
* Crusaders Quartet	Seventy Six	1935-50
Egypt Hollow Quartet		1954-64
Fairland Gospelaires	Fairland	1970-75
Farmer Family	Albany	1946-49
* Farmer Sisters	Albany	1949-54
Good News Trio	Albany	1984-
* Gospel Servants	Albany	1967-68
Harmony Masters	Albany	1983-
Heavenly Harmony	Albany	1985-
Highway Quartet	Highway	1949-51
Last Chance Quartet	Albany	1948-49
* Lowhorn Family	Albany	
* Lowhorn Trio	Albany	1956-
* McWhorter Trio	Albany	1954-71
Mills Quartet	Albany	1949-81
Mullinix (Ray) & Messengers	Albany	1972-76

Northside Nazarene Quartet	Albany	1987-
Peanut Quartet	Albany	1945-54
* Rhythm Masters	Albany	
* Seventy Six Quartet	Seventy Six	1946-50
* Singing Lord's Five	Albany	1981-85
Smith (Bob) Family	Albany	1973-
Travelers Quartet	Albany	1961-65
Walnut Grove Singers		1979-
* York Quartet	Albany	1947-49

CUMBERLAND COUNTY

Baise Chapel Quartet	Burkesville	1942-53
Craft Family	Bow	1982-85
Cumberland Co. Gospel Singers	Burkesville	1974-77
Cumberland River Boys	Bow	1987-
Gloryland Express	Burkesville	1987-
* Gospel Three	Bow	1972-
* Gospelettes	Bow	1978-82
Happy Five	Burkesville	1971-75
Happy Praisers	Peytonsburg	
Jones Family	Spears	1935-
* Marrowbone Quartet	Marrowbone	1982-
Messengers	Bow	1987-88
New Believers	Burkesville	1989-
Norris Brothers Quartet	Bow	1932-40
Norris Family	Kettle	1968-
Norris Quartet	Bow	1940-60
Of One Accord	Burkesville	1986-
Riddle Quartet	Bow	1942-?
Seminary Quartet/Trio	Seminary	1977-
Sunshine Singers	Burkesville	1986-
Tri-County Quartet		1952-58
Winfrey Quartet	Irish Bottom	
* Wright Family	Burkesville/	
	Louisville	c.1969-1972

EDMONSON COUNTY

Alvey Singers	Chalybeate Springs	1940s
Annetta Singers	Annetta	
Bee Spring Quartet	Bee Spring	1974-86

Bowman Brothers Quartet		1985-86
Carrier Quartet	Brownsville/	
	Bowling Green	1968-76
* Commanders	Brownsville	1967-75
Davis Family	Lindseyville	1938-
Fairview Quartet		1938-41
Gospel Four	Huff	1972-77
* Gospel Lights	Bee Spring	1972-
Green River Quartet	Brownsville	
Green River Quartet	Brownsville	1987-
Green River Trio	Mammoth Cave	1987-
Hall Family	Lindseyville	1982-86
Happy Hitters	Lindseyville	1950-51
Harmoneers	Cedar Springs	1950s
Heritage Singers	Lindseyville	1974-82;
		1990
Holly Springs Quartet	Holly Springs	c.1928-c.1938
Hopewell Quartet	Huff	1941-
Lindseyville Quartet	Lindseyville	1943-65
Madison Brothers Quartet	Brownsville	1979-
* Madison Family	Poplar Springs	1955-81
Melody Echoes	Lindseyville/Brooklyn	1977-81
* Midway Quartet	Midway	1965-68
Minyard Family	New Grove	1971-
Poplar Springs Quartet	Poplar Springs	1937-41
Renfro Quartet	Chalybeate Springs	1946-57
Sego Family	Lindseyville/	
	Louisville	1968-
Skaggs Family	Chalybeate Springs	1984-
Stockholm Baptist Quartet	Stockholm	1984-
Tomes Brothers	Ollie	1930s-40s
* Tomes Four	Brownsville/	
	Louisville	1970s-
Union Light Quartet	Union Light	1961-72;
		1984-
Vaughan Kentucky Quartet	Brownsville	1936-38
Vincent Family	Lindseyville	1956-71

GREEN COUNTY

* Aarons	Greensburg	1983-
Chapel Aires	Greensburg	1958-64

* Christian Heirs	Thurlow	1965-77
* Conquerors	Greensburg	1980-84
Dobson Four	Summersville	1979-87
* Durret Family	Summersville	1962-
Evangels	Greensburg	1970s
* Glory Road Singers	Summersville	1973-
Gospel Echoes	Greensburg	1974-79
Gospel Four	Greensburg	
Gospel Three	Greensburg	1976-78
Gospel Tones	Greensburg	1945-80
Holly Grove Quartet		1959-
Homeward Bound	Greensburg	1987-88
Houk Family	Greensburg	1962-
Inspirational Four	Greensburg	1978-83
* Joymakers	Greensburg	1967-
* King's Crusaders	Greensburg	1981-83
* Little Barren Quartet	Little Barren	1937-79
Little Barren Trio	Little Barren	1961-64
Marr Family Duet	Greensburg	1981-
* Marr Family Trio	Greensburg	1941-80
McCubbin-Henderson Quartet	Summersville	1915-19
McCubbin-Peace Quartet	Summersville	1923-25
Milby Family	Greensburg	1975-
Oak Forest Quartet	Gabe	1948-60
Oak Grove Quartet	Oak Grove	1975-78
Redeemed	Greensburg	1984-86
Shuffetts and Ann	Greensburg	1979-82
Singing Echoes	Greensburg	1974-77
Singing Redeemed	Summersville	1987-
Sounds of Joy	Greensburg	1983-
Squires Quartet	Bramlett	1930-83
Tonesters Trio	Greensburg	1965-68
Trammel Creek Quartet		
Trinity Singers	Little Barren	1981-82
Young Family	Little Barren	1982-

HART COUNTY

Bon Airs	Bonnieville	1956-61
Bonnieville Quartet	Bonnieville	1959-67

Bowman Brothers Quartet	Bonnieville	1970-84
* Campground Quartet	Campground	1935-41
Cave Hill Singers	Cave Hill	1979-84
* Cavelanders	Horse Cave/Cave City	1975-88
Children of Light	Bonnieville	
* Christian Sounds	Horse Cave	1971-78
* Cook Family	Bonnieville	1971-
Cottrell Family	Bonnieville	1935-60
Crossbearers	Horse Cave	1986-
Donna's (Stanton) Bunch	Bonnieville	1970-71
Dorsey Family	Munfordville	1975-
God's Ambassadors	Horse Cave	1982-
Gospel Servants	Horse Cave	1972-74
* Gospel Voices	Horse Cave	1971-74
Happy Four	Bonnieville	
* Harlow Singers	Hardyville	1983-
Hart County Five	Munfordville	1952-59
Hart County Quartet		1945-51
* Hensley Family	Canmer	1978-
Hensley Quartet	Canmer	1953-
Joyful Echoes	Bonnieville	
* Jubilaires	Bonnieville	1960-72
Little Harmony Quartet	Horse Cave	1956-60
London Quartet	Horse Cave	1944-54
Mabe Quartet	Bonnieville	1928-61
Master's Trio	Hardyville	1966-71
McCubbins Brothers	Munfordville	1949-57
* McCubbins Family	Munfordville	1958-
Poynter Family		
Scrap Iron Quartet	Munfordville	1947-49
* Sextons	Hardyville	1984-
* Singing Stantons	Bonnieville	
Sun-Rays	Munfordville	
* Stewards of the King	Hardyville	1979-84
Sullivan-Vincent Quartet	Munfordville	1986-
Sunday Aires	Bonnieville	1976-79
Templeman Children/Sisters	Munfordville	1966-
Templeman Family	Munfordville	1953-70
* Templeman Quartet	Horse Cave	1934-53
* Vincent (Jack) Trio	Munfordville	1972-74
Voices of Faith	Munfordville	1972-75
Waddell Quartet	Cub Run	1952-58
Wells Family	Horse Cave	1955-
Wood Family	Bonnieville	1957-65

LOGAN COUNTY

A-Team	Adairville	1980-83
Adairville Quartet	Adairville	1936-37
Allen-Costello Quartet	Adairville	1981-82
* Ambassadors Quartet	Russellville	1980-87
Armistead Family	Adairville	1979-84
Armistead Family (Kevin)	Adairville	1987-
Campbell Quartet	Homer	1918-38
Cavaliers	Russellville	1972-77
* Challengers	Russellville	1971-
Chapel Aires	Chandlers Chapel	1972-
Chapel Five	Chandlers Chapel	1961-64
* Crusaders	Lewisburg	1962-
Forthcoming	Adairville	1986-
Galileans	Auburn	1986-
Glory Road Singers	Lewisburg	1975-81; 1986-
Good Intentions	Russellville	1976-80
Gospel Ramblers	Lewisburg	1986-
Gospel Ramblers, Jay Anderson and the	Auburn	1980-
* Gospel Six	Lewisburg	1968-75
* Gospel Tones	Adairville	1960-72; 1987
Gray Family	Lewisburg	1920-29
Happy Aires	Chandlers Chapel	1965-72
* Harmoneers	Lewisburg	1982-
Harmony Masters	Russellville	1985-86
Harvesttime	Russellville/Auburn	1980-
Jericho Band		1920s
Joyful Noise	Auburn/Woodburn	1977-
Kedron Quartet		1922-37
* Kentucky Harmoneers	Lewisburg	1957-82
Kindreds	Russellville	
Kingsway	Russellville	1982-
Lack Family	Homer	1973-
Logan Aires	Auburn	1952-61
Masters Quartet	Russellville	1979-
Master's Blend	Adairville	1984-84
* McKinney Quartet	Deer Lick	c. 1920-c. 1942
Messengers	Chandlers Chapel	1985-
Moore Family		

Morgan Family	Lewisburg	1960-70
* New Freedom Singers	Auburn	1987-
New Hope Quartet	New Hope	1941-47
Pioneers	Russellville	1982-84
Reid Brothers Quartet	Adairville	1932-33
Revelators	Russellville	1977-
* Searchers	Russellville	1974-77
Simmons Quartet	Oak Grove	1926-35
* Singing Hopes	Russellville	1975-79
Singing McClellans	Auburn	
Smith Family	Russellville	1983-
Smotherman Quartet	Homer	1912-18
Sounds of Love	Russellville	1976-78
Southern Aires	Lewisburg	1957-59
Spirituals	Russellville	1975-78
Stuart Quartet	Stuarts Chapel	1925-50
Stuart-Hall Quartet	Russellville	1948-51
Sunshine Girls Trio	Auburn	1935-38

METCALFE COUNTY

Antioch Quartet	Knob Lick	1947-82
Beaumont Quartet	Beaumont	1946-65
Beaumont Trio	Beaumont	
Beechville Harmoneers	Beechville	1980-84
Bowles Family	Summer Shade	1935-43; 1985-87
Brotherhood Gospelaires		
* Cassadys	Edmonton	1986-
* Conquerors	Edmonton	1989-
Crenshaws	Edmonton	1985-87
Dickson Family Quartet	Price's Creek	1954-
* Edmonton Quartet	Edmonton	1952-85
* Faith Singers	Edmonton	1973-
Foundation	Edmonton	1983-83
Gospel Way Quartet	Edmonton	1981-85
* Grace Union Quartet	Edmonton	1946-73
Hallelujah Gloryland Singers	Edmonton	1980-84
Happy Family Gospel Singers	Summer Shade	1990-
Happy Harmonizers	Knob Lick	1933-57
Harmony Echoes	Edmonton	
* Harvest Singers	Edmonton	1975-

Janes Quartet	Edmonton	1948-50
Jesus Mission Hallelujah Gloryland Singers	Edmonton	1987-
Joyful Four	Edmonton	1981-82
Lone Star Quartet	Beaumont	1972-
Missionary Mound Quartet		1951-54
Parrish Family	Summer Shade	1945-54; 1965-72
Pink Ridge Quartet	Sulphur Well	1938-52; 1963-65
Red Lick Quartet	Edmonton	1987-
Sacred Sounds	Edmonton	1984-
Savoyard Quartet	Savoyard	
* Seekers	Center	1965-75
Seekers	Edmonton	1983-84
Singing Believers	Edmonton	1985-86
* Spirituals	Edmonton	1974-
Thompson Family	Edmonton	1987-
* Thrasher Family	Summer Shade	1978-

MONROE COUNTY

Bartley Family	Sulphur Lick	?-?; 1983-
Bartley Trio	Sulphur Lick	1956-64
Beautiful Home Quartet	Beautiful Home	1959-63
Berea Quartet	Berea	1941-48
Butler Family	Forkton	1962-70
* Christianaires	Fountain Run/ Lafayette	1963-
Coffelt Family	Beautiful Home	1948-49
Country Gospel Singers	Forkton/ Sulphur Lick	1955-62
* Echoes of Athens	Tompkinsville	1981-86
Family Ties (Coffelts)	Beech Grove	1988-
Freedom Singers	Fountain Run	1981-88
Gamaliel quartet	Gamaliel	1945-47
Golden Keys	Tompkinsville	
Gospel Harmony Boys	Gamaliel	1963-68
* Happy Day Singers	Gamaliel	1972-75
Hume (Archie) Quartet	Ebenezer	1925-36
Jubilations	Lamb	
* Jubilee Singers	Lamb	1985-

Key Masters	Gamaliel	1960s
Kingrey Family	Persimon	c. 1932-c. 1943
Melody Singers	Mt. Hermon	1967-80
Mt. Poland Singers	Mt. Poland	1978
Rock Bridge Quartet	Rock Bridge	1914-17;
		1965-87
Smith Family	Hestand	
* Strode Family	Lamb	1980-85
Tompkinsville Quartet	Tompkinsville	1938-50
Wheeler Family	Lamb	1963-69

Pulaski County

Adams (Lewis) Quartet	Science Hill	1939-45
* Ambassadors Quartet	Somerset	1974-77
Ansel Quartet	Ansel	1948-64
* Baker Family	Somerset	1977-
* Baker Quartet	Somerset	1957-75
Bethlehem Quartet	Nancy	1983-
* Bethany Quartet	Somerset/	
	Indianapolis	1946-
* Bluegrass Meditations	Somerset	
* Brothers Quartet	Somerset	1983-
Buck Creek Quartet		1955-65
Builders for Jesus	West Science Hill	1988-
* Carter (Oscar) Quartet	Valley Oak	1930-79
Chitwood Quartet	East Somerset	1923-65
Cook Quartet		1950-54
* Counsellors'	Somerset	1984-
* Crusaders Quartet	Somerset	1982-86
Cumberland Four	Nancy	1939-50
Cumberland Quartet	Eubank/Somerset	1932-40;
		1942-62
East Somerset Quartet	Somerset	1946-50
Edwards Quartet	Somerset	c. 1945-c. 1965
Farris Family	Science Hill	1934-45
Fellowship Quartet	Somerset	1968-71
Fellowship Quartet	Somerset	1982-
* Firm Believers	Science Hill	1981-
Flat Lick Quartet	Shopville	1958-78
* Glory Way Travelers	Somerset	1976-87
Glory Ways	Somerset	1987-

Godby Quartet	Science Hill	1952-85
Gospel Melodies	Somerset	
Gospel Messengers	Somerset	
Gospel Sounds	Eubank	1980-87
Gosser Sisters	Nancy	1965-69
Gossett Family	Somerset	1985-
Greatway Singers	Somerset	1983-84
* Harvesters	Somerset	
* Harvest Time Trio	Somerset	1975-80
Heavenly Crusaders	Science Hill	1976-78
Jacksonville Quartet	Science Hill	1972-82
Joyful Singers	Science Hill	1975-
Joyful Sounds	Somerset/Eubank	1977-82
Keith Sisters	Eubank/	
	Science Hill	1977-
Lake Cumberland Quartet	Nancy	1965-81
Lake Cumberland Quartet	Valley Oak	1953-68
McKinney Quartet	McKinney	1954-65
* Mt. Lebanon Quartet	Nancy	1972-84
Nancy Bunch	Nancy	1948-52
* New Covenant Quartet	Somerset/	
	Burnside	1985-
New Foundations	Nancy	1986-
Old Country Church Quartet	Valley Oak	1948-51
Randall (Charles) Trio	Somerset	1960-75
Science Hil Quartet	Science Hill	1928-55
Science Hill Methodist		
Male Quartet	Science Hill	1964-
Sears Quartet	Whetstone	1929-31
Somerset Quartet	Somerset	c. 1933-48
Southern Harmony Quartet	Somerset	1961-64
Starlighters Quartet	Somerset	1951-53
Tarter Trio	Nancy	1978-83;
		1988
Thompson Quartet	Eubank	1931-60
Trinity Quartet	Science Hill	1983-
No Name Quartet	Jacksonville	1980-
West Somerset Quartet	Somerset	1931-33
Whetstone Quartet	Whetstone	1924-28
Whittaker (Burt) Quartet	Nancy	1940-50
Whitter Family	Science Hill	1965-
Woodstock Quartet	Woodstock	1945-58
* Wooten Four	Eubank	(1957) 1962-

RUSSELL COUNTY

Burtons	Sano	1989-
* Cedar Springs Quartet	Cedar Springs	1963-73
* Chordsmen	Russell Springs	1979-84
Coffey's Chapel Quartet	Eli	1956-
Coffey Family	Russell Springs	1956-84
Columbian Quartet	Russell Springs	1930-32
Cumberland Mountain Boys	Russell Springs/	
	Cincinnati	1942-47
* Cumberland Valley Trio	Jabez	1956-81
Deliverance Quartet	Bethlehem	1975-76
* Dixie Aires Quartet	Russell Springs	
Dixie Four	Russell Springs	1937-41
* Dixie Melody Boys	Russell Springs	1948-58;
		1961-68
Freedom Ridge Quartet	Sewellton	1979-
Glory Bound Singers	Eli	1984-
God's Children	Russell Springs	1983-
Gospel Defenders	Russell Springs	1971-74
* Gospel Echoes	Russell Springs	1977-
Gospel Harmoneers	Russell Springs	1946-56
* Gospel Messengers	Russell Springs	1971-79
Gospel Servants	Russell Springs	1972-74
Harmony Quartet	Russell Springs	1939-39
Harmony Trio	Russell Springs	1952-56
Jamestown Quartet	Jamestown	1948-53
* Joybell Singers	Russell Springs	1973-85
Macabees Quartet	Russell Springs	
Mission Harmoneers	Russell Springs	1955-60
Mt. Hope Singers	Russell Springs	1984-
New Friendship Quartet		1940-49
* Notesmen	Russell Springs	1976-79
Parks Ridge Quartet	Russell Springs	1932-36
* Perkins Family	Jabez	1965-85
* Polston Family	Jabez/Russell Springs	1940-
Rexroat Family	Russell Springs	1936-36
* Rock of Ages Quartet	Russell Springs	1974-
* Roy Family	Russell Springs	1953-
Russell County Boys	Russell Springs	1983-
Salem Quartet	Salem	1928-31
Salemaires	Salem	1983-86
Singing Temples	Russell Springs	

Sons	Russell Springs	1979-84
Starlighters	Russell Springs	1949-50
Sunny Valley Boys	Webbs Cross Roads	1947-49
Three B's	Salem	1961-62
* Twilight Singers	Russell Springs	1979-
Webbs Cross Roads Quartet	Webbs Cross Roads	

SIMPSON COUNTY

Eaton Trio	Salmon	1945-50
Glorybound Singers	Franklin	
Gospel Angels	Franklin	1957-70
* Gospel Five	Franklin	1950-68
Gospel Harmonettes	Franklin	1986-88
Gospel Tones	Franklin	1946-48
* Greater Desire	Franklin	1988-
* Harmony Echoes	Franklin/	
	Bowling Green	1973-83
Hillsdale Quartet	Hillsdale	1973-74
* Journeymen and Jan	Franklin	1983-90
Messengers	Franklin	1988-
Moyers Family	Franklin	1990-
Mt. Vernon Quartet	Gold City	
New Beginnings Trio	Franklin	1986-
New Journeymen	Franklin	1990-
* Pathfinders Quartet	Franklin	1973-88
Patterson Family	Franklin	1940-41
* Patterson Family Quartet	Drake's Creek	1952-
Patterson Quartet	Drake's Creek	1940-41
* Pattersons	Drake's Creek/	
	Indianapolis	1947-
Providence Quartet	Providence	1949-50
Salmon Quartet	Salmon	1950-55
* Soul Winners Gospel Singers	Franklin	1975-
Southern Melody Quartet	Franklin	1969-76
Steps of Faith	Franklin	1971-
Stevenson Trio	Stevenson	1970-74
Sunday School Boosters		
Quartet	Salmon	1950-55

TAYLOR COUNTY

*Believers	Campbellsville	1973-74
Bertram Family Quartet	Campbellsville	1978-
Buck Creek Boys	Campbellsville	1975-87
Cochran Family	Campbellsville	
Feathersburg Church of God Singers	Feathersburg	1974-
Full Gospel Five	Campbellsville	1973-
*Good News Quartet	Campbellsville	1974-
Gospelaires	Palestine	1963-76
*Gospel Carriers	Campbellsville	1981-88
*Gospel Lovers Quartet	Campbellsville	1969-
Harmonettes	Mannsville	
Hays Family	Campbellsville	1930-48
Heavenly Highway Sunlighters	Campbellsville	1982-84
Inspirational Quartet	Campbellsville	1966-69
Johnny and Wig and the Harmony Boys	Campbellsville	1962-82
Messengers	Campellsville	1960-62
New Edition	Campbellsville	1987-
Newsmen	Campbellsville	1970-72
*Pittman Valley Boys	Campbellsville	1972-
Revelations	Campbellsville	
Robinson Family	Campbellsville	1984-89
*Servants Quartet	Campbellsville	1965-89
Speck Ridge Gospel Train	Elkhorn	1960-89
Speck Ridge Trio	Elkhorn	1950-60
Sunshine Girls	Campbellsville	1948-77
White's Ridge Singers	Campbellsville	1989-

WARREN COUNTY

Allen Quartet	Bowling Green	1960-76
Ante-Room Harmonizers	Bowling Green	1935-37
Beginners	Bowling Green	1982-84
Bow. Grn. Police Dept. Q.	Bowling Green	1980-83
Bowling Green Quartet	Bowling Green	1928-30
Bowling Green Quartet	Bowling Green	1946-46
Bratcher Family		
Burton Memorial Quartet	Bowling Green	1943-48
*Burch Family	Bowling Green	1980-88

Called Out Ministries	Bowling Green	1981-
* Chordsmen	Bowling Green	1976-78
* Cockriel Family	Bowling Green	1972-
Crossbearers	Bowling Green	1983-85
Divine Faith	Bowling Green	1988-
Dixie Aires Quartet	Bowling Green	1959-65
* Dusty Road Boys	Bowling Green	1986-
Faithful Aires	Bowling Green	1964-66
Faith Gospel Singers	Bowling Green	1970-76
Fellow Aires	Bowling Green	1984-86
Fellowship	Bowling Green	
Firm Believers	Bowling Green	
Forest Park Quartet	Bowling Green	1958-60
Friendly Five	Bowling Green	1948-55
Friendly Spirits	Smiths Grove/	
	Oakland	1981-87
Friendship Gospelaires	Oakland	1982-
Full Gospel Singers	Smiths Grove	1981-
* Gennie and the Redemptions	Bowling Green	1984-86
Gloryland Five	Bowling Green	
Glory Road Express	Bowling Green	1984-85
* Good News Edition	Bowling Green	1982-
Good Will Quartet	Bowling Green	1936-43
Gospel Echoes	Bowling Green/	
	Franklin	1958-62
Gospelettes Trio	Bowling Green	1959-62
Gospel Lamplighters	Rockfield	1972-73
Gospel Melody Quartet	Bowling Green	1960-63
Gospel Revelators	Bowling Green	
Gospel Singers	Bowling Green	1948-58
Gospel Tones Quartet	Bowling Green	
Gospel Voyagers	Bowling Green	1986-
Gospelettes Trio	Bowling Green	
Happy Four	Oakland/Merry Oaks	1983-86
Harmony	Bowling Green	1990-
Harmony Echoes	Bowling Green	1974-78
Harmony Echoes	Bowling Green	1985-
Harmony Singers	Smiths Grove	1982-85
* Harvestime Singers	Bowling Green	1978-82
Hendrick Family	Sunnyside	1960-68
Homeward Bound	Bowling Green	1985-88
* Howard Family	Bowling Green	1979-
Hudson/Thomas Quartet	Richardsville	c. 1941-c. 1945
Jordan River Boys	Bowling Green	1986-87

Joyway Sounds	B.G./Sm. Grove/	
	Glasgow	1978-84
* Joyway Singers	Smiths Grove	1969-86
King's Four	Bowling Green	1986-86
* Kinsmen Quartet	Bowling Green	1961-76
Kirby Family	Bowling Green	1983-89
Lighthouse Singers	Bowling Green	1982-
* Madison Family	Smiths Grove	1978-88
Majestics	Bowling Green	1965-69
Martha's Chapel Singers	Boyce	1986-
Martinsville Lights	Oakland	1987-
* Melody Makers	Bowling Green	1946-79
Melody Masters	Bowling Green	1957-62
Messengers	Bowling Green	1967-67
New Spiritual Singers	Bowling Green	1985-
New Vision Singers	Bowling Green	1990-
Old Union Trio	Bowling Green	1960-60
One People		
Overton Trio	Bowling Green	
Parables	Bowling Green	1986-86
Peacemakers	Bowling Green	1984-
Plano Quartet	Plano	1945-63
Promised Land Quartet	Bowling Green/	
	Louisville	1985-89
Putman Family	Bowling Green/	
	Scottsville	1984-
Revelations	Bowling Green	1981-82
Rhythmettes		
Richardsville Trio	Richardsville	c. 1943-48
Rocky Springs Melody Makers	Claypool	1985-
Rountree Family	Bowling Green	1934-48
Sacred Five	Bowling Green	1936-49
Seekers	Bowling Green	1981-87
Sentinels	Bowling Green	1980-80
Shades of Blue	Bowling Green	1987-89
Southern Harmonaires	Bowling Green	1989-
* Southern Harmony Boys	Bowling Green	1949-71
* Southern Harmony Quartet	Bowling Green	1977-
Spiritual Five	Green Hill	1949-58
Starlighters	Bowling Green	1985-
* Stuart Sisters Trio	Bowling Green	1955-65
Stuarts	Bowling Green	1962-81
T.K.I. Boys	Bowling Green	1954-56
Tonettes	Alvaton	1953-61

Travel Masters Quartet	Bowling Green	1964-70
* Trinity Trio	Bowling Green	1979-82
True Gospel Singers	Bowling Green	1986-
* Turner Family	Bowling Green	1965-
Victory Voices	Bowling Green	1978-
Voyagers	Richardsville	1986-
Watchmen	Bowling Green	1987-

WAYNE COUNTY

Anderson Family	Oil Valley	1960-
Bertram Family	Hidalgo	1950-60
* Bertram (Bobby) Family	Alpha	1973-
* Bertram Sisters	Monticello	1975-
* Bradshaw Family	Monticello	1960-
Calvary Singers	Monticello/Parnell	1981-84
Corder Family (Hubert)	Monticello	1949-
* Davis Family	Monticello	1972-
Fall Creek Quartet	Monticello	1951-58
First Methodist Quartet	Monticello	1980-82
Fumbling Four	Monticello	1949-53
Gap Creek Quartet	Gap Creek	1983-
Glorybound Singers	Hidalgo	1983-85
Gloryland Singers	Monticello	1984-
* Guffey Sisters	Murl/Flat	1966-76; 1989
Happy Travelers	Windy	1979-80
Harvest Time Singers	Monticello	1982-
King's Trio	Monticello	1975-
Melody Trio	Monticello	1955-57
Oak Grove Singers	Oak Grove	1987-
Phipps Family	Coopersville	c. 1925-c. 1938
Powell Quartet	Monticello	1920-70
Rector's Flat Church Quartet	Murl	1949-52
Selvidge Family Quartet	Spann Hill/ Steubenville	1940-74
* Victory Singers	Monticello	1982-
Wayne High Boys	Monticello	1954-56
Williams Quartet		
Wilson Quartet	Frazier	1935-45
Zion Singers	Monticello	1980-

APPENDIX B
SHAPE-NOTE TEACHERS

The list of shape-note teachers from south central Kentucky contains the names of men and women who were dedicated to the task of improving congregational singing in the local churches. Names of most of these teachers are household words even to this day among those people who attended the shape-note singing schools years ago. The following teachers have been identified.

ADAIR COUNTY: Lafe Akin, J.W. Dudley, Emmit T. Ferrell, Brother Grimsley, Johnny Janes, O.L. Rich, Charlie Tucker, L.J. Tucker, Walter B. Wells, and John Wolford.

ALLEN COUNTY: Erlis D. Austin, Everett J. Butrum, L.E. Butrum, Garnet Cassaday, T.W. Crowe, Sr., Andrew J. Dixon, Clyde Farris, B.C. Frost, Daily C. Gaines, Durwood Hinton, Melvin Hinton, Hughes Holland, Vesper Jones, Tim C. Kisselbaugh, Charlie Lamb, Mrs. Walter Lambert, Felton Landers, Alfred Lyles, Orvel Lyles, Bishop Mayhew, Virgil McGuire, Elzie Meador, Perkin Meador, Bascom Napier, Dr. Hoy Newman, Spencer Pope, Rev. L.S. Spann, Clair Thomas, Lazarus Thomas, Wesley Tucker, Price Weaver, Palmer Wheeler, Abraham Willoughby, and Fletcher Wolf.

BARREN COUNTY: J.T. Light and W. B. Walbert.

BUTLER COUNTY: Willie Byers, Ed Dye, Hershel E. Dye, Ellis Embry, Cal Felty, Adam Flener, and Wradon Flener.

CASEY COUNTY: Ches Ashley, Andrew Haste, Huston Haste, Jim Frank Haste, Willie Haste, Thomas Judd, Denny Moore, Rice Ware, and Virgil Ware.

CLINTON COUNTY: Elmer Butler, Sen. Claude Farmer, Dillard Shelley, and Rheul Thomas.

CUMBERLAND COUNTY: Lum Ashlock, Virgil Ashlock, Jim Capps, Henry Flowers, Mack Garner, Cary Hume, (Miss) Glee Hume, William Keen, D. Meredith, Albert Norris, Leonard Norris, Troy Spear, Grady Spear, Vanus Watson, Bee Wells, Judge J.W. Wells, and Dan Wray.

EDMONSON COUNTY: Willie Barbee, Marshall Browning, Georgie Childress, Lowell Davis, C.E. Deweese, Emmons Kinser, Theodore Lane, Elzie Lindsey, E.L. "Man" Meredith, Charlie Sturgeon, Sherman Tomes, McNeal VanMeter, and Fred T. Webb.

GREEN COUNTY: R.D. Cabell, Simon Finn, R.A. Jeffries, Stant Lile, Joe McCubbins, Loren Patterson, Richard D. Pepper, _____ Shreve, A.L. Thompson, and W.A. Wade.

HART COUNTY: Noble Cottress, Lon Craddock, Audie Dennison, Frank Elliott, Jackie Gardner, Raymond Gardner, Willie Mabe, Jim Riggs, Guy Templeman, and Hollis Templeman.

LOGAN COUNTY: J.T. Blue, Clarence Campbell, Henry Campbell, Rayburn Campbell, Taylor Chapman, Watt Gilliam, Wythe Jenkins, Jim McKinney, Sr., Jim McKinney, Jr., William Clay Neal, Curtis Savage, Duff Smotherman, Stuart Smotherman, Willie B. Smotherman, Otis Spencer, Roy Stuart, and Chester Whitescarver.

METCALFE COUNTY: _____ Brandy, Jim Hardy, J.W. London, and John G. Salmon.

MONROE COUNTY: "Big Jim" Hagan, Merwyn Hagan, Archie Hume, Sam Ray, John Steen, W.A. Turner, and Tom Yates.

PULASKI COUNTY: Lewis Adams, Sid Beasley, Victor Bryant, Oscar Carter, Jonah Fry, Waldo Fry, Odolphus Hamm, Tom Hale, Alta Beasley Hallmark, Jimmy Martin, Clyde McReynolds, James Mercer, Johnny Phelps, Wallace Proctor, Odus Reynolds, Glen Roy, Robert L. Roy, Tolbert Roy, James A. Sears, Willis Sears, Frank Spencer, Carlos Stephens, Fred Thompson, George Thompson, Everett Todd, Willie Voiles, Cass Wallin, Chapel Wallin, Jeeter Wallin, Jonas Ware, and Joseph Wares.

RUSSELL COUNTY: A.G. Coffey, Edgar Coffey, Gilbert Coffey, Leo Crisman, Robert Foley, Frank Hughes, C.L. McKinley, Ernest McKinley, Hollis Mitchell, Edward Phelps, Doyle Rexroat, Forest Rexroat, Huburt Rexroat, Lyle Rexroat, Ivis Roy, Oscar Tucker, Luther Turner, and Millard F. Upton.

SIMPSON COUNTY: Cager Gammon, J.B. Howser, and Thomas Patterson.

TAYLOR COUNTY: Flora Landis and J.B. Thompson.

WARREN COUNTY: Virgil P. Cassaday, Edd Hudson, and George Moulder.

WAYNE COUNTY: Harley Anderson, John M. Barnes, Ephriam Bell, Millard Fillmore Bell, Johnny Bertram, Omar D. Bertram, Alfred Corder, Jim Floyd, Rollie Lair, Jim Mills, Eula Morrow, Ephriam Phipps, Millard Phipps, Jesse Rector, William Rexroat, and James Granville Young.

In 1954 seven of the above listed persons were still actively teaching for the James D. Vaughan Music Company. Listed in *Vaughan's Family Visitor* were the names of C.E. Deweese, Cager Gammon, Perkin Meador, E.L. Meredith, Charlie Sturgeon, J.H. Templeman, and Fred Webb.

NOTES

INTRODUCTION

1. Feintuch, "Noncommercial Black Gospel Group," 37.

2. Lornell, *"Happy in the Service of the Lord,"* 129.

3. While singing activity in adjacent Grayson, Hardin, Muhlenberg, Ohio, and Todd counties is no longer as prominent as it was through the 1950s, those counties could justifiably have been included in this study.

4. Horsley, "Spatial Impact of White Gospel Quartets," 91.

5. Davidson, *Dictionary of Protestant Church Music,* 135-36. Citation obtained from Brobston, "Brief History of White Southern Gospel," 4. Brobston, 35-36, also includes a discussion of the first uses of the term "gospel song," dating from the 1830s.

6. Examples of these noncontroversial lyrics include the following couplets that were drawn from four songs current in the late 1980s: "When I move on up to Glory, / I'm gonna have a shoutin' time"; "Here's another empty vessel, / Fill it Lord another time"; "The sun's coming up in the morning, / Every tear will be gone from my eyes"; and "I have heard about Heaven, / And I want to go there."

7. In Appendix A, all trios, quartets, and family groups are listed by name, home community, and years of active service. This information was obtained over a five-year period from one or more persons familiar with each of the groups listed. Statistics quoted throughout the study are based on these data. I feel strongly that the list—with approximately 840 groups documented—comes within 5 percent of representing the total number of small ensembles spawned in south central Kentucky from 1900 to 1990.

8. Brobston's unpublished doctoral dissertation, "Brief History of White Southern Gospel Music" is in many ways a pioneering study in this regard and it proved very helpful in connection with my own study.

9. Eighty-two tape-recorded interviews were conducted with singers, musicians, and composers. Seventeen of these interviews were conducted by my students. Archival release forms were signed in all instances except when I was negligent in asking. These interviewees talked willingly and gladly. I conducted an additional 600 to 700 brief interviews with pencil and pad, some of which were done by telephone. All

materials amassed in this manner, including available group photographs, appointment books, home recordings, commercial tapes and albums, and other types of memorabilia, have been donated to the Manuscripts Division of the Kentucky Library at Western Kentucky University. A special category for Gospel Music has been created there.

1. THE SHAPE-NOTE ERA

1. Works that deal at some length with the origins of shape-note music include Horn, *Sing Me to Heaven*; Cheek, "Singing School and Shaped-Note Tradition"; McLemore, *Tracing the Roots*; Bruce, *And They All Sang Hallelujah*; Blackwell, *Wings of the Dove*; Stevenson, *Story of Southern Hymnology*; Sutton, "In the Good Old Way"; Caswell, "Social and Moral Music," 47-71; and Eskew, "Shape Note Hymnody."

2. The practice of lining out hymns is described briefly in Clements, "The Folk Church," 140-41. Analyses of responsorial singing are offered in Patterson, " 'Going Up to Meet Him' "; and Sutton, "Speech, Chant, and Song." For an excellent account of the influence of recent gospel music on earlier church musical forms, see Patterson, "Psalms, Hymns, and Gospel Songs."

3. Lewis Adams, West Science Hill, showed me a copy of *The Harp of Zion*, a figure-face hymnal that his father had used at one time. It was published in Lexington in the 1860s.

4. Cited and described in Jackson, *White Spirituals*.

5. McLemore, *Tracing the Roots*, 23.

6. Jackson, "Story of the Sacred Harp," v-xx, examines the roots of the Sacred Harp tradition and explains the sounds of this music genre. Another good description is Cobb, "Fasola Folk."

7. Quoted by Tuttle, *Simpson-Cook Autobiographical Sketches*, 8.

8. Wright, *Autobiography of Rev. A.B. Wright*, 30.

9. Brobston, "Brief History of White Southern Gospel Music," 71; Brobston also cites invaluable sources in tracing the later history of southern gospel music, 24-26.

10. Mrs. J.B. Reynolds, born in Hart County's Wildcat community, described this early singing school to William McDonald of Hardyville, Kentucky, in late 1971. This and other details she provided may be viewed in the Folklore, Folklife, and Oral History Archive in the Kentucky Library, Western Kentucky University, Bowling Green. File 1971-103. Jackson, "Did Spiritual Folksong Develop in the Northeast?" talks about the New England origins of folk hymns in Kentucky and Tennessee.

11. Edna Hume Kingrey, Louisville, Ky., to author, Nov. 7, 1987.

12. It may be that singing schools were held in Logan County at an even earlier date. A 1947 story in the Russellville *News-Democrat* dates shape-note singing schools as early as the late nineteenth century. And Julia Neal of Bowling Green provided me with a photograph showing her uncle, William Clay Neal, teaching the round notes c. 1890. It is highly likely that he offered shape-note instruction as well.

13. Reputedly, the first songbook issued by James D. Vaughan was *Golden Chimes* (Cornersville, Tenn., 1900). While a copyright exists for the publication, no extant copies are known to scholars, according to Charles K. Wolfe, Oct. 29, 1989.

14. In describing the teaching methodology employed by his father, Andrew Phipps of Muncie, Ind., provides a portrait of how many of the early teachers most likely approached their teaching. "Eph Phipps taught mainly in Wayne and McCreary counties," wrote Andrew, Sept. 7, 1987. "He always put his music on a dark, long piece

of cloth or board. He used chalk to put in such things as scale, lines and spaces, key signature, notes, time quotients, and lines of music to indicate the diatonic major and minor scales."

15. Mrs. R.C. Weddle, Liberty, Kentucky, to author, Apr. 10, 1987. In two subsequent letters, she supplied two photographs of singing schools taught by Virgil Ware at Rich Hill, Casey County, sometime between 1914 and 1925. She also provided me with a long list of names of those persons in attendance.

16. Adams led his final singing at age eighty-three at the West Science Hill Methodist Church, Sunday evening, Apr. 3, 1988. A widower who lived alone, he was found dead at home the next morning.

17. Brobston, "Brief History of White Southern Gospel Music," 165, observes that shape-note instruction declined significantly when consolidated public schools brought improved opportunities for musical training of young people.

18. In answer to the question of whether the singing school was a secular or a religious institution, Allen P. Britton, in "The Singing School Movement" (1961), asserts that it was both. Not only did these schools play crucial social roles for the people of the community, but, he contends, they educated people to fill important worship roles in the church. Cited by Brobston, "Brief History of White Southern Gospel Music," 53.

2. THE SINGING CONVENTION MOVEMENT

1. Stanley, "Gospel Singing Convention," 11.

2. Brobston, "Brief History of White Southern Gospel Music," 154, cites a reference indicating that early Alabama conventions were sometimes referred to as "all-day singings."

3. See Brobston, "Brief History of White Southern Gospel Music," 121, for specific mention of and citations for the New England singing societies.

4. Stanley, "Gospel Singing Convention," 3.

5. The first known singing convention in Kentucky occurred in 1884 in Benton, a small town in extreme western Kentucky. That history-making event was of the four-note (Sacred Harp) variety, however, and is thus not germane to the county conventions in south central Kentucky that featured seven-note music exclusively.

6. Lawrence, "Look at a Final Generation," 57.

7. Scottsville Citizen-Times, June 3, 1971, 4.

8. Earlis D. Austin recalled on January 18, 1989, that his father and uncle helped to split the shingles used to cover the building, and that Mr. Crowe, a former funeral director, told him that, as a boy, he had carried drinking water to the construction crew.

9. Vaughan's Family Visitor, 43, 6 (June 1954).

10. Much of the information about the Logan County Convention was obtained from Beisswenger, "Singing Schools."

11. Creason, "Inspiration from a Songbook."

12. Under the leadership of Rex Agers, Barren County also pursued the notion of instituting a gospel music association to take the place of the county convention there. The Barren County Gospel Singing Association has operated quite successfully since its inception in 1978, featuring top quartet groups from southern Kentucky and northern Tennessee. The Association does not meet in churches, but at either the Lura B. Mitchell Clubhouse or in the parking lot outside Louise's Bible Bookstore in Glasgow.

13. Stanley, "Gospel Singing Convention," 7.

14. Brobston, "Brief History of White Southern Gospel Music," 230-31, comments that professional quartets began to appear at local conventions elsewhere in the South about this same time.

15. For similar thoughts, see Wolfe, "Gospel Goes Uptown," 84.

16. By the 1960s all county conventions had been discontinued except those in Allen, Barren, Green, Hart, Logan, Pulaski, and Russell, where they have successfully withstood changing times and musical tastes. Even in these counties, however, church choirs and song leaders are things of the past. Only small ensembles, mainly quartets and trios, along with occasional duets and soloists, perform at the conventions these days. Martin, "Cumberland County Singing Convention," describes one of that county's final singing conventions.

17. The Kentucky State Singing Convention has been held in one of the counties of south central Kentucky every year except six since its founding in 1946.

18. Information courtesy of C.E. Deweese, singing master, who was Salmon's secretary-treasurer both years. A feature story in Bowling Green's *Park City Daily News*, September 25, 1946, stated that between five thousand and six thousand persons were present at the first big state singing. Wesley Tucker, a Western Kentucky University student from Scottsville, served as the Convention's first pianist. Bowling Green groups present at the first State Convention included the Sacred Five, later heralded as the finest ever to come out of the Bowling Green area; the Rountree Quartet; the Sunshine Quartet; the Plano Quartet; and the Sunbeams, directed by Marie Lyles.

19. Information about Butrum was provided by his son, Everett Jewell, who taught music schools and private piano lessons, and played piano for numerous quartets and trios across the years.

20. These informal convention procedures in some ways resemble the rules and etiquette for southern fiddling contests.

21. The question of changing musical styles and performance aspects is dealt with at some length in chapters 7 and 8.

3. Shape-Notes and Early Gospel Quartets

1. The West Allen Quartet name soon reappeared and continued to be used until 1941, involving such local notables as Louis McElroy and Wilbur and Harold McCleary in the process.

2. A second Allen County group calling itself the Liberty Quartet sang from 1944 to 1947. Mautie Reynolds also played piano for this group, composed of T.Y. Tabor, Brodus Tabor, Glen Conner, and Clara Helen Reynolds. The group's name was changed in 1947 to the Melody Makers, which was one of the quality groups to come out of south central Kentucky.

3. Vaughan, "History of the Twenty-Five Years of the National Singing Convention," 5.

4. Beisswenger, "Singing Schools in South Central Kentucky," 19, writes that Jim McKinney was taught the shape-notes around the turn of the century by Wythe Jenkins.

5. Wolfe, "Early Gospel Quartets," writes about the inceptive years of certain professional gospel music groups.

6. Wolfe, *Kentucky Country*, 84.

7. The 78s were six and one-half inches in diameter and contained a second

spindle hole about 1" to the right of the center hole. The other seven songs included "I'll never Forget," "Pray the Clouds Away," "Redeemed," "Somebody Calling My Name," "The Old Home Place," "Turn Your Radio On," and "Little Pine Log Cabin." The only four known extant records cut by the Campground Quartet are now on deposit in the Kentucky Library, Western Kentucky University, courtesy of Mr. and Mrs. Lee Caswell.

8. Carrier's gospel music career has been chronicled by Daniel, "We Had to Be Different to Survive."

4. THE TRANSITION YEARS

1. The York Quartet cut a 45 rpm lacquer-on-metal album on June 5, 1948, using the facilities of a small recording studio in Albany. The two songs they recorded were "At Sunset, I'm Going Home," and "Way Down Deep in My Soul." Johnny Howard later sang with the Travelers Quartet of Albany; the Highway Quartet of Clinton County; and the Heartland Singers of Elizabethtown.

2. It was a tearful occasion for audience and singers alike when all of the original Southern Harmony Boys except M.B. Fleming sang as a group again on Oct. 16, 1989. Mae Fleming once again played piano for them. The event that brought them together was a special session of the 1989 Kentucky State Singing Convention billed as Heritage Sunday.

3. Wolfe, "Gospel Goes Uptown."

4. For additional commentary about the quartet–publishing company conflict, see Wolfe, "Gospel Music Goes Uptown," 96-97; also Wolfe, " 'Gospel Boogie.' "

5. THE BEGINNINGS OF A NEW ERA

1. One of the readers of this book while it was still in manuscript commented on the importance of the post–World War II years (1945-53) for the recording industry, as follows: "The record industry saw the rise of hundreds of independent labels and regional studios, and this made it much easier for local gospel groups to record. Many were able to produce custom pressed 78s on their own label; others paid regional companies like Rich R Tone and Acme to issue their records. There are hundreds of these 78s around the upper and deep south (and even Midwest), and since they were all done to order, there are no definitive files or lists of them; they are a discographical nightmare, but a wonderfully democratic means of spreading the music. One label, Bibletone, would custom press, creating a different numerical series for each group."

2. Virtually all local groups used only the piano until about 1960 when the Lefevres of Atlanta made an appearance in Bowling Green, according to both Frank Weaver and Brodus Tabor. The Lefevres' influence was felt locally overnight, as some area groups immediately attempted to copy the new electric sound.

3. For an informative account of this pioneer group, see Calloway, "The Rangers Quartet."

4. Melloan, "Dragging Their P.A. Systems Behind Them," 6.

5. Country music historian Malone, "Chuck Wagon Gang," 4, writes of the Gang's sound: "The enduring and widespread popularity of the Chuck Wagon Gang is owed in large part to the fact that their style has successfully wedded both the country and gospel traditions. Like such groups as the Blackwood Brothers, they chose the

quartet format, sang in a style drawn from the singing schools, and performed songs taken from the shape-note hymnals."

6. By way of illustrating the Chuck Wagon Gang content of the Egypt Quartet's radio programs, the broadcast of March 24, 1963, included the following songs: "Just as the Sun Went Down," "Ride On God's Careworn Children," "Higher, I'll Sail away Home," "Anchored in Love," "Remember the Child," "Dreamboat," "Walk in the New Jerusalem Way," and "Drifting Too Far from the Shore," all songs performed and recorded by the Gang.

6. Present Times

1. Information on the Imperials was provided during a telephone conversation with Jake Hess, their founder and promoter, Feb. 7, 1990. Ron Hamm was the Imperials' first drummer. It was also during that summer, 1965, that the Imperials first added an electric bass and electric rhythm guitar to their act.

2. These a cappella groups were the Gospel Four, Bee Spring Quartet, Madison Brothers, Stockholm Quartet, Sullivan-Vincent Quartet, Green River Trio, Cave Hill Singers, and the Jacksonville Quartet. Four of the eight were actively singing in early 1990, and all four are in Edmonson County, along with the still-active Union Light Quartet.

3. Some of the area's a cappella groups obtain their songs from sheet music and by listening to the recordings of selected professional ensembles. By and large, however, these fine groups still mine the shape-note hymnals in quest of their songs. In this regard, they are continuing in the same tradition that early quartets here established decades ago. The songsters they use are typically new publications, indicating that a cadre of song composers are still at work churning out lyrics set to shape-note music. Arlis O. Harmon of Allen County ranks among the more prolific old-time song composers. His work is dealt with at some length in chapter 8.

4. These numbers do not include the country gospel, bluegrass gospel, or full band ensembles that sprang up during the same twenty-year period.

5. The very fine Dusty Road Boys of Bowling Green were having a bit of the same identity crisis at the time of this writing. When these defenders of traditional four-part southern harmony decided to relinquish the piano and bass guitar in favor of certain string instruments, people began immediately to use the term bluegrass when referring to them.

6. The Twilight Singers still use some Chuck Wagon Gang songs on occasion. Their departure from the sound of the Gang did not deter other groups in the Lake Cumberland region from continuing on in that distinctive style, however. Among those that did or still emulate it are the Jones Family of Kettle, Cumberland County; the Country Church Singers, Middleburg; the Glory Way Travelers and the Gospel Melodies, Somerset; God's Humble Servants, Knifley; the Harvesters, Edmonton; the Rogers Family, Clementsville; the Sunshine Quartet, Columbia; the Trinity Quartet, Science Hill; the Victory Quartet, Monticello; and the Walltown Quartet, Casey County. No Chuck Wagon sound-alikes exist in the study area west of Metcalfe County, located at midpoint.

7. The Conquerers originated in Greensburg. It was there that youthful Kent Humphrey, the group's lead singer, signed a contract in 1981 to sing lead for the Dixie Melody Boys of Kingston, North Carolina.

8. The Thrasher Family features Mary Thrasher and her daughters, Amy, Beth,

and Becky. Becky's husband, William, is drummer for the group. The Thrashers have traveled many miles to sing praises to their Lord and to witness to others. Under Mary's leadership, they've aired over radio and television numerous times and have recorded several tapes and albums. One of their albums bore the title of one of Mary's many song compositions, "I Am Determined."

9. Other low-profile full band gospel groups, some of which were country style, that were still active at the beginning of the 1990s included the Aarons of Greensburg; the Brown Family of Albany; the Burch Family and the Fellowships of Bowling Green; the Cassadys and the Faith Singers of Edmonton; the Davis Family of Monticello; the Glory Road Singers of Lewisburg; the Glory Ways, the Bakers, and the New Covenant Quartet of Somerset; the Good News Quartet of Campbellsville; and Greater Desire, Franklin.

10. Among the current groups that utilize the full band sound and/or are known for using contemporary lyrics are the Spirituals of Edmonton, the Joymakers of Greensburg, and the Singing Martins of Scottsville.

11. Class acts that were still active in 1990 and still producing the older four-part harmony sound included the Happy Travelers of Bethelridge, the Travelers of Morgantown, the Kentuckians of Scottsville/Bowling Green, the Cross Roads Quartet of Russell Springs, the Canaanland Quartet and the Liberty Quartet of Glasgow, the Jubilee Singers of Lamb, the Union Light Quartet of north Edmonson County, the Dusty Road Boys of Bowling Green, the Brothers and the Counsellors' of Somerset, the Challengers and the Harmoneers of Lewisburg, the Melody Aires of Columbia, the New Freedom Singers of Auburn, the Harmony Echoes of Bowling Green, and Greater Desire, Franklin.

7. Walking Straighter and Narrower

1. Dinwiddie, "Can Gospel Music Be Saved?" 19, agrees with this position. He contends that the term "gospel music" should be reserved for music that is related to the gospel of Christ and to man's response; it should not be used to identify a music that merely "expresses positive feelings," 16. While not addressing the question of whether or not the gospel can be sung, and if we can assume that shape-note songs and more recent gospel songs are in the same music stream, Beary, "Stylistic Traits of Southern Gospel," 26, offers a controversial explanation for the origin of the problem: "Gospel songs of the seven-note tradition . . . are not songs for worship service," she writes. Instead, they are "songs with religious words to be used for singing conventions and singing schools. They are intended for semireligious activities outside the structured church program."

2. In 1984, Loryn Atwell took Randy Swaffer in as his business partner under the corporate name of RS Recording Studio. Atwell, native of Metcalfe County, Kentucky, was a pioneer in the recording business in the Upper South. He began in 1958, then ten years later he opened a record-pressing plant.

8. Singing the Glory Down

1. The term "singing" is used in this chapter to designate trio and quartet performances only.

2. All-night singings are virtually things of the past these days. Such events are

still held at Red Lick Cumberland Presbyterian Church, home of the Red Lick Quartet, and Pink Ridge Baptist Church. Both churches are located in Metcalfe County.

3. By way of illustrating the extent of singing group involvement on New Year's Eve, radio station WGGC, Glasgow, carried announcements of thirty-one such events scheduled for Dec. 31, 1986, all of which involved local quartets.

4. The performance of white gospel music has largely been ignored by scholars. Black gospel music has received some attention in this regard. For a good representative description of the latter, see Patterson, " 'Going Up to Meet Him.' "

5. Of interest in connection with emotion-charged worship services is Lawless, *God's Peculiar People*.

6. Allen, "Spiritual Entertainment," 1, and "Singing in the Spirit."

7. See Malone, "Chuck Wagon Gang," 4.

8. See Brobston's "Brief History of White Southern Gospel Music," 311. Marshall, "Keep on the Sunny Side," 29, observes that bluegrass lyrics have five recurring themes. These are individual salvation, life's rocky road, the maternal hearth, grief for the deceased, and good Christian "action orientation."

9. Hall, "Editorial," (June 1970).

10. Hall, (Nov. 1973).

11. Musicologist Beary, "Stylistic Traits of Southern Gospel," 27, observes that "almost any experience of life could provide [song] writers with the basis for a song text."

12. Wolfe, *Kentucky Country*, 148.

13. Attention should be called here to an interesting article, Knight, "Perceptions of Landscapes in Heaven."

14. Song composers were held in highest public esteem, and at about the same level as the music teachers. Allen County alone produced a long list of published composers, including L.E. Butrum, who saw at least thirty-four of his songs published by Vaughan, Winsett, Hartford, Stamps-Baxter, Bateman Bros., and his own L.E. Butrum Music Company of Bowling Green. His son, Everett, composed about three dozen songs, many of which were included in quartet books published by the late John Daniel of Nashville, Tennessee. Perkin Meador had at least twenty-nine songs published; Virgil P. Cassady about one dozen; Wesley Tucker twice that many; and Harold West published at least seven. W.B. Walbert from the Allen-Monroe border near Fort Run may have been the most prolific song writer of all Allen County composers. He joined the Vaughan Music School staff and eventually married Vaughan's daughter. His noted accomplishments have been chronicled in *Vaughan's Family Visitor* and elsewhere.

The Adair County hillcountry spawned such composers as Walter B. Wells, while Casey County is the place of birth of teacher and composer Jonas Ware and his extremely talented and widely known son, Virgil Ware, as well as composers Jason Haste and his cousin, Andrew Haste.

C.E. Deweese, the area's best known survivor of the old-time teachers/singers/composers, and who has written words and music to approximately forty published songs, spent much of his youth and early adult years in Edmonson County, which also lays claim to Edsel Denison. The latter, acclaimed to be one of the finest tenor singers in the Mammoth Cave region at mid-twentieth century, wrote the words and music to "I'm Going to Live up There," published by Vaughan in 1950. Their Warren County neighbor, Edd Hudson of Richardsville, saw eight of his songs published by Stamps-Baxter and Vaughan between 1937 and 1960.

CONCLUSION

1. Written descriptions of the "degradation" to which commercial gospel music has gone in destroying the quality of church music include Dinwiddie's, "Can Gospel Music Be Saved?" and McFarland's "Looking for the Gospel at a Gospel Concert."

2. "Living the Life We Sing About" is the title of a documentary film on the Cross Family Singers of Russellville, Kentucky. The film was produced by Burt Feintuch in 1979. In 1980, Feintuch published an article about the Cross family: "A Noncommercial Black Gospel Group in Context: We Live the Life We Sing About." Perhaps the title, which is a quote from the Cross family itself, derives from Mahalia Jackson's famous song of the late 1940s "I'm Gonna Live the Life I Sing about in Song."

BIBLIOGRAPHY

INTERVIEWS

Unless otherwise specified, all tape-recorded interviews were conducted by the author. Hundreds of brief, non-recorded interviews were conducted as well.

Adams, Lewis. West Science Hill, Jan. 29, 1988.
Atwell, Loyrn. Lafayette, Tenn., May 27, 1989.
Austin, Erlis D. Scottsville, Jan. 31 and Feb. 6, 1986.
Bale, Iona. Greensburg, Apr. 17, 1986, by Phillip Smith.
Basham, Gennie. Bowling Green, Apr. 26, 1986, by Lynne Roberts.
Bennett, Christell. Horse Cave, Apr. 11, 1987.
Bowles, Maude. Summer Shade, July 7, 1984, by Shirley Bowman
      Hammer.
Britt, Depp and Mary. Scottsville, May 12, 1988.
Bryson, Hazel. Bowling Green, May 1, 1986, by Deborah Harp; Feb. 16
      and Mar. 12, 1989, by the author.
Butrum, Everett Jewell. Madison, Tenn. Mar. 17 and May 12, 1989.
Cassaday, Garnet. Settle, Feb. 10 and 12, 1986.
Caswell, Lee. Munfordville, June 18, 1989.
Childress, Georgie. Mammoth Cave, Apr. 19, 1986.
Cockriel, Lonnie and Toby. Bowling Green, Apr. 29, 1986, by John
      Lawless; Aug. 21, 1986, by the author.
Cooley, Calvin and Mary. Columbia, Apr. 4, 1987.
Cooper, Rick. Liberty, Feb. 11, 1987.
Curry, Paul. Columbia, Dec. 4, 1987.

Davis, Lowell and Wilma. Park City, June 17, 1986, by Chad Berry; July 3, 1986, by Berry and the author.

Denison, Rick and Joanna. Lindseyville, June 17 and July 7, 1986, by C. Berry.

Deweese, C.E. Park City, Oct. 8 and 15, 1984, by Drew Beisswenger; June 16, 1987, by the author.

Durrett, Mike. Summersville, Apr. 17, 1986, by P. Smith.

Dye, Edwin. Bowling Green, Dec. 11, 1984, by D. Beisswenger.

Feese, Earl. Columbia, July 25, 1986.

Foley, Grace. Russell Springs, Apr. 19, 1987.

Foster, Bob and Mathael. Somerset, June 27, 1988.

Gaskin, Morris. Russell Springs, May 13, 1988.

Gibbs, Buell. Holland, Mar. 31, 1987.

Gilpin, Lewis H. Breeding, Mar. 1, 1988.

Godby, Charles Ray and Joan. Somerset, June 27, 1988.

Hall, Bernie and Joyce. Lindseyville, June 9, 1986, by C. Berry; July 7, 1986, by Berry and the author.

Harmon, Arlis O. Adolphus, Apr. 27, 1986, by Bentley Tittle; May 2, 1987, by the author.

Haste, Hobart. Bethelridge, Feb. 11, 1987.

Haste, Jason. Bethelridge, Dec. 4, 1987.

Hodges, Hartsell. Columbia, Nov. 25, 1987.

Howard, Johnny and Doris. Elizabethtown, Nov. 22, 1986.

Hurt, Jack and Patty. Edmonton, Sept. 16, 1985.

Hurt, Sherman and Mary. Edmonton, July 7, 1984, by S.B. Hammer; Sept. 5, 1985, by the author.

Johnson, Kemble. Bowling Green, Apr. 21, 1986, by Gayle Kindred.

Jones, Bill and Margaret. Glasgow, Mar. 11, 1986 and May 14, 1988.

Light, J.T. Glasgow, Apr. 22, 1986, by Teresa Hollingsworth; Aug. 19, 1986, by the author.

Lindsey, Johnny and Chloie. Lindseyville, Jan. 27, 1987.

Lyle, Bobby and Genell. May 4, 1986, by Chip Woodson.

Madison, Dit. Huff, July 12, 1987.

Martin, Hazel. Elizabethtown, Nov. 10, 1986, by Kelly Lally.

McCubbins, Haskell and Annette. Munfordville, Jan. 16, 1989.

McGaha, Vernie. Russell Springs, July 10, 1986.

McKinley, Ernest. Russell Springs, Sept. 18, 1986.

McKinney, Jim. Elkton, Nov. 12, 1983.

Meredith, Cora and David. June 17 and July 3, 1986, by C. Berry.

Mullinix, Libby. Albany, Sept. 26 and Dec. 14, 1987.

Muncie, Imogene. Campbellsville, Feb. 12, 1987.

Napier, Corbin. Holland, Mar. 31, 1987.

Neely, Mary F. Campbellsville, Feb. 12, 1987.

Newton, Linda. Somerset, June 27, 1988.

Oakes, John and Margaret. Scottsville, May 12, 1988.

Parker, Donald. Campbellsville, Mar. 10, 1986, by Cheryl Fraim.

Polston, Garry. Greensburg, Feb. 25, 1987.

Ponser, Elma. Somerset, June 27, 1988.

Reece, Debora. Glasgow, June 12, 1988.

Rexroat, Doyle and Reva. Russell Springs, June 28, 1986.

Rexroat, Forrest. Russell Springs, June 28, 1986.

Rose, Anne. Russellville, Apr. 17, 1987.

Roy, Glen. Nancy, Sept. 19, 1988.

Roy, Ivis and Thelma. Russell Springs, Sept. 19, 1986.

Savage, Curtis and Rosa. Pembroke, Nov. 9, 1987.

Sears, Norma and Bobby. Somerset, Oct. 14, 1987.

Sego, Eva. Lindseyville, July 8, 1986, by C. Berry.

Shores, Willis. Auburn, May 4, 1988.

Smith, June. Valley Oak, Oct. 14, 1987.

Strode, Wayne. Lamb, July 1, 1984, by S.B. Hammer.

Stuart, Howard. Bowling Green, Apr. 14, 1986, by Jack Hodges.

Stuart, Noble. Bowling Green, Dec. 12, 1984; Dec. 16, 1988.

Swift, Edna. Franklin, Feb. 16, 1989.

Syra, Stanley and Lourine. Edmonton, Sept. 27, 1985.

Tabor, Brodus. Bowling Green, Jan. 9, 1986 and Mar. 17, 1986.

Webb, Thomas and Audrey. Russellville, Sept. 12, 1988.

Wells, Lucille L. Horse Cave, Apr. 11, 1987.

Wethington, Maurice. Campbellsville, Feb. 12, 1987.

Whitescarver, Chester. Russellville, Feb. 23 and Nov. 9, 1983, by D. Beisswenger.

Wilson, Curtis. Columbia, Mar. 17, 1986.

Wilson, Frank. Bowling Green, Jan. 9, 1986.

Wilson, Woodrow. Jabez, Dec. 18, 1987.

PUBLISHED SOURCES

Allen, Ray. "Singing in the Spirit." *Rejoice: The Gospel Music Magazine* (Summer 1988): 7-14.

———. "Spiritual Entertainment: Faith and Aesthetics in African American Gospel Performance." Paper presented at the annual meeting of the American Folklore Society, Baltimore, 1987.

Beary, Shirley. "Stylistic Traits of Southern Shape-Note Gospel Songs." *The Hymn* (Jan. 1979): 26-33.

Beisswenger, Drew. "Singing Schools in South Central Kentucky." Master's thesis, Western Kentucky Univ., 1985.

Blackwell, Lois S. *The Wings of the Dove: The Story of Gospel Music in America.* Norfolk: Downing, 1978.

Brobston, Stanley H. "A Brief History of White Southern Gospel Music Singing Groups in Rural Georgia." Ph.D. diss., New York Univ., 1977.

Bruce, Dixon D., Jr. *And They All Sang Hallelujah: Plain-Folk Camp-Meeting Religion, 1800-1845.* Knoxville: Univ. of Tenn. Press, 1974.

Burt, Jesse, and Duane Allen. *The History of Gospel Music.* Nashville: K & S, 1971.

Calloway, Jack. "The Rangers Quartet: The First Decade (1936-1946)." *Precious Memories: Journal of Gospel Music* (Sept.-Oct. 1989): 5-10.

Caswell, Austin B. "Social and Moral Music: The Hymn." In *Music in American Society: From Puritan Hymn to Synthesizer,* ed. George McCue. New Brunswick, N.J.: Transaction, 1977.

Cheek, Curtis L. "The Singing School and Shaped-Note Tradition: Residuals in Twentieth Century American Hymnody." Ph.D. diss., Univ. of Southern Calif., 1967.

Clements, William M. "The Folk Church: Institution, Event, Performance. In *Handbook of American Folklore,* ed. Richard M. Dorson. Bloomington: Indiana Univ. Press, 1983.

Cobb, Buell E., Jr. "Fasola Folk: Sacred Harp Singing in the South." *Southern Exposure* (Summer and Fall 1987): 48-53.

Creason, Joe. "Inspiration from a Songbook." Louisville *Courier-Journal Magazine* (Nov. 18, 1956): 7-9.

Daniel, Wayne W. "We Had to Be Different to Survive: Billy Carrier Remembers the Swanee River Boys." *John Edward Memorial Foundation Quarterly* (Spring-Summer 1982): 59-83.

Davidson, James R. *A Dictionary of Protestant Church Music.* Metuchen, N.J.: Scarecrow, 1975.

Dinwiddie, Richard D. "Can Gospel Music Be Saved?" *Christianity Today* (May 21, 1982): 17-19.

Eskew, Harry. "Shape Note Hymnody." In *Groves Dictionary of Music and Musicians,* 6th ed. 20 vols. (Washington, D.C.: Macmillan, 1980).

Feintuch, Burt. "A Noncommercial Black Gospel Group in Context: We Live the Life We Sing About." *Black Music Research Journal* (1980): 37-50.

Hall, Connor B. "Editorial." *Vaughan's Family Visitor* (June 1970 and Nov. 1973).

Harmon, Arlis O. "Allen County Pioneer Singers." Scottsville *Citizen-Times,* date unknown.

Horn, Dorothy D. *Sing Me to Heaven.* Gainesville: Univ. of Florida Press, 1971.

Horsley, A. Doyne. "The Spatial Impact of White Gospel Quartets in the U.S." *John Edward Memorial Foundation Quarterly* (Summer 1979): 91-98.

Jackson, George P. "Did Spiritual Folksong Develop in the Northeast?" *Southern Folklore Quarterly* (Mar. 1939): 1-3.

_____. *White Spirituals from the Southern Uplands.* Chapel Hill: Univ. of North Carolina, 1933; rpt. New York: Dove, 1965.

_____. "The Story of the Sacred Harp, 1844-1944." In *The Sacred Harp,* ed. Benjamin F. White and E.J. King. Nashville: Broadman, 1968.

Knight, David B. "Perceptions of Landscapes in Heaven." *Journal of Cultural Geography* (Fall/Winter 1985): 127-40.

Lawless, Elaine J. *God's Peculiar People: Women's Voices and Folk Tradition in a Pentecostal Church.* Lexington: Univ. Press of Kentucky, 1988.

Lawrence, Sharon S. "A Look at a Final Generation: The Shape-Note Singing School Tradition in South Central Kentucky." Master's thesis, Eastern Kentucky Univ., 1982.

Lornell, Kip. *"Happy in the Service of the Lord": Afro-American Gospel Quartets in Memphis.* Champaign: Univ. of Illinois Press, 1988.

Malone, Bill. "The Chuck Wagon Gang: God's Gentle People." *Journal of Country Music* (1985): 4-12.

Marshall, Howard W. "Keep on the Sunny Side of Life: Pattern and Religious Expression in Bluegrass Music." *New York Folklore Quarterly* (Spring 1974): 3-43.

Martin, Kathleen R. "Cumberland County Singing Convention." *Kentucky Folklore Record* (Spring 1974): 29-32.

McFarland, John R. "Looking for the Gospel at a Gospel Concert." *Christian Century* (June 18, 1986): 579-81.

McLemore, B.F. Tracing the Roots of Southern Gospel Singers. Jasper, Tex.: privately published, 1988.

Melloan, Joan. "Dragging their P.A. Systems Behind." *Gospel Reaching Out* (Nov. 1973): 6.

Melloan, Johnny. "From the Editor." *Gospel Reaching Out* (July 1974): 2.

Patterson, Daniel. " 'Going Up to Meet Him': Songs and Ceremonies of a Black Family's Ascent." In *Diversities of Gifts: Field Studies in Southern Religion,* ed. Ruel Tyson, Jr., James L. Peacock, and Daniel W. Patterson. Urbana: Univ. of Illinois Press, 1988.

Patterson, Beverly. "Psalms, Hymns, and Gospel Songs: Changes in

Primitive Baptist Singing." Paper presented at the annual meeting of the American Folklore Society, Philadelphia, 1989.

Stanley, David H. "The Gospel Singing Convention in South Georgia." *Journal of American Folklore* (Jan.-Mar. 1982): 3-12.

Stevenson, Arthur Linwood. *The Story of Southern Hymnology.* Salem, Va.: Stevenson, 1931.

Sutton, Brett. "In the Good Old Way: Primitive Baptist Tradition." *Southern Exposure* (Summer and Fall 1977): 97-104.

―――. "Speech, Chant, and Song: Patterns of Language and Action in a Southern Church." In *Diversities of Gifts: Field Studies in Southern Religion,* ed. Ruel Tyson, Jr., James L. Peacock, and Daniel W. Patterson. Urbana: Univ. of Illinois Press, 1988.

Tuttle, Betty Waddle. *Simpson-Cook Autobiographical Sketches and Lineage.* Unpublished manuscript, undated.

Vaughan, Stella Benton. "History of the Twenty-Five Years of the National Singing Convention." *Vaughan's Family Visitor* (Oct.-Nov. 1961): 3-8.

Wolfe, Charles K. "'Gospel Boogie': White Southern Music in Transition." *Popular Music,* vol. 1. Cambridge: Cambridge Univ. Press, 1981.

―――. "Gospel Goes Uptown: White Gospel Music, 1945-1955." In *Folk Music and Modern Sound,* ed. William R. Ferris and Mary L. Hart. Jackson: Univ. Press of Mississippi, 1982.

―――. "Early Gospel Quartets: The Case of the McDonald Brothers." *Mid-American Folklore* (Summer and Fall 1982): 70-78.

―――. *Kentucky Country.* Lexington: Univ. Press of Kentucky, 1982.

Wright, J.C., ed. *Autobiography of Rev. A.B. Wright of the Holston Conference, M.E. Church.* Cincinnati: Cranston and Curts, 1986; rpt. Jamestown, Tenn.: Fentress County Historical Society, 1977.

INDEX